THE SCIENCE OF RUGBY FOOTBALL

The Science of Rugby Football

Mike Davis and Donald Ireland

PELHAM BOOKS

First published in Great Britain by
Pelham Books Ltd
44 Bedford Square
London WC1B 3DP
1985

British Library Cataloguing in Publication Data

Davis, Mike
   The science of rugby football.
   1. Rugby football
   I. Title   II. Ireland, Donald
   796.33'32   GV945

   ISBN 0 7207 1597 0

Printed in Great Britain by
Butler & Tanner Ltd, Frome

We dedicate this book to Jenny and Monica who have, over the years, constantly put up with the absences of their husbands due to the call of rugby, but who still give tremendous support.

Contents

Contents

Acknowledgements

We are indebted to the following for their assistance.

Mrs Penny Tommis for her detailed and clear line illustrations.

EJ Rees and RJVS Simpson of Sherborne School for their ability to produce such excellent photographs.

Sherborne School, for the boys who so ably demonstrated individual and unit skills for the photographs.

Mrs MA Hull who, because the authors were working to last minute deadlines, became the fastest typist in the West, besides having to decipher illegible handwriting.

Foreword by Bill Beaumont

It was something of a surprise to be asked by Mike Davis to write a foreword for this excellent publication. But, I hasten to add, a very pleasant surprise.

Without doubt Mike Davis was the outstanding reason why England were successful in the early 1980s. He came to an England set-up full of old lags like myself, who had seen coaches come and go – and we thought we knew it all.

We were all very sceptical about this guy who had come from coaching schoolboys, but I, along with the rest of the lads, very quickly pricked up my ears when he started on the training field.

Mike had the great ability of always planning the training sessions, and he was always able to pick up things in matches that we were not doing well and then have practices ready for us to work on these things on the training field. All his training was geared to match situations – and this is of great importance.

This book is full of useful exercises that a coach can use in planning his training sessions. There are far too many to go into, but all aspects of the game are covered by the very comprehensive practical drills, which are excellently illustrated.

In the future I feel that this book will become an essential part of any coach's training sessions.

It has been a privilege to write this foreword and may I wish both Mike and Don much success in one of the most comprehensive and informative coaching books that I have ever read.

Bill Beaumont

Introduction

Our reasons for writing this book are to enable the player to get the most possible enjoyment out of his game but, more importantly, to realize his potential. However, rugby football is a team game and any one player is only one fifteenth of the entity; a coach is needed to weld a successful team.

We have attempted to produce a book that will convince both the individual and the coach that they are complementary to each other. Players must be encouraged to think for themselves, use their initiative and, above all, not to become stereotyped in their approach or ideas. To achieve this, both player and coach accept that success requires supreme competence at the basic skills of the game, knowing what has to be achieved, and perhaps most important of all *to be able to read the game*. There is no substitute for imagination, creativeness or improvisation, but these ideals require a platform. That platform consists of basic skills, both individually and as a unit.

We have endeavoured to produce a book in which both the player and the coach will be provided with the right techniques, individually, as a unit, and then as a team. More importantly, we hope to guide all to the only philosophy of the game which really is *the scoring of tries*. To achieve this a team must have possession or be seeking to regain possession.

Techniques and general principles are laid out before the practices are illustrated. These build up from **individual** basic skills to **unit** basic skills to **team** basic skills. There are many headings and subheadings so that the reader can easily pick up the theme he wishes to develop. Both coach and player can use the book as a reference, helped by numerous drills in all sections, as they plan a session for the field.

These principles must be understood and they apply to the rugby player be he ten, twenty, or thirty years of age. As a player develops his skills and techniques, the greater will be his appreciation of the game.

And last but by no means least, when the basic skills have been acquired and put into action by the individual, unit and team alike, we should seek to develop the dedication of the New Zealanders, the doggedness of the English, the fire of the Irish or Scots, not to mention the flair of the Welsh and the improvisation of the French – which together epitomize all that is best in this wonderful game of rugby football.

Key to the symbols used in the line drawings

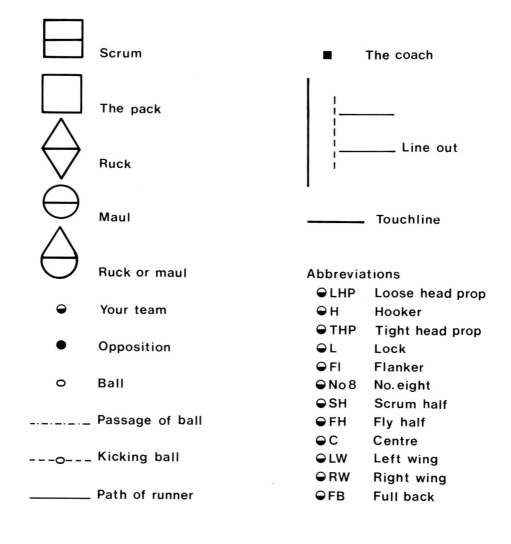

Scrum

The pack

Ruck

Maul

Ruck or maul

Your team

Opposition

Ball

Passage of ball

Kicking ball

Path of runner

The coach

Line out

Touchline

Abbreviations

LHP   Loose head prop
H   Hooker
THP   Tight head prop
L   Lock
FI   Flanker
No 8   No. eight
SH   Scrum half
FH   Fly half
C   Centre
LW   Left wing
RW   Right wing
FB   Full back

PART 1

General Principles

1. Philosophy

ATTITUDE
Concentration; no mistakes
Be positive; go forward

FITNESS
Speed; stamina; strength; suppleness
Mental hardness

POSSESSION
Basics; individual skills
Unit skills; technique
Communication; tighten

PRESSURE
Territorial advantage
Keeping possession
Variety of attacks
Disrupt their possession
Cut down their options
Tight defence

CONTROL
Communal pace
Hang on
Continuity and patience
Discipline

THE BALANCE
Good selection
Decision makers
Flexible tactics
Simplicity
Know your limitations

ATTITUDE

The right mental approach is so important in a game like rugby that depends on other attributes apart from skill. Such qualities as concentration, courage, tenacity, awareness and discipline are highlighted in this game. **Concentration** is probably one of the most important of all the qualities in a game with so many different facets that the team plays as one.

So a player must be mentally prepared for the game and build up in a cool and calculated way. Each player has his own personal approach to this mental preparation so words and actions of leadership must create an atmosphere to sharpen this concentration, focus the mind and emphasize the particular preparation that the game ahead requires.

It is important that each player should be cool from the neck up as he takes the field. Psyching-up is a complete waste of time if it makes a player react in an irrational manner as he starts his game; such an attitude would only last for a few minutes. The player must prepare in a constructive manner and be able to sustain his approach throughout the game. Concentration must continue throughout the game so that each player can perform his specialist role to his full potential.

No mistakes It is essential that a player has the intention of eliminating mistakes in the game ahead. Obviously, mistakes will be made during the course of a game, but the mental approach of cutting down errors will instil a discipline into the player.

Be positive It is very difficult to get the balance right between eliminating mistakes and expanding your game. The limitations of a team and individuals must be assessed and within that framework it is important for the team to try new approaches. This is an attitude of mind.

Go forward All ploys must ultimately go forward even if ground is initially sacrificed. It is important to have this ultimate aim no matter which team has the possession.

FITNESS

The four Ss of speed, stamina, strength and suppleness, added to a mental discipline and hardness, are essential requirements if a player is to prepare properly for the demands of the game.

Speed Quickness off the mark can be put to advantage in ball-getting, attack and defence. It is very difficult to compete against pace.

Quickness of thought is just as important. Quick reactions can secure loose and untidy balls and a realistic team will realize that this type of possession can be well used if coupled with that powerful weapon, the element of surprise.

Reaction to the ball-carrier can sustain many movements that would otherwise have died. This type of support needs physical speed to be near the breakdown or link with the ball-carrier. It needs mental speed to calculate angles of support running and what role to take as a support runner when called upon.

Stamina It is well known that the skill factor breaks down as fatigue sets in, so it is important to postpone this state as long as possible.

A running stamina is required for the demands of support, covering and chasing. Conditioning is also required for the physical contact part of the game. There is also a mental stamina that can be helped by concentration.

Strength Different types of strength are required for the different roles of each team member, but the word, power, which is an explosive strength, makes sure that every team member regardless of position on the field, or size, is involved.

Suppleness Training for the three Ss already mentioned can be hindered in a most marked way if the fourth S is neglected. Some of this training will tend to tighten up the muscles of a player and may possibly result in the loss of manoeuvrability, fluent speed and flexibility. This is sad because only ten minutes a day is necessary to solve this problem. If suppleness exercises are not added to a fitness programme a lot of hard work can be wasted. But perhaps more importantly, suppleness prevents injuries. In rugby, players will find themselves in physical positions that are not normally met in their everyday life, or in other sports.

Mental hardness The psychological limit is always reached before the physiological limit and the gap varies tremendously depending on the dedication and temperament of the individual. A lot of training can be geared to improving the mental discipline of a player and this is important preparation; there is no point in reaching a high standard of physical fitness if the player is not prepared to use it.

The game itself has many stoppages, so it is important for the player to gear his training to improving his recovery rate after exertion. This may be purely wind recovery or physical contact recovery, but he must realize that as rugby is a game of stops and starts, maximum effort is needed when the game is in progress.

It also helps to build up confidence knowing that the background of fitness work has been thorough. This confidence is built on the knowledge that in a game lasting nearly one and a half hours your opponent can be eventually out-paced, out-thought, out-lasted and physically dominated.

POSSESSION

The basics As a pianist would first master his scales and arpeggios and then still practise them as he becomes more advanced, so must a player master the basics and continually 'freshen up' these skills until they become instinctive. Handling, running and kicking skills need constant revision, especially as particular units in a team would have to associate with particular techniques of handling and running. Also, each player will have to adjust his handling, running and kicking skills depending on the situation that he is confronted with.

Individual skills A team has a variety of specialists, some of these widely contrasting, so each player must aim to be a craftsman or tradesman for his particular role. Self-pride should motivate him to learn the skills that his position demands.

Unit skills There are three key words for this section: technique, communication and tighten.

Technique – joint techniques have to be practised in smaller groups, usually to form a collective physical presence, or to work out timing off each other. Support for the ball-carrier is immediately improved.

Communication – liaison between backs and forwards is the first priority; lack of communication within these two groups can be a problem. The more sophisticated a system the more codes can be used, but basically the system needs communication so that all fifteen men are aware of what is being attempted. There is an old rugby saying that it is better for all eight members of the pack to carry out a wrong tactic than four of the pack to do it right while the other four are doing it wrong.

Tighten – Loose play can weaken the advantage of any possession gained. As a forward, if your scrum-half's play is hindered due to scruffy possession you are at fault.

Forwards must be aware that they should never be empty-handed in any situation that involves producing the ball. Mauls should see no daylight between pack members. Rucks should leave the ball neatly for the person who is going to use it. Scrums

5

should be a solid platform, lineouts need sweeping up. Backs and forwards must be aware of wayward passes and adjust their lines of running and weight of pass accordingly.

PRESSURE

Whoever has the ball, pressure on the opposition can force them into errors that should be taken advantage of.

Our possession

Territorial advantage A team should be able to relax more as they play deeper into their opponents' half and be more adventurous because if a mistake is made there should be more chance to recover from that mistake. At the same time, the defenders are probably more tense as they defend closer to their own try-line.

Other factors regarding the opposition must be taken into account before a team decides how to play against them, but gaining territory is certainly a way to keep pressure on the opposition.

Kicking must be varied and accurate if a team wishes to gain ground and pin the opposition in their own half. There is no justification in hopeful kicks by players to give themselves 'thinking time'.

Keeping possession Having the ball should put pressure on the opposition, especially if a team goes forward with this possession, but keeping possession will certainly put on pressure. It is very tiring continually defending, especially if players end up chasing shadows.

Variety of attacks A team must not become predictable as this will help the opposition to get into a rhythm of defence. This should only be accepted if the tactics are to lull the opposition into a false sense of security before the killer stroke. The opposition must be kept guessing and be made to hesitate by the variety of moves they face.

Their possession

Disrupt their possession The aim must be to deny the opposition clean possession. If the opposition gain possession try and make it as untidy as possible and this should make it easier to regain possession.

Cut down their options This means giving the opposition less time and space. An opponent must not have the time and space to decide whether to kick, pass or run at his leisure. The aim must be to make an opponent with the ball jink because he can only do this sideways and no progress is made. However, defensive support is necessary to take advantage of forcing this man sideways. The same can be said about chasing kicks by your own team. Hurrying the catcher can force him into errors. Chasing kicks in pairs is very effective. The aim should be to nip all moves in the bud, which will motivate defenders to fill up space quickly and not allow moves to develop and snowball.

Tight defence A good system of defence needs both plenty of communication and a confidence in your fellow defender to carry out his role. This will frustrate the opposition, and frustration can make them desperate or reckless. It may also make them more limited in their ambitions and easier to cope with. They may even lose confidence in their ability to attack. This defence must be aggressive. There is no room for 'duty' defence because it is easier for the opposition to retain possession. Aggressive defence can produce spilled balls which can be regained.

CONTROL

When you first learn to drive a car there is always the danger that the car is controlling the speed and not you. Rugby is the same: it is easy to run out of control, in attack and defence, through not controlling the pace of the game. A player, unit or team must be in complete charge of a situation by not being rushed in thought or deed.

Communal pace A player must try to avoid being isolated from his support. There are, of course, situations when a player feels that he must pin his ears back and go, but much of an attacking build-up would be more effective if the player controlled his pace and therefore was more balanced to feed the support, beat the man or be tackled on his own terms.

Forwards in particular are closer to each other as a unit, but it follows that the opposition are also closer so it is important to make sure that the ball remains secure, even after physical contact.

Backs can unnecessarily eat up ground in their attacking build-up, meeting the opposition before the thrust has been developed. There are many occasions when a back has to delay his run in order to get the maximum advantage when he receives the ball.

Hang on For pressure on the opposition, never hang off. In attack, hang on. If a player has had physical contact on his own terms he should be balanced enough to stay on his feet. The hanging-on is requested for one to two seconds so that the ball can be presented to the support.

There are different methods of keeping the ball available depending on the way the opposition tries to stop you, but even if the ball is loose there should be the confidence in the support to assist if the first player only has the time to anchor or secure the bobbing ball.

Continuity and patience Once this ball is kept available on contact and is used again, patience is required to keep this control until an opening appears. It is no good a ball-carrier trying to force a gap, it will eventually appear if possession can be retained. If control is maintained in the close-contact work of forwards it is easier to feel where the weaknesses are by probing in different areas against the opposition pack.

Discipline Mental control is required as well as physical control and this includes not giving away penalties. Lack of technique, lack of concentration, frustration, ignorance of laws, fatigue and sheer pressure are factors that contribute towards giving away penalties. Most penalties can and should be avoided.

The ideal of always playing the ball and not the man will bring about a more positive attitude, and remember that you have to be exceptionally tall to stop a penalty!

THE BALANCE

The successful side gets the balance right in their approach and tactics. And the first thing that is required is good selection.

Good selection It is probably a good sign if a team consists of people of differing sizes, heights and shapes. There must be a mixture of different specialists with ball-players and ball-handlers combining. Combinations of players are also necessary.

Decision makers The main decision makers are the No. 8 and the half-backs. One hundred per cent decisions are essential, with confidence being built up because of those decisions.

Flexible tactics It has to be decided: when to keep the ball close or play it wide; when to kick and when to run; when to decoy and when to penetrate; when to vary alignment from deep to flat with

7

other variations; when forwards release the ball as they drive forwards; when to ruck and when to maul.

These decisions can only come naturally if game situations have been presented to the players in practice so that in the game they recognize them and react accordingly.

Simplicity The more complex a move is, the longer time it takes to perform, and this means more scope for mistakes and more time for the defence to cope. The principles are straightforward and simple, so should be the executions.

Know your limitations Knowing the limitations of individuals and team can save embarrassing situations. It is realistic to practise the things in which the players have confidence so these will have a chance of success. Preparations should be thorough and the strengths in a team should be used. Confidence is boosted by thorough preparation.

PART 2

Obtaining Possession

2. Scrums

SCRUMMAGING AS A BASE

The mechanics of scrummaging

The most efficient drive from each player is if it is directed parallel to the ground, so the best place to get the feeling of efficient pushing is to be on the ground.

It is obviously not desirable to start scrummaging eight against eight so the build-up may as well start gradually with a one-against-one situation. This is where it can start on the wrong foot. Forwards push against each other as shown in the photograph and their main concern is keeping their balance and not falling down. This means that a proportion of their effort is concerned with keeping on their feet when in fact their whole effort should be used driving forward parallel to the ground.

... nor this ...

Drill 1 – in pairs
Start facing one another on hands and knees and go through these progressions.
1 See if the players can wiggle their back-sides. This is the easiest way to see if they have an arched back if the movement is coupled with chin as high as possible.

Not this way ...

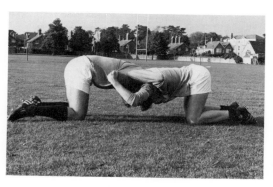

... but this way

2 To emphasize the chin again (which will in turn flex the neck), make the pairs push against each other, still on their hands and knees, and in turn one of the pair will lift the other by pushing up his chin. See the photo below.

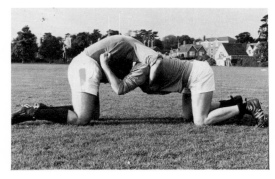

Lifting using the chin

3 One of the pair will lift the other again with his neck by raising his chin, but he will also take his knees off the floor for about 8 cm (3 ins).
4 The pair in contact pushing on their hands and knees will organize a bind on each other that will allow them both to bring their knees off the ground together. Firm feet positions and strong binding are necessary for this strong position. See the photo below.

Binding to lift knees off the ground

Basics

The following basic points would have been emphasized for efficient pushing in the scrum:

1 Arched back
2 Chin up
3 Low knees so low buttocks
4 Strong binding
5 Firm feet positions

Drill 2 – a pack with an opposition pack
Let the pack organize themselves into a scrummage until every member is comfortable. If a member is not comfortable find out why; there is no reason why every member of the pack should not be comfortable.

Drill 3 – a pack with an opposition pack
Let the pack scrummage with the ball left in the tunnel so that both packs have to settle down with equal drive against each other. The coach will say to one pack only one of three words: 'Knees', 'Tighten' or 'Chins'.

On the command 'Knees' the whole pack will be expected to lower their knees and get used to them being slightly off the ground.

On the command 'Tighten' the whole pack will tighten their binding, no matter what their position is. The coach should see the knuckles whiten.

On the command 'Chins' the whole pack will raise their chins and flex their necks.

On each of these commands there should be a positive reaction and drive for the scrum carrying out the actions.

Drill 4 – a pack with an opposition pack
The coach will show the ball at each end of the tunnel when the packs are scrummaging. Every member of the pack should be able to see the ball from his scrummaging position. The coach will then walk around

the opposition pack and every member of the back five of the scrum should be able to see his feet.

Can they see?

The important thing about the back five of the scrum being able to see the feet of the opposing scrum-half in particular, is first of all comfort again, because if the neck can rotate the pressure must be on the shoulders.

Secondly, valuable seconds can be gained if the back five of the scrum break off the scrum when they have possession. There is no need to stand up, look, then go in the direction of the ball. This waste of time can be converted into distance if one second is averaged out as five metres. If the toes of a scrum-half are pointing a certain way there is a very good chance that he will run or pass that way. A five- to ten-metre start by a lock forward to next breakdown could indeed be a bonus.

Binding and feet positions

There is not a recognized standard size for each position in the front five, in fact there are some pretty irregular shapes and sizes that end up in these positions. Therefore, there are going to be variations in binding mainly for physical reasons.

However, apart from the laws, there are some logical reasons why certain positions should stick to guidelines on binding and feet positions.

Problems for a loose-head prop

1 Opposing tight-head will try to split the loose-head prop from his hooker.
2 Opposing tight-head will try to put pressure on the neck of the loose-head.
3 Opposing tight-head will try and dominate the loose-head because he is pushing with one shoulder.

The problem of splitting should be solved by a strong right-arm bind around the hooker. The onus is on the loose-head to force his right shoulder under the hooker's shoulder and pull the hooker as close to him as possible. His grip should be high up and as far around the hooker as possible, not only for a tight bind but also for a straight arm (not bending at the elbow). This will allow his own tight-head to bind below him but also be fairly high himself. This binding cannot be strong if the loose-head is happy to take the 'armpit by-pass', ie to bind outside the right shoulder of the tight-head, escaping any pressure on the neck. The back of the head with the chin up must aim at the sternum in the middle of the chest of the tight-head; only here, or slightly off-centre, can the loose-head be in a pushing position to inconvenience the tight-head.

Head in sternum

Armpit by-pass

Obtaining Possession

To stop the tight-head putting pressure on the neck of the loose-head and for the loose-head to start scrummaging with a straight back, he must 'attack the armpit' with his left arm. The loose-head can then get a good grip on the back of the tight-head with a high elbow action. This is important for two reasons:

(a) The high elbow tenses the shoulder and neck muscles together as the scrummage begins. This will mean that the neck muscles are not taking the weight on their own.

(b) Once the scrummage assembles it is very difficult then to raise the elbow because it is surrounded by tight-head arm and shoulder exerting downward pressure which is mechanically easier. The law demands that the tight-head cannot pull down, but he can still exert this downward pressure that is tiring for the loose-head, because then he has to virtually hold up his opposite number.

This high elbow action should be with a bent arm if the loose-head wants to drive upward as the ball comes in. A straight arm gripping further around the back of the tight-head will ensure a good locking position to make sure that the loose-head is not moved. If he reaches the shorts a better grip is possible, with the chance of pulling and twisting the tight-head round to an ineffective position. The loose-head can also bind on the front of the shorts of the tight-head and lever up as the ball comes in – if the tight-head allows him to do this! The loose-head is also allowed to put his hand on his own knee. This is purely a survival technique because the feet can only be in a position to stop the player falling down and cannot be in an effective position for driving.

Hand on knee

His feet positions are determined by the desire to drive forward and help the hooker channel the ball. His left foot should be far enough back to drive, open up a wide tunnel and be stable. There will be a certain amount of adjusting depending on the priorities for each scrum, but whatever the foot position it is important that the thigh should be perpendicular to the ground so that the flanker can push against it without sliding up past the hip.

His right leg, although he wishes to drive and be stable, is placed where the hooker wants it. The position is determined by channelling and leaving enough space for the hooker to reach across the tunnel. Sometimes the hooker wishes to 'sit on' the loose-head prop's hip, so it is important for the thigh to be further back so that the lock-forward has space to push with his left shoulder (with space for his head). Sometimes the hooker kicks the prop's right foot into position – there is not much conversation in the front row!

Drill 5 – front row with opposition front row
Loose-head prop synchronizes driving upwards as scrum-half puts ball in tunnel.

Drill 6 – front row with opposition front row
Loose-head prop starts with low scrum-

maging, he drives upwards for a few seconds and during this time scrum-half and hooker go through their routine of putting the ball in to strike.

Drill 7 – front row with opposition front row
Consecutive put-ins alternating between channel 1 ball and channel 2 ball, so that the loose-head prop can adjust his right foot.

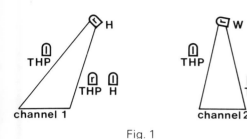

Fig. 1

Problems for a hooker

1 Forced backwards away from the ball.
2 Opposing hooker putting pressure on neck.
3 Opposing tight-head will try and split loose-head prop from hooker.
4 Not being able to get across the tunnel for his own put-in.
5 Only being able to deflect the ball.
6 Not being able to manoeuvre freely.

The hooker should always bind over the top of the shoulders of his two props: it puts him closer to the middle of the tunnel, but also makes it possible to 'hang' his weight over whatever prop he wants. A variation is used, that of binding over the shoulder on the loose-head prop and under the shoulder of the tight-head prop for the hooker's own put-in. This may help the hooker get across the tunnel easier, but he will not have the combined muscles of neck and shoulder on the right-hand side to combat solid scrummaging from the opposition.

The neck will be exposed by the opposition hooker. Even if the hooker is of small build he must not bind under the shoulders of his props. As a demonstration, it can be pointed out as the front row bend down how easy it is to push the hooker back further, by the coach just pushing the shoulders of the hooker alone and just watch him slide back from his props.

The hooker's left arm must have a strong bind on his loose-head prop. As shirts are fairly elastic it is an idea for the hooker to grip the collar (near the V shape) of the loose-head prop. The hooker may even walk around his loose-head prop for a special tight grip.

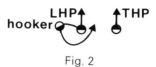

Fig. 2

This strong grip coupled with the loose-head's strong grip should show little gap and the appearance of a two-headed monster! They should act as one, making it very difficult for a tight-head prop to split them.

The hooker cannot expect to have an equally tight grip with both props and, in fact, it is undesirable from the tight-head prop's point of view as well as the hooker. In this section, however, we will only deal with the hooker's problems.

A tight grip on the tight-head prop would hinder progress across the tunnel. It is important to have a grip to satisfy the law, but the closer the hooker is to the tight-head prop, the further he may be from the loose-head prop. Also, for looking down the tunnel, keeping pressure off his neck and turning hips towards the tunnel to assist clean striking, most of the front of the hooker's body will be turned away from the tight-head prop. The only real contact is the hooker's right arm, so it is very much a 'duty bind'.

Obtaining Possession

The feet positions of the hooker are important if the strike is not to become 'wooden', depending on deflection alone. The hooker should be able to get his right foot in a position where the outside of the lower leg is nearly parallel to the ground on the strike and the ball is 'caressed' back with the heel and the lower calf. The hooker can then determine which channel he wants.

Before the strike the hooker should have his feet together as near to the middle of the tunnel as the law allows, but with the weight on his left leg. It is important for him to bind with his hips facing his scrum-half before he goes down to scrummage.

As the scrummage is formed, his right shoulder would exert more pressure on the opposition, and that would mean on the opposition hooker. This twisted position means that he has a good view down the tunnel and with the weight on the left leg, and the opposition hooker providing support for his right shoulder, the hooker's position is stable after the strike.

The hooker must be given a little rectangle to work in and nobody should be pushing against him from his own team. His hips downwards should have no contact whatsoever from any other member of the scrum from both sides.

Drill 8 – hooker pushing against one passive scrummager
Ball is dropped vertically from a metre above the hooker. He strikes and caresses the ball back.

Drill 9 – hooker pushing against one passive scrummager
A tennis ball is dropped vertically as in drill 8. Same action required.

Drill 10 – front row against opposition front row
Rhythm needed from tap signal because of

reaction delay. On the signal, both scrum-half and hooker shout aloud as they put the ball in: 'Tap and strike.' The timing of the 'and' is important as the pause is needed for the scrum-half to react to seeing the tap and putting the ball in.

Drill 11 – front row with opposition front row
Hold front row down low. Signal loose-head to drive up and hold, then give tap signal.

Drill 12 – front row with opposition front row
Be driven back by opposition, come back to mark and then give tap signal.

Drill 13 – front row with opposition front row
Practise rhythm with contact of front rows: 'Contact and strike.' As in drill 10, the timing of 'and' is important because the hooker has to go down into the scrummage in a striking position.

Problems for a tight-head prop

1 Compression from both sides of the scrum.
2 Being twisted around and lifted.
3 Pressure upward on right-hand side of the chest.

There is so much pressure from in front and, hopefully, from behind the tight-head prop that it is important that the basic techniques of scrummaging are understood and implemented as the scrum is being formed. The arched back, low buttocks, chin up and thighs perpendicular to the ground must be in evidence before the pressures of the scrum begin.

The tight-head prop must think all the time of pushing square. If he starts off by trying to get a tight grip on his hooker, there is a danger that his hips will be facing towards the middle of the tunnel and there is a greater chance of him being twisted around. The tight-head prop should have a grip that satisfies the law but allows him to emphasize the left shoulder. Tight-head props used to pull down with the right shoulder, twisting their body at the same time; because of the danger of collapsed scrums this is not allowed now. In fact, this right hand has to be bound on the back of the loose-head now, which can expose the right-hand side and centre of the chest, and there is the possibility of being lifted. So it is even more important to emphasize the left shoulder and put the onus on the loose-head prop to get under the chest of the tight-head. The tight-head can now be driven higher on the right-hand side without feeling that his feet will leave the ground.

With this compression on the tight-head prop, he is dependent on the locks and flankers to keep his hips straight so that he is not twisted around. This will be dealt with later in this chapter, but the tight-head can help himself to square up again by pushing with the right arm to drive the left shoulder and left hip around.

Although the thighs will be perpendicular to the ground, the tight-head's feet can be as far back as he wants, because mechanically it is up to the opposition to hold him up. He should take advantage of this and use his feet position to transmit shove from behind and drive himself.

Drill 14 – a tight-head prop against 2 opposition
The tight-head packs against the other 2 opposition. He dips his hips and knees to drive upward, making sure that his back is arched throughout. Continue this for 4 or 5 drives.

Drill 15 – a tight-head prop against 2 opposition
The tight-head prop lets the opposition

push against him, enough to bend his back and lower his chin. He then drives upward to straighten his back and raise his chin. Continue for 4 or 5 drives.

Drill 16 – all front row players in pairs
The opposition twist one of the other prop's shoulders downwards with enough resistance to make the prop work hard to rotate his shoulders back to a square position again. Trunk and lower back rotation will be required to bring the prop to a square position again. See the photos below.

Twisting the shoulders: back view

Twisting the shoulders: front view

Problems for a lock

1 Lack of tightness with fellow lock.
2 Packing too high by riding up back of prop.

3 Not being able to get head between hooker and prop.

4 Holding own prop in.

5 Holding own prop down.

As the name suggests, these two men must lock the scrum together, so they must be tight together themselves. There is a school of thought that suggests that the locks should grab each other's shorts for a tight position but in fact nothing could be worse, for a variety of reasons.

The drive, holding on to the shorts, pushes forward the inside shoulders. These would push against the hooker and he does not want his movement hindered by contact of this sort. One of the lock's jobs is to tighten up the front row. If they are not tight themselves at the point of contact they cannot affect the front row. Also, locks are usually different heights. If there is tight contact at the shoulders the shoulders are in one line and only the No. 8 has to make his own arrangements. The final reason affects the No. 8, who will be the last to go down so he must find it easy to slot his head into the gap between the hips of the locks. If the 'hinge' of the locks is at the shoulder, the No. 8 will find it easy to pull open their hips, place his head there and pull back the hips.

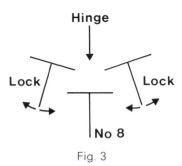

Fig. 3

The right-hand lock should bind under the armpit or even further around the body of his fellow lock, over the shoulder of his fellow lock. The left-hand lock should also bind under the armpit or further round the chest, but obviously under the arm of the right-hand lock. The reason for this affects the hooker again. The right-hand lock will be slightly twisted, with his right shoulder lower than his left because he will be looking down the tunnel; the left-hand lock will be squarer but emphasis will be on his left shoulder. (This is to make sure that the hooker is not touched.)

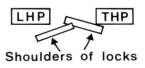

Shoulders of locks

Fig. 4

This will also help solve the problem of the locks getting their heads in the gap between prop and hooker, but this has to be coupled with the height at which the locks are prepared to scrummage. The props have to scrummage with thighs perpendicular to the ground to help the locks and flankers transmit their shove. The locks and flankers should push with their shoulders at the top of the thighs. Any lower and there is too much pressure on the knee. It should be difficult to slide up any higher when the lock pushes against the top of the thigh, because even props have rounded buttocks especially made so locks and flankers cannot pack any higher if they start in the right place.

Another of the lock's duties is to bind the prop in and stop his hips drifting out, and also to keep the prop on the ground if the opposition front row decide to drive upward. The tight binding of the lock's inside arms helps and if each lock aims at both his arms pulling inwards towards himself, with correct binding, the problem of the props' hips drifting out should be solved. For really effective pulling in of the prop the locks should bind on the outside hips of the props. Unfortunately, most locks are not really strong enough to hold this position so they opt for the more compact style of binding between the props' legs. Another argument put forward against packing on the outside hip of the prop is that there is no pushing space for the flanker, but if the elbow of the lock is held high, not only is there a guideline for the flanker to aim at driving under, but the high elbow helps the lock to pull inwards.

Not this way . . .

Lock binding outside hip – elbow high

. . . but this way

If the locks do bind between the props' legs, there is no need to hang on to the shorts or shirt in the middle. The aim is to keep the prop in as well as holding the prop down, and a high elbow with the arm wrapped around the leg until the fingers are in the pocket of the props' shorts has a dual-purpose role. Locks should remember to **bind round not down**.

Both feet should be well back and both in a position for driving. The only reason for a foot to be under the lock's body would be to hold the body up. This would be such a waste, because correct binding would ensure this anyhow. From a negative point of view – if the knees are 8 cm (3 ins) from the ground and if the lock feels insecure about packing so low, he only has to drop a little way to the secure position of being on his knees before he steadies himself again.

The feet can be splayed sideways for greater surface area with the ground and the chance to dig the heels in. This can be useful if the pack is 'locking out', but the legs with the inside of the knee facing the ground are in no position to drive forward and upward. It is also difficult to get the thighs perpendicular to the ground, so the No. 8 would be in a worse position not only for pushing but also for driving off the scrum in attack or defence. Pushing off the sole of the boot puts all the drive in one line, and this counter-drive is probably the best way to deal with the drive from the opposition.

Problems for the flankers

1 Helping keep own props from drifting out.
2 Protecting scrum-half.

3 Seeing the ball in the set scrum.
4 Getting off the scrum quickly.

Flankers generally do not realize how important they are, by stopping their own prop from drifting out at the hips. They must remember that they each have one whole buttock to push against (if they pack 3-4-1), which is no less than the locks. The only advantage that the lock has is stronger binding on the prop and an attitude of mind that this facet of the game is important to them. This is also coupled with a loyalty to the scrum-half who the flanker feels he must protect. If the flanker feels that the best way to shield his scrum-half is by packing at an angle and hoping that his passive hips are going to protect the scrum-half, his scrummaging will be less effective and could be a hindrance.

By binding with the lock and pulling in with his inside arm, this tight binding with his lock will allow him to keep in the hip of the prop with the side of his face. This can be more helpful to the prop if he goes down at the same time as the locks. It is one of those aspects of the game when the flankers *have* to say that there are four players in the second row of each pack, and they should go down together.

It is also good protection for the scrum-half because the left flanker in particular can be an important contributor to the channelling by pushing straight. So any ball that inadvertently comes out of channel 1, he can control when it comes out or push it across for channel 2, which *really protects the scrum-half.*

By binding strongly with the inside arm and resting the outside arm with the knuckle-bent joints of fingers on the ground, the flanker should be low enough to see up the tunnel and study the feet of the opposition. Boots and socks have their own distinctive markings, and a flanker should be able to identify the positions of the opposition before the game is very old.

This means that he can use his 'sprint start' position off the scrum to advantage most of the time, as he is able to drive forward from this low stable position. There are, of course, times when he will want to stand off the scrum and wait, but this position with the outside arm on the ground should not be wasted as it puts pressure on the opposition by driving forward.

Problems for a No. 8

1 Not being able to transmit shove.
2 Not being able to get head in scrum.
3 Not breaking up quickly enough.

The No. 8 forward should not worry about transmitting shove because the power would be soaked up by the locks and props before it reached the opposition. With a good body position and firm base he can become a good 'starting block' for his locks to drive off. If he sees himself in this role, he will concentrate on good positional technique.

Low buttocks – knees low – arched back – chin up are particularly important because the locks should already be in this low position and they can drive off the No. 8.

The feet should be well back but slightly more apart so as to get into a position to control the ball when it is channelled.

If the locks bind with each other high up at the shoulders, the No. 8 should have no problem grabbing the outside pockets on the shorts and pulling their hips open to slot his head into the gap. This binding by the No. 8 around the hips of the locks should also ensure that the No. 8 can break away quickly and see the progress of the ball in the scrum for and against the head.

OTHER IMPORTANT POINTS IN THE MECHANICS OF SCRUMMAGING

Distance apart of front rows

The locks and flankers are expected to have their heads and shoulders in position before the front row go down. All seven should be bound together before they go down to scrummage; only the No. 8 can justify having a final look at the situation before the ball is put into the scrum. Locks and flankers will start on their knees, so it is important for the front row to be a consistent set distance away from the opposition before every scrum. The front row could use an arm's length as a guideline so the locks and flankers can adjust from their kneeling position before the scrum forms to a driving position when the scrum forms. This means that feet positions can be dug into before the scrum forms.

The hooker is not important for scrum mechanics

There is no shove transmitted through the hooker, except for an 8-man shove.

Find the hooker

Drill 17 – a pack with an opposition pack
Let the two packs scrummage. When they are steady, one hooker lets go his binding

and crawls out of the scrummage. It will be seen that the two packs minus one hooker can carry on with the scrummage, despite the hole in the middle!

Confidence in the binding

For the bullet-style sprint start in athletics, a basic test to make sure that the weight is over the arms is to knock an arm away. The athlete should fall over because the legs are only in a position for driving parallel to the ground. The scrummager should have the same confidence in his binding to hold himself in position so that the powerful legs can be used exclusively for driving forward. Hips should be used more for lowering the body or getting under an opponent, and if the thighs are perpendicular to the ground, the scrummagers packing behind are not disrupted by this lowering action.

Driving on your own ball

The hooker wants a steady scrum, but a nudge on his own ball should soak up any pressure from the opposition. The scrum naturally wheels to the left, because of the duties of the loose-head prop in particular lifting up to maintain a clear tunnel. The opposition tight-head is in the ideal viewing position to time any exaggeration of the wheel by pulling the loose-head on. So it is even more important for the tight-head prop to realize that a drive on his side may stop the natural wheel and retard the manufactured wheel created by the opposition. Obviously, the right-hand lock and flanker must follow suit. The tap signal between hooker and scrum-half makes it difficult to time a drive, but it also makes it difficult for the opposition as well. Studying your own scrum-half in action should help timing.

The double shove

With 2 evenly-matched sides, the initial drive from both packs is soaked up by the other side. The effective drive is the second one with the ball at the No. 8's feet. There is the element of surprise, also the chance that the opposing back row would have detached by then, making the second drive easier. This can also take the pressure off the backs because the back row will be less willing to fly off the scrum if they know that the pack may attempt a double shove. The hooker or No. 8 should call the timing of this second shove.

The hooker is in an ideal position to feel when the pressure from the opposition pack is off. The disadvantage is that he cannot tell if the ball has been properly controlled at the base of the scrum. The No. 8 is the one who knows when (and if) the ball is controlled so the timing of the shove could come from him. The No. 8 calling seems to have better reasons.

Locking out

This is a desperation tactic to be used if a pack is hopelessly dominated by opposition drive. The props place their feet as far back as possible, but they must remember that the thigh must be near the perpendicular to the ground or the 4 pack members in the second row cannot assist. The locks and flankers can place their feet so far back that the legs and back are in one continuous line. The No. 8 does not have an ideal base to work off and in this case he may feel happier binding on the inside legs of the locks.

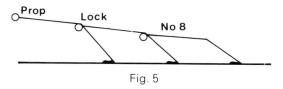

Fig. 5

Driving on their ball

Houdini used to flex his muscles as the chains were put on him. As he disappeared from view he relaxed his muscles and the chains loosened, making it easier to slip them off. The drive against the opposition ball is a concerted forward and upward drive by 8 men. The comparison with Houdini is that a pack should go down in a scrum with flexed muscles. Once the scrum is bound, relax those muscles, even have slightly bent backs, and flex the muscles again as the ball comes in. This will give a greater range for driving.

It must also be remembered that an 8-man shove is not a 7- or even 7½-man shove with the hooker thinking that he can sneak a ball against the head. Apart from his contribution to the drive, especially the upward movement, it means that the locks can push with both shoulders from a square position.

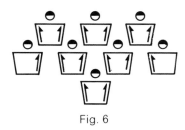

Fig. 6

Another method of 8-man shove involves different feet positions by the front row to help drive upwards.

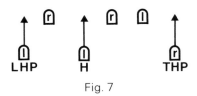

Fig. 7

The inside feet of the props and the right foot of the hooker are ahead of their other feet.

The props take a step forward as the ball comes in and that helps to raise the shoulders. The hooker can work in unison with the tight-head prop and place his left foot in a possible deflection position, if the opposing hooker cannot strike.

Drill 18 – a pack with an opposition pack
Put in for opposition pack. Get all the other pack to shout as they drive. On the parade ground you can always tell what the soldiers' reaction is going to be like by the way the commands are barked out: a crisp command will get a crisp reply. Similarly the coach can tell what the drive is going to be like by the tone of the shout: the more aggressive the shout, the more aggressive the drive.

Scrum formations

The most common formation these days is the 3-4-1. The main advantages are that the props have more support and channelling is helped. These two factors must be remembered when experimenting with different formations to release moves at the base of the scrum. Good back-row moves depend on a good front row. They must be able to hold firm.

If the front row can take the pressure, different formations can be useful for attacking and defensive moves, and they will be mentioned later in this chapter.

Wheeling the opposition

The aim is to isolate the opposition scrum-half from his fly-half, not to isolate your back row from their half-backs. So if the path of the ball from left to right wants to be handicapped, a wheeled scrum is useful. It can stop the path of scrum-half to fly-half, scrum-half to blind-side wing, back row moves going right, so there is no par-

ticular side of the field where it is more appropriate. Scrums naturally wheel to the left anyway.

The mechanics of wheeling are straightforward. As their loose-head drives on his ball, the tight-head pulls him onto him, stepping back. The right-hand lock and flanker also allow this stepping-back and the other side of the pack at least holds firm. It is important for the back row to detach, especially the right flanker and No. 8. If they don't, only the scrum-half is there to counter any alternative attack by the opposition.

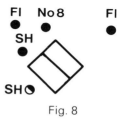

Fig. 8

Wheel and drive
Opposition packs often counter wheeling by breaking off through the back row, or by feeding the scrum-half standing back. This takes time to set up, so a wheel and drive can be effective as they are organizing themselves.

The lock-forward is probably the best to call this difficult timing because he has to adjust his feet from wheeling to driving. After the initial wheel, the left-hand side of the scrum has just held firm and will be ready for the drive quicker than the right-hand side, who have been stepping back. Obviously they must not wait too long or the opposition will have organized themselves, so a good rhythm is needed: 'Wheel, wait, and drive', the rhythm being as long as it takes to say the phrase. The drive will be sideways across the pitch, which should be disruptive.

Obtaining Possession

Countering the wheel

The loose-head prop cannot stop himself being pulled round unless he can anticipate that the opposition are going to wheel. If he guesses wrongly he could be pulling back himself when the opposition have decided to drive. That could be embarrassing. The tight-head could retard the wheel by driving, giving the back row more time to organize. A list of alternatives is necessary.

1 The No. 8 drives off, as the scrum is still turning. This can be most penetrating if it is possible because the opposition back row have been swung round initially. The reason it is not possible most times is that the strike has not reached the No. 8's feet in time.

2 No. 8 calls right-hand flanker. The scrum has been turned through 90 degrees, the No. 8 calls the right flanker to drive into him as he picks up the ball like a rolling maul, or the No. 8 pops up a pass to the flanker coming round.

3 Packing 3–3–2. The No. 8 packing on the left calls the right flanker who is packing in the usual No. 8 position.

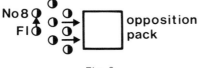

Fig. 9

This is the same move as in 2 above but it can be quicker for two reasons: the No. 8 is packing between the left flanker and left lock so the quicker channel-1 ball can be used; the right flanker has his feet at the same level as the No. 8 so he does not have to wait for the No. 8 to break first as the hindmost feet of the scrum.

4 The scrum-half stands back to take a pass from the No. 8.

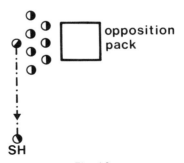

Fig. 10

The scrum-half has to stand directly behind because the No. 8 will be tackled as soon as he touches the ball, so he will not have time to look for his scrum-half. Therefore the scrum-half must be in the same place relative to the No. 8 every time.

5 As the scrum wheels, the tight-head prop turns inwards.

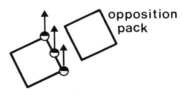

Fig. 11

The tight-head has to be strong enough to turn inwards after the wheel and face up the field again. He will then drive, still attached to his own front row, who will detach from their opposite number or take them along. The ball will still be in the scrum, the pack will walk forward with it and the opposition pack will be in disarray.

Drill 19 – a pack against an opposition pack. Let the pack have their own put-in for 8 scrums. The opposition work out a sequence of drives or wheels: let us say, 1st 4th, 5th and 7th are wheels, 2nd, 3rd, 6th and 8th are drives. The pack with the put-ins has to react to each scrum and either counter the drive or work off the wheel.

If you have to collapse, collapse properly

Quite rightly, the law committees have tried to eliminate the collapsed scrum with heavy penalties. It had reached an alarming state when it was being used as a tactic by club and international sides; schoolboys tried to mimic their adults and because they lacked the physical attributes to carry out techniques, frightening neck injuries resulted. So it is a duty to put forward some guidelines if a player **cannot help** collapsing:

1 Try to keep chin up high throughout.
2 Try to hang on to binding of opposite number if in the front row.
3 Don't spreadeagle, try to go down on knees.
4 Try to keep hips below level of shoulders.
5 Stop driving forward if men in front of you have collapsed.

FORWARD UNIT SKILLS

Back-row moves

For most back-row moves to be successful the scrum must remain square or, ideally, wheeling slightly to the right to shield the move from the opposition back row.

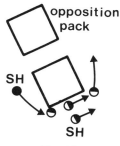

Fig. 12

Most back-row moves go to the right. It is the natural running path of the scrum-half, which would also mean running away from the most dangerous opponent of back-row moves, the opposing scrum-half. Dangerous because he can follow the ball through the scrum so is naturally closer when it comes out.

There is little time available once the ball is released, so the simpler the move the more chance there is of getting across the gain line. The main runners are the scrum-half and the No. 8. The right-hand flanker is useful as a support or a pivot.

Any scrum close to their goal-line on the right-hand side of the post should create a 2 against 1 situation if the blind-side winger is included. The important factor when working out back-row moves is that there are two or three options with every move. The following examples are only shown because they have options. The circumstances will determine which option is used.

1 No. 8 pick up.

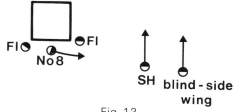

Fig. 13

a) feed scrum-half outside him
b) feed flanker inside him
c) feed blind-side wing outside him
d) feed flanker standing off (after packing 3-3-2)
e) feed scrum-half standing off
f) dummy and go himself

2 Scrum-half run.

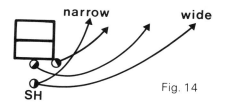

Fig. 14

25

Obtaining Possession

a) feed No. 8 inside him
b) feed flanker inside him
c) feed blind-side wing inside scissors
d) feed blind-side wing outside
e) feed flanker standing off as support
   (after packing 3–3–2)
f) dummy and go himself

3 Right-hand flanker as pivot – packing 3–3–2.

Fig. 15

The pivot takes one step towards the opposition, purely to interest them, not to make contact.

a) Pivot back to scrum-half outside him
b) Pivot inside to No. 8
c) Pivot out to blind-side wing
d) Scrum-half misses pivot and passes straight to blind-side wing

Formation to protect scrum-half run

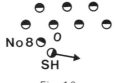

Fig. 16

Quick channel and maximum protection by No. 8 allows scrum-half to run this ball.

Back row moves going left

Because players are meeting the opposing scrum-half, moves going left are difficult, but if they are successful the element of surprise gives more penetration.

The wheeled scrum can force the back-row moves already mentioned. A 3–3–2

formation can manufacture a wheel for the attacking side.

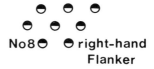

Fig. 17

The right-hand flanker blocks off the No. 8 and the left-hand flanker does the same on the other side. A pop-up pass from this base to the right-hand lock gives him a chance to drive forward.

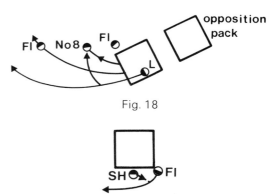

Fig. 18

Fig. 19

The scrum-half feeds the right-hand flanker going left.

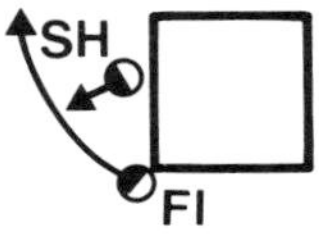

Fig. 20

The scrum-half takes channel 1 ball right away and feeds the left-hand flanker packing 3–3–2, ie packing on the lock.

The problem with back row moves going left without a wheel is finding options. The element of surprise is the only real weapon on this side.

Defence from scrums

Always work on a system that there must be two men on each side instantly ready for any attack from the base of the scrum or the half-backs, on their put-in.

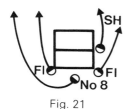

Fig. 21

A pincer on the first man with men going forward on him to cut down his options is better than hanging off and waiting for him. This does not mean that the back row cannot detach if it is a slow ball, as long as they go forward into the tackle once the ball has emerged from the scrum.

Defence against back-row moves

Quick ball opposition going right from their scrum. The left-hand flanker takes the first man. The No. 8 takes the second man.

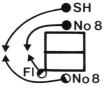

Fig. 22

Quick ball opposition going left from their scrum. The scrum-half takes the first man. The right-hand flanker takes the second man; or, if the scrum-half has been caught up, the right-hand flanker takes the first man. The No. 8 takes the second man.

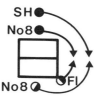

Fig. 23

Delayed ball. If the ball has been held in the back row, the No. 8 will have time to push out the flanker and take the first man himself. There are two main advantages. First, the two defence as a pair tend to 'psych out' the first runner as a penetrator. Secondly, the flanker is usually the quicker man and can be more useful covering the wider spaces if the opposition decide to move the ball.

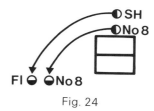

Fig. 24

Defence against half-backs

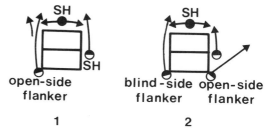

Fig. 25

The pincer on the scrum-half is important no matter which way the scrum-half means to pass the ball. The left-hand flanker and the scrum-half must make the scrum-half their first target (Fig. 25 (1)). Only if the ball is delayed coming out of the scrum can the No. 8 take the scrum-half and push the flanker further out.

The right-hand flanker can be prepared to fly out to the backs if the ball is passed on his side (Fig. 25 (2)) because their scrum-half should not be able to cut back with his opposing scrum-half marking him closely.

The pushover try

The pushover try differs from the 8-man shove and the double shove because the element of surprise is lost. The opposition usually expect the pushover try as one of the attacking options because of the position of the scrum on the field of play.

Again, an upward lift by the attacking front row would be required when the drive came. If this drive came immediately after the ball was heeled, a dominant pack could afford to keep the ball at the feet of the locks to drive over the line. However, this is not recommended for two reasons. First, from the safety point of view, the lock dropping on the ball to actually score the try would leave the front row and his fellow lock in an unstable position. A counter shove by the opposition could injure any of the attacking pack. Secondly, when the ball is over the try line, anybody can dive on the ball, either to score a try or save a try. The ball at the feet of the attacking lock is easier and closer for the opposition to save a try, especially the defending scrum-half who can follow the path of the ball and is, of course, not binding.

It is important to get the ball to the attacking No. 8's feet by a channel where the ball is not impeded en route. This means that the No. 8 could control the ball over the line off an initial shove or hold the ball waiting for a second shove. This also

gives the No. 8 time to note how the opposition have reacted to this pressure. If the opposition seem to be holding the drive, the attacking pack can continue to hold the ball, hoping that the defensive pack will detach its back row covering a No. 8 pick-up and drive or a scrum-half run for the line. If the defensive back-row do detach, obviously yet another drive is possible against less men in the opposing pack.

If the defensive flankers and No. 8 are determined to 'dig in' and help stop the pushover try, a slick back-row move or scrum-half break could finish the job. The attackers must also observe how much the defensive mid-field have been dragged towards the scrum. A threequarter over-lap situation is another possibility on the open or the blind side.

While these observations and decisions are being made by the No. 8 and scrum-half, the positioning of the scrum-half is important. The No. 8 with the ball at his feet does not want to be hampered by the opposing scrum-half, so the attacking scrum-half must stand to the left of the scrum, shielding the opposing scrum-half from the attacking No. 8 and also being in a position to pick up and drive himself.

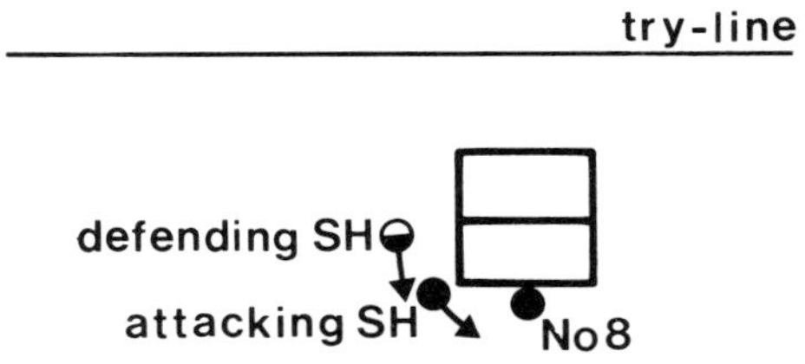

try-line

Fig. 26

When opposing a pushover try it is important for the flankers to stay down, but make sure that they are in a position to see the ball at the No. 8's feet of the attacking scrum. The defending flankers must be prepared to dive on the ball if it goes over the try-line, especially the left-hand flanker who will not be impeded by the attacking scrum-half.

If the ball is released the left-hand side defending flanker must drive forward and take the first man with the ball, hoping to drive him backwards or spill the ball. The defending scrum-half will already be in a position to disrupt and complete a pincer on the attacking No. 8 and scrum-half.

3. Rucks and Mauls

How and when to ruck and maul

It is unfortunate to hear a side say that they are a rucking side or that they are a mauling side. There are many situations of ball-getting in a match when one would logically ruck or one would logically maul, and a side must decide instantly what is required for each situation. Fortunately, most of the general principles required are the same for ruck and maul.

General principles for both ruck and maul

Both need:

1 A focal point
2 A solid base
3 Good body position
4 To stay on feet
5 To keep driving legs after contact
6 To never go in empty-handed
7 No daylight between team-mates when performing the mechanics
8 To 'take out' opposition fringes
9 To continue to drive forward as the ball is presented

The main differences between the ruck and maul

1 On approaching the focal point
for the ruck: use outstretched arms – wide shoulders
for the maul: burrow in for the ball – narrow shoulders

2 Body position
for the ruck: all backsides end up facing their own half-backs
for the maul: some backsides will be facing opposition, in particular the initial ball-carrier.

3 Going beyond the ball
for the ruck: the focal point with ball will be by-passed and left for somebody to pick up
for the maul: the focal point with ball will be by-passed, bound on and 'blocked off' only if the area is heavily populated. As the ball is played wider, the focal point is then driven into by the first man.

Clutch and accelerator

For changing gear, as the accelerator pedal is driven forward, the clutch pedal is brought backwards.

For rucking and mauling to be efficient, it is so important for the ball-winning side to continue driving as the ball is being presented. So many promising ball-getting situations are wasted because the pressure is taken off as the half-backs are given the ball, and the opposition have a chance to adjust their position and set up a defence. This does not only apply to the defending players involved in the ruck and maul. The outside defence have to readjust if only to stay in an onside position, so the more the defence can be forced back on their heels, the more the attack can use this type of ball in a running way.

The players must be sensitive to the 'clutch and accelerator' situation, that the best use of the ball will be when it is laid back *as* they are driving forward. Players must also be sensitive to the fact that a static maul produces neat, methodical but slow ball with the opposition set up in their starting blocks ready to knock the backs over. The static maul has to generate a forward drive or a drive around the fringes, or the ball presented has to be kicked.

The basic mechanics of ruck and maul are the same

So for the practices, the only real difference between the ruck and the maul is that the ball is at a different level.

When to ruck and when to maul

As a general guideline:

Backsides facing own scrum-half = ruck.
Backsides facing opposition = maul.

THE RUCK

Focal point

The ball must be static so that the ball-getters, who will be coming from varying distances and angles, have something to home in on.

Drill 20 – 4 attackers, 4 defenders

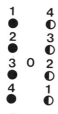

Fig. 27

4 attackers and 4 defenders, each having an allotted number, line up against each other

with the ball in the middle. A number is called and the 2 players with that number dive on the ball to secure it. If the player has time he can 'persuade' it back, if not he secures the ball and steadies it. It must be pointed out that he must release the ball as soon as he is touched by the opposition. But, he is quite entitled to initially dive on that ball because he has not been tackled and the ball is loose. He must, however, play the ball immediately.

Drill 21 – the pack
The coach dribbles the ball in all directions and nominates one man to fall on the ball and steady it. The rest of the pack drive over it, remembering to loop around the ball if it is secured behind them.

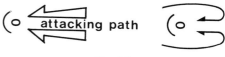

attacking path

Fig. 28

Solid base

It is easier to ruck with opposition than without opposition because they become your solid base. The opposition must be used to help the attacking side keep their balance and if possible set up an instant set scrum.

Drill 22 – attacking pack, defending pack

The defenders form an arrowhead formation and remain upright. The ball is placed 10 metres in front of them. The coach calls numbers to the attacking side as they are waiting lying on their fronts. This will ensure that the pack arrives at different times as in a game situation.

An example: Shout 7 – pause – shout 5, 2 – pause – shout GO – the remaining five follow.

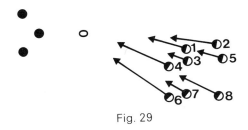

Fig. 29

The first man (No. 7 in the example) picks up the ball but dives to the ground 2 metres from the opposition.

The next two (numbers 5 and 2 in the example) drive past the ball (the first there taking the far side of ball) and into the upright opposition, forming a solid base for the following 5 to add to the drive. Different numbers are shouted for each situation.

Make sure that the attacking pack runs from an angle, so that driving in parallel to the touchline can be emphasized.

Good body position

Players realize that they have to drive low, but most of them 'swallow in' from about a metre away; this is ineffective. They must pick their spot from 5 metres away and get used to running in the position that they hope to be in on impact. This is where the outstretched arms (or wide shoulders) are so important. It helps the player keep his balance and also gives him the opportunity to bind with a team-mate as they converge on the same focal point.

Players should aim at gaps between opponents at rib level, because the upward drive that is required for this level should off balance the opposition if they come in too high. Ideally the shoulders make contact with the ribs, but the player cannot get away from the fact that his head will be in front of his shoulders. So if the head has to make contact first it makes sense to hit something relatively soft and the midriff and rib areas seem more inviting.

The head position is particularly important because the neck is vulnerable. The chin must be up so that the player's neck is tensed. The player can also see what he is aiming at!

Drill 23 – the pack
One man jogs slightly ahead of the other 7. On the command 'RUCK ON' the front man braces himself and the others converge on him usually in a 2-3-2 formation. They continue driving him for 5 metres and must stay on their feet. Another man then jogs slightly ahead of the other 7 and the sequence starts again.

Stay on feet

It seems a strange thing to say, but the main reason why players cannot stay on their feet is because they watch the ball!

A player can start off with the right body position and drive in a determined and powerful way, but as soon as he by-passes the ball he looks at it, which means that he has to dip a shoulder. This puts him off balance and he falls over. So the message is: concentrate on the mechanics of rucking and forget about the ball.

Drill 24 – a pack and an opposing pack

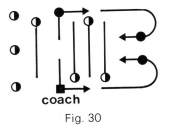

coach

Fig. 30

The working pack link in pairs to drive over 4 parallel prostrate bodies before making contact with 3 upright opposition at the other end. Their footwork will be good because the prostrate bodies will soon tell them if it isn't. Their body position will be good because the coach with an assistant will be travelling in the opposite direction with an outstretched inside arm to catch anybody who is not driving in a low enough position.

Drive legs

Players either forget to continue driving when impact is made or feel that the energy used would be of little significance. Short paces with an upward drive by all of the pack would find out the areas that the opposition are 'laying on of hands' and, in most cases, even if the ball did not emerge, the set scrum would be awarded to the side going forward, and most sides should depend on getting their own ball from the set scrum.

Drill 25 – in threes
2 men bind loosely and wander walking in different lateral directions. The other man drives between them, binding on and forcing them back 5 metres by pumping his legs. So that he has to use his legs, he must never start more than a metre away from the pair.

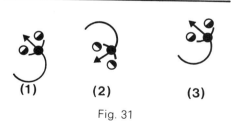

Fig. 31

Because of the lateral wanderings of the pair, it is important to emphasize that the drive is always parallel to the touchline.

The impact should always be to the front of the practice opposition, because the practice opposition is usually upright and a drive into the back tends to rick the back or strain a muscle because the impact is not expected. At least from the front the opposition can jack-knife to cushion the blow.

Drill 26 – in pairs
From 3 metres away, drive into a man who will tackle passively in an upright position. Drive him initially, put the ball on the ground and continue driving. See photos below and overleaf.

Drive into upright man . . .

. . . who will tackle passively

Put the ball on the ground . . .

. . . and continue driving

By-pass ball

Ideally, it would be nice to step over the ball with one pace, set up a solid base and heel the ball when the others arrive and bind. Unfortunately, this is spoilt by the opposition who seem to have the same idea. So if a team aim to set up a base one metre past the ball, they will end up 3 metres be-

hind it. If they aim 5 metres past the ball, they will then end up 1 metre past the ball. It is a much more healthy approach. It also means that the ball is left for the scrum-half and does not have to be heeled, which would weaken the forward drive position.

Drill 27 – the pack with 6 opposition

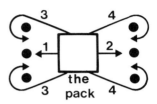

Fig. 32

The pack have to instantly react to one of four of the coach's orders: 'RUCK LEFT'; 'RUCK RIGHT'; 'RUCK BEHIND LEFT'; 'RUCK BEHIND RIGHT'.

The pack drive the 3 upright opposition for 3 metres and return to the middle. Body lean, binding and driving have to be organized instantly, but also emphasize head and neck position.

Opposition will always face the contact.

Drill 28 – the pack with opposing pack

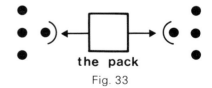

Fig. 33

Another motivation for a pack to by-pass the ball is to 'expose' any opposition flopping over and killing the ball.

One opposition in turn flops on the ball with the other 3 upright behind the ball. He flops on the ball as soon as he hears the coach call 'RUCK LEFT' or 'RUCK RIGHT' to the pack. The pack will drive over the flopping man then continue driving into the 3 upright opposition.

Never be empty-handed

Forwards have to be continually nagged about grabbing shirts in all aspects of possession-seeking. It is the simplest way of tidying up possession before the ball is presented to the scrum-half.

A forward cannot be fussy about whom he grabs, his team-mate or opposition, when there are a lot of people in close proximity, but he must be sensitive to being empty-handed in those situations. Apart from his own strength he must develop techniques of grabbing that ensure that the elbows are close to his own body, a short lever is stronger than a longer one.

If players remembered never to go in empty-handed there would be less scrappy play, and scrum-halves, referees and spectators would be more grateful. If a scrum-half is caught in possession his own pack should wince; it is an attitude of mind.

Drill 29 – a pack with 2 opponents

Fig. 34

The pack grab shirts, *not* link arms, and the 2 opponents try to break out. (The reason for grabbing shirts is to test grip strength which needs power from fingers, wrists and forearm.)

The opposition do not try to crawl through their legs.

Drill 30 – a pack and 3 opponents

Fig. 35

All players weave in and out in a restricted area. On a command, the 3 opponents try and escape from that area but should be grabbed by the pack and held in.

No daylight

Instant binding and driving tends to overcome this problem, but players must be sensitive to being too loose, for the opposition will try and exploit any gaps that exist and also try and sabotage your possession.

Probably the best way to get this message across is to set up the opposition in a loose way and let the pack take advantage of their looseness.

Drill 31 – a pack and 4 opponents
One opposition has the ball, the other 3 opponents stand fairly close to him. The pack drive low and knock the ball from his hand to the floor. Depending on how wide the ball bounces, the pack either dive on the ball to secure it and drive over it, or instantly drive over the loose ball, binding and taking all 4 opponents with them.

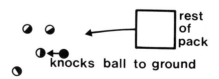

Fig. 36

Drill 32 – a pack and 4 opponents
The 4 opponents stand fairly close to each other passing the ball to each other, as if it is a hot potato. Forward passes are permitted. On a command, the pack get in amongst them as the opposition continue this hot-potato passing. Inevitably, the ball will go loose and the pack will react as in Drill 31.

Take out fringers

One advantage for the wide-shoulder position and never going in empty-handed, is that fringers who are hanging off the sides can be swallowed up into the existing ruck. The edges are tidied up and it gives latecomers a specific role. The weakness is that the ruck then becomes too lateral without the depth to give it its powerful thrust forward. Latecomers have a decision to make on what is more important: take out the fringers on the side of the ruck, or drive on to the existing ruck.

Drill 33 – a pack and 5 opposition
Make the pack come from an angle but end up driving parallel to the touchline, collecting up upright opposition en route.

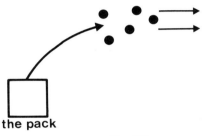

the pack

Fig. 37

THE MAUL

Focal point and solid base

Players should be able to make the decision whether they are going to drive into the ball-carrier initially, to transfer the focal point, or 'block off' the ball-carrier and allow the next man to transfer the focal point. Their decision should be determined by how heavily populated the area is at the time. If the ball-carrier is in relatively wide open spaces, it makes sense to drive in on him and transfer the ball quickly giving the support so many more options. If the opposition are in a position not only to hinder the initial ball-carrier but to get at the support as well, it would be better to block off the ball carrier so the transfer can buy time to work out the ball.

As a general rule, if forwards are confronting forwards the ball-carrier would be expected to be blocked off first. If any threequarter is involved the ball-carrier can be driven into first, to transfer the ball.

The important thing to emphasize with both methods is that the ball must only be transferred through the one pair of hands. Once the ball goes through more than one pair of hands, the initial impact of the drive will be lost.

Drill 34 – a pack with an opposing pack
The coach holds a ball and wanders in and out of the attacking pack. He places the ball in the stomach of one of the attackers. He is immediately blocked off and the fourth man drives in on the ball-carrier to transfer the ball, the rest of the pack pick their positions to drive. The opposition try to get at the ball, but with the initial advantage that the coach has given the attacking pack this should not be possible.

Drill 35 – a pack with an opposing pack
The two packs are more spread and the coach throws the ball to someone at the edges. This means that the first man there must take the far side to block off the ball-carrier. The rest of the pack then follow on as in Drill 34.

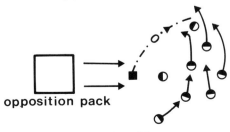

opposition pack

Fig. 38

Drill 36 – a pack with players in threequart-ers and opposing pack

Set up a simple maul that guarantees poss-ession (make the opposition passive). The scrum-half passes the ball out to the three-quarters. The coach calls 'TACKLED', or a scissors is executed and then 'TACKLED' is shouted. The threequarter waits to be 'picked up' by the pack who set up a maul. The backs realign waiting for the next ball.

Body position and stay on feet

As it is important to keep the ball off the ground in the maul, it is essential for the ball-carrier to stay on his feet. Obviously, this is not important for the ruck.

The ball-carrier tends to be in a more upright position controlling his own pace so that he can make contact on his own terms. The various methods of fending off men-tioned in Part 3 should help him to stay on his feet or use the opposition to help him stay on his feet. However, if he is to set up his support, he will need to take a final extra-long pace and present a hip, thus making it difficult to knock him over. This will mean that when the time comes for the ball-carrier to wrench himself to face his support, he is in a strong position to turn without losing balance or losing the ball.

Drill 37 – in threes

Let a semi-passive opposition hold the ball-carrier in an upright position when they are facing each other. With one ag-gressive wrench the ball-carrier should be able to adjust his body position so that he is facing his support, who will take the ball from him after he has turned.

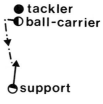

tackler
ball-carrier

support

Fig. 39

Drill 38 – pack with opposition pack

The build-up is the same as drill 22 in the rucking practices, except that the ball is closer to the opposition and the first man picks up the ball and drives into the first opposition, who is further away from the rest of the opposition than he was in the rucking practice.

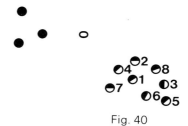

Fig. 40

The calling of the numbers determines whether the ball-carrier is blocked off or driven into first.

Blocked off example: shout 7 – pause – shout 3, 4 – pause – shout go (rest of pack follow).

Drive in on ball-carrier example: shout 5, pause – shout 8 – pause – shout 1, 6 – pause – shout go (rest of pack follow).

Drive legs

The reasons given for driving in the rucks hold true in the mauls. The defence will find it difficult to counter the attack if they are back on their heels, but there are differ-ences. If the ball-carrier is to be a solid focal point he will not be able to drive himself, but it will be important for him to be

37

driven, even used as a battering-ram. Also, the static maul is a base to work on other options, but if a team want to make the most of their backs from this source of possession, the 'clutch and accelerator' technique is necessary. As a pack, driving legs initially, using short paces, is important.

Drill 39 – in fours
One behind the other, the ball-carrier runs ahead, turns as if setting up a maul after being tackled (imaginary) and is driven 5 metres by support before he takes the ball and carries on the movement. The support will also set up ball to the next supporting player.

Drill 39a – in fours, 4 opposition
Opposition in a line, one behind the other, 12 metres apart. Same drill as the one before, but with opposition.

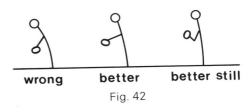

Fig. 41

Drill 40 – pack and opposition pack
Set up a static maul, the pack with the ball well shielded and the opposition pack binding on fairly upright. On the command, the pack start driving their legs with short paces and react to any weakness that should appear in the opposition pack, whether that weakness is on the fringes or through the middle.

Never be empty-handed; no daylight

The approach to the maul is different from the ruck. It is less 'full frontal' and the players tend to lead with one shoulder into a maul. Thus the maxim: 'wide shoulders for the ruck, narrow shoulders for the maul'. The players tend to burrow and lead with their arms into a maul, aiming to take the ball with the armpit as they continue driving. Therefore it is important how the original ball-carrier presents the ball. In certain situations the ball-carrier can force the ball away from his body, but he must be aware of the dangers of holding the ball too low. Geometrically the ball is closer to his body and can be disrupted far easier, even if the arms are outstretched.

Fig. 42

Holding the ball away from the body is not a strong position and the transfer can cause problems of having too much daylight. If the ball-carrier can secure the ball near his body, the support can drive him as he takes the ball.

Not like this . . .

... but closer to the body, like this

Continue driving

Drill 41 – in pairs
Pairs facing each other very close together.
Both are trying to get their elbows on the

inside of the other's elbows, and if a player succeeds he give his partner a friendly dig in the stomach to let him realize that he has succeeded!

Drill 42 – 6 against 2 opposition
The ball-carrier drives towards 1 of the 2 opposition, the base is set up and the 6 try to keep possession against the 2, even if it means retreating. The important thing is to make sure that the transferring of the ball is done in such a tight way that the two opposition cannot touch the ball.

Drill 43 – pack and opposition pack
Set up the pack with the ball, but hold back one member of the pack in turn. As the opposition is trying to get at the ball, release the one member to burrow and dig out the ball.

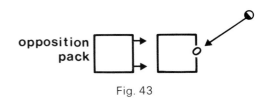

Fig. 43

4. Lineout – as a Base

In theory, a lineout should enable the team throwing in to jump and catch the ball and bring it down cleanly for the scrum-half to feed the backs. They will have width to work in and their opposition backs will be initially 20 metres away.

The realists will quickly note that the ball is not often caught cleanly, and the service to scrum-half is not always ideal. The 20-metre gap becomes closed up, or else the 20-metre gap is not used profitably. However, lineout skills must still be at the top of a list of priorities and a team must also learn to cope with situations that are not ideal.

REQUIREMENTS FOR THE LINEOUT

The catcher must be able to jump forward and attack the ball, jump vertically and also jump falling backwards. He must be able to offer firm parts of his body to withstand contact that could knock him off course. He must also be able to twist in the air so that the ball is protected as his feet land on the ground.

The thrower-in must be able to throw a short or long ball with the same action. He must be able to throw a hard flat ball or the slower lobbed ball.

The catcher should be able to see the ball held by the thrower-in at all times.

Catching the ball

Although physique is important when it comes to staking a claim in the jungle of the lineout, the competition at about 3 metres off the ground should depend upon whose wrists and hands are highest in the air. So the spindly character can do quite well against his better-built opponent if his fellow pack members are well-drilled, and the timing and technique of the lesser-built man can put him higher in the air. Of course good throwing-in is essential, but the important factor is how high the man can jump. Natural spring can be improved by learning how to 'hover' and by using the arms to add to the upward lift.

Drill 44a – individual
Leap in the air, raising the arms at the same time and twist through 360° to land on feet on the same spot. The jumper has to jump high enough to allow time to complete the action. Another good preparation for a jumper is having to twist through 90° in the air so that the ball is protected as he lands.

Drill 44b – individual
Practise jumping and twisting in the air through 90° to land with back to the opposition, feet on a wide base.

Drill 44c – individual
Use a basketball ring or cross-bar to hang flat objects at the required heights to suit the jumper. (The objects can be clothing

draped over cross-bars.) The player jumps with arms by the side and then lifts his arms outwards and upwards to slap an object with both hands. He has to 'hover' again to give himself time to complete the action.

A jumper tends to stretch forward or back before jumping to fill an area before his opponent does, and if it is his throw-in he should have the advantage through being able to anticipate where the ball is going to be thrown. This stretch forward or back is a split-second before his jump, so there is a danger of over-reaching, or hurrying the jump and jumping off one leg. If the jumper can 'gather' himself after filling the area he is going to jump from, he will be able to jump off two legs – which must be more powerful.

If the jumper takes off from one leg, his body will be propelled diagonally across the gain line, whether he is jumping forwards or backwards. He can do a lovely impression of a dying swan, but will be out-of-control and cannot contribute after touching the ball.

Jumping forward

A shot-putter is told as he travels across the circle and eventually releases the shot, 'SHIFT AND LIFT'. The lineout jumper, particularly if he is standing at 2, 3 or 4, must think of this athletic expression if he wants to perform this powerful jumping movement.

The jumper is allowed to take one step forward and/or diagonally before jumping. This step should be with both feet at the same time. The jumper starts in a low position with bent legs and keeps his legs bent as he takes a shallow step forward with both legs.

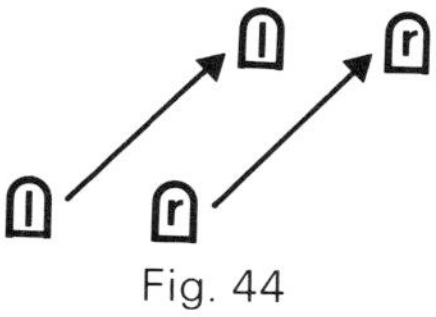

Fig. 44

Drill 45 – individual

The coach shouts 'SHIFT' and the players, with bent legs, drive diagonally left or right. It is not a hop, the soles of the feet hardly leave the ground, but just enough to travel quickly a distance of about half a metre to a metre. The distance is determined by how far the jumper wishes to go forward to sideways, making sure that he does not cross the gain line.

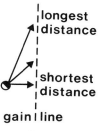

Fig. 45

As the feet are taking this diagonal path, the rest of the body will lead with the inside shoulder. This will immediately present a back to the opposition and thus protect the ball if caught. It will also allow the jumper to twist his 90° easily. The hip, which is hard, will automatically make contact with the opposition as the jumper twists, so he need only focus his eye on the ball and not on the opposition.

The jumper cannot afford to wait for this hard flat throw to hit his chest and gather it there. He must attack the ball and meet its flight or it may never reach him. That is why leading with the inside shoulder is essential, because the inside hand can touch the ball with fingertips and allow it to roll up to the palm of his hand before the other hand reaches it. The jumper usually finds that twisting one way is easier than the other, so on his 'bad side' he can start with his back more sideways on to the opposition.

The jumper in the middle of the lineout may prefer to stand with his inside arm already up. It acts as a guide for the thrower-in to obtain accuracy. It also starts the upward movement of one arm and although the lack of full range of swing upwards cannot help the jump, it does stop the opposition hampering the upward swing as arms from both sides flay around. The upward hand can also be used for signals between jumper and thrower-in for variations in throw.

Middle jumper stance

Variation in lineout signal

The rhythm of the thrower-in with the jumper is as important as the rhythm of the scrum-half with the hooker in the set scrum. Fortunately, most throwers-in are hookers so they will appreciate the importance. If the jumping action is 'shift and lift', the thrower-in should adapt to this, even using the same theme for his rhythm. That is holding the ball above his head initially, taking it back on the shift and hurling it in on the lift. Some jumpers like to take the rhythm from the thrower-in and other jumpers like to jump forward and hover while the ball is thrown at them. It does not matter, as long as the thrower-in is familiar with the rhythm of the jumper and even says it under his breath as he throws the ball in.

The same jumping action can be used for the deflection. This is a quicker ball if deflected directly to the scrum-half. This must be done with two hands reaching, even if it is only touched with one hand, because the angle of meeting the ball will be more accurate, and the ball must be guided on the open side of the scrum-half. The ball on the blind side of the scrum-half is difficult to get away, especially with the opposing thrower-in in the corridor of the 5-metre line ready to pounce, plus the inconvenience of the scrum-half having to twist his body around in order to get his pass out. It must be remembered that there is no variation on the deflection and as soon as the ball leaves the lineout the defence can advance.

Jumping backwards

Opposition jumpers are very eager to jump forward on your ball and with a disguised throw and a well-timed drill your jumper can sometimes find himself with a free jump if he takes the ball behind his opposition.

Again, there must be a rhythm and it is essential for the thrower-in to know this rhythm because it takes more time for the jumper to gather himself for his jump. The front jumper may wish to entice his marker forward first. He does this by taking a short pace forward with his inside foot, a large pace back with his outside foot, a gather and a jump. The combined action between thrower-in and jumper would be something like this:

Jumper – inside step forward;
thrower-in – take ball back.
Jumper – outside step back;
thrower in - delay ball in back position.
Jumper – bring right foot back to gather.
Thrower-in – throw lobbed ball
Jumper – catch.

The jumper should then forget the players around him, concentrate on his rhythm and therefore keep his eye on the ball throughout.

If the player stands with arms stretched upwards, he will realize that he can reach higher by raising one shoulder and hand. However, this does not mean that he must deflect the ball. It has already been pointed out that the deflection can be used as variety, but continually used will allow the opposition to stream out and put pressure on the half-backs. The one-handed leap can allow the jumper to meet the ball and cushion it down to the other hand which will be a shoulder width away and slightly lower.

This lead with the inside arm will emphasize the protrusion of the hips for contact again, which is important if the jumper wants to stay on course.

Drill 46 – individual with helper.
As the jumper is dealing with a lobbed ball, it will come down nearly vertical. It is difficult to time a jump to meet the ball at the highest point possible.

The helper stands on a chair or something similar and holds the ball for the jumper to jump and take it. This will progress to the helper being high enough to drop the ball. The jumper will leap to meet the ball and catch it, or meet it with one hand to guide it to two hands.

Jumping vertically from standing position

Sometimes it may be an advantage for the jumper not to hover but to leap straight up, collect the ball and bring it down quickly, or to deflect it. The throw-in is fast but fairly high and rising, so the catcher really intercepts the ball on its path. This means that he has little time to stop and gather, so he has to develop a technique that can give him a powerful jump from a bent-leg position without a step first. The absence of the step will mean that the jumper will be further away from the gain line and will have to leap across the line. As he will be more unbalanced, he will depend on his support to keep him on his feet. The role of the support will be dealt with later.

Drill 47 – individual
Player jumps from a box onto the ground. As soon as he lands he bends his legs and leaps straight back onto the box. More than one box can ensure different heights for individual practice. This exercise will improve the standing jump.

The ball must not end up in no man's land

If the jumper catches the ball, he must release it at the top of his jump or bring the ball down immediately. The ball has to be forced down low but away from the body. If the ball is low and close to his lower legs it can easily be interfered with. The wide foot positions with the body in a half-squat position should be a barrier, protecting the ball if it is held at arms' length or taken away by a support player, as in a maul.

The ball must not be held between the upward-outstretched position or above the waist. It would then be exposed in no man's land and would be difficult to distribute.

Drill 48 – the pack split into 2 sets of 4
Form a mini lineout, 4 each side. The coach throws the ball anywhere in the lineout and any man can act as a jumper. The ball is thrown in a biased manner so one side must be able to catch it. The catcher immediately brings the ball down and it is immediately taken away from him by one of the other three.

Throwing in: balance

THE THROWER-IN

Although the New Zealanders bowl the ball in and the French sometimes throw the ball from between their legs, the advantage of the torpedo throw is that the players participating in the lineout can always see the ball. This is easier for the players who either jump or support.

It is an advantage to be able to grip the ball but not essential. The ball must be taken above the head so that the eyes are in line with it. The little finger touches the lace and the other hand steadies the ball until the thrower-in takes it back. The reason it is not essential to grip the ball is that the hand and arm try to spin it so that it travels through the air aerodynamically. This means that the fingertips are the last thing to have contact with the ball. The hand and arm go across the body but are still in line with it. For balance, a right-handed thrower would start with his left foot forward and would face the lineout fully.

Ball in line with eyes

For the flat hard throw the thrower-in must imagine where the jumper will be as he catches the ball and must throw to that spot. This takes getting used to because he is throwing into empty space.

For the lobbed throw, again the thrower is aiming at a space because the jumper will be there eventually. The thrower does not think so much about getting the ball to his own jumper as getting it over the reach of the man marking him. The action for this lob has to be slower and more fluent than for the flat ball.

The quick rising throw needs a fast punchy action, as does the flat hard throw. All types of throw, like most actions in sport, need a follow-through. This means, in the throwing action, that the hand and arm must follow the ball as if the hand was going with it. This is particularly important for the longer throw, because a change of action through trying to throw the ball too hard usually results in a ball that does not spin through the air correctly. It either drops short or goes off-course or both.

The thrower must also remember that the right-handed throw tends to drift to the right, so the thrower must adjust to which side his team is jumping from.

LINEOUT SUPPORT

Jumpers can stand where they like from No. 1 to No. 7 in the lineout, but they do like to concentrate on keeping their eye on the ball and only having to be concerned with the man opposite them. A player does not want to be hindered or marked by players in front of or behind him so normally he would like support to 'block him off' and take care of these problems for him. Ideally, the jumper would like to jump high, collect the ball and enter a slot flanked by his support.

Usually the man standing at No. 1 in the lineout is a support man. He should stand

bent forward facing the opposition for four reasons:

1 Being bent forward, the jumper has a better view.

2 He can watch the ball throughout its flight.

3 Facing the opposition leaves more room for his jumper to jump forward to his head, instead of being stopped by his hips or his backside if he was facing the touchline.

4 It allows him to 'attack the armpit' of his opposite number with a straight arm (the one nearest the touchline), making sure that he does not slide around the fringes and menace his scrum-half. He can also drive his opponent towards mid-field, plugging gaps between No. 1 and No. 2, especially if his jumper is jumping backwards.

Fig. 46

The man behind the jumper usually stands at No. 3 in the lineout. Ideally, he should be a bulky man with no pretences as a jumper because he has two jumpers to support usually and a middle of the lineout which needs blocking off constantly. Not only must he know where the ball is being thrown, he must know what kind of jump his player is about to execute. These two pieces of information determine his role.

1 Front jumper goes forward – support from the No. 3 with head facing opposition drives diagonally forward, binding on his jumper and attacking the armpit of his opposite number with a straight arm (the one nearest mid-field). The No. 4 takes a diagonal pace forward and is also ready to jump if the ball is missed by the No. 2.

2 Front jumper goes back – support can stand square facing opposition and drive straight, binding with No. 2 as he comes back and No. 4 as he comes forward, jumping as a double jump. Or he can face the touchline and take a diagonal pace forward, shielding the No. 2 jumper from any marking behind. It will be essential for the No. 4 to jump forward in a double jump because there will be a big gap behind the No. 3 man then.

3 Middle jumper goes forward – stance by No. 3 very much the same as the No. 1, allowing the No. 4 to jump forward to his head. The No. 2 watches the ball then turns to face the No. 4 to 'clean up' any ball knocked forward. The No. 2 must not leave the line for his support.

4 Middle man goes back – the No. 3 drives diagonally mid-field, this time attacking his opposite number's armpit on the touch-line side. The No. 2 must also stand his ground and make sure that his opposite number cannot break through.

The jump in the middle of the lineout should not need a sweeper, so the lineout is compressed from both ends towards the middle jumper. This makes the role of the No. 1 man simple: he continues to drive his opposite number in-field as he did when the front jumper jumped backwards. However, if a side felt that it was absolutely essential to have a sweeper for the middle jumper, it would be the No. 1 in the lineout who would be sacrificed to do this job. There would, of course, be a gap left, but the opposing No. 1 is usually less instinctive about breaking through. Also the hooker may be able to plug that gap and at least the path of the ball from scrum-half to fly-half has not been threatened from this position at the front of the lineout.

The task of the man standing at No. 5 in the lineout is a most important and skilled one. Gaps are exaggerated by forward jumping and a pack is confronted with per-

sonalities in this area who are primed and expert in hounding loose ball and half-backs. The No. 5 must assist the No. 4 jumper, but must also realize that he is in the ideal position to clean up ball thrown to No. 2. Apart from having the decision of when to clean up for the No. 2 jumper, he must be aware of the whereabouts of his opposing No. 5. He can support his No. 4 jumper by standing his ground or timing a double jump with him. A lot depends on the success of the No. 4 jumper, but as a general rule:

1 No. 4 jumping forward – the No. 5 takes a diagonal pace forward with his inside leg and stands his ground, trying to fill as big a gap as possible. If the ball was missed by the No. 4, the reaction time needed to catch the loose ball is better suited to the No. 6 in the lineout than the No. 5.

2 No. 4 jumping backwards – the No. 5 can offer a double jump with the No. 4 to obtain the ball or stand behind the No. 4 to protect him from interference behind. Although the No. 5 may have the physique of a jumper he may have to sacrifice himself as a support player for the No. 4 or No. 6 in the lineout.

Role of a No. 6

Apart from the ball aimed at the No. 6 in the lineout, it is amazing how much ball this man will pick up from ball meant for No. 2 or No. 4, depending of course on his reactions and catching ability.

Drill 49 – 2 packs
Practise 'baulking' the No. 2 and No. 4 jumpers to help the No. 6 jumper react to collecting the ball that is missed by the No. 2 and No. 4.

The ball is usually lobbed to the No. 6 in the lineout. It is important for him to keep his eye on it because it will be in the air

longer and with players around him mis-
timing their jumps and making early physical contact he must not be hurried into
jumping. He must also realize that the
thrower-in has had to use more force to
reach the back of the lineout, so a tap-down
could ricochet too far, if the ball is not
guided down with a wrist movement. The
No. 6 should aim to use the wrist to guide
the ball close to his face and chest. Of
course, with the force of the throw, the ball
will rebound about a metre from the face
and chest, which will be ideal for the support to gather. The No. 1, 2 or 3 can be
used for this support.

Role of a No. 7

The law allows this man to stay detached if
a maul or ruck follows the lineout and the
No. 7 should take full advantage of this. If
he is used as a jumper it is usually having
to run back to a ball thrown over the lineout. It is important that he is not still
running as the ball reaches him. He must
give himself time to check and gather. This
will certainly give him an advantage over
the opposing No. 7, who probably started
after him and will be still running backwards as your No. 7 is gathering himself to
jump. So a controlled jump with height is
essential.

the ball. The No. 6 can also deflect into the
No. 4's hands or even the No. 5. It is more
difficult for the No. 2 to deflect forward
because the No. 1 would have to step back
to take the ball and weaken the defensive
wall, or an alert thrower-in would have to
collect the ball.

However, it is easier for the No. 2 to deflect backwards. He would have to abandon
the double footstep and lift for the 'dying
swan' attacking jump described earlier in
the chapter. That is a one-leg step that allows him to dive further forward. He ends
up out of control, but it allows him to reach
the ball earlier than the opposition and
change the path of it enough to come down
on his own side of the lineout – to be collected by the No. 4, 5 or 6 without them
leaving the line.

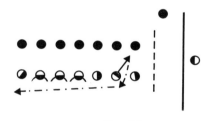

Fig. 47

This dive allows the ball to hit the fingertips and alter the course slightly. The
No. 4 can also deflect for the No. 6 or 7 to
collect.

SECOND-TOUCH BALL

If the ball has to be deflected to drive again
or secure, it is not desirable to deflect into
the scrum-half's hands. The 'second touch'
should go to another forward in the lineout.

The No. 4 can jump forward and deflect
down into the No. 2's hands. The No. 2
should not leave the line but should stand
with his back to the opposition but slightly
inclined facing the No. 4 in order to collect

Peeling

This is a penetrating type of second touch
where players leave the lineout to attack
around the extremes of the lineout. If the
peel is around the back and the ball is
initially thrown to the No. 6, he needs an
'umbrella' of players to guide the ball down
to. He cannot be expected to pin-point the
ball down to one player.

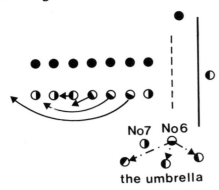

the umbrella

Fig. 48

The further back the No. 7 runs, the more chance there is of pushing the ball forward to a supporting forward, as the gap in front is wider, or using the scrum-half as part of the umbrella.

It must be remembered that the No. 7 catching the ball and driving forward can be very effective. It saves a pair of hands in setting up the drive and there is instant support.

As it is difficult for the thrower-in to pin-point the long ball, he must have the confidence to overthrow rather than under-throw the ball. His own team know the signals and should be quicker to the ball through anticipation, but they will hesitate if they think that it will not be thrown far enough. Even if the ball ends on the ground near mid-field, the anticipation through knowing the signals will ensure that the team that threw in will have more players to the breakdown.

Another effective peel around the back uses the No. 7 as the jumper. He will usually run back to collect this ball, so the No. 2, 3 or 4 cannot be expected to be in a position to receive the deflection; the No. 5 or 6 is better suited for this task. An umbrella can still be formed, but it depends how far back towards the middle of the field the No. 7 wishes to go whether a 2- or 3-man umbrella is possible.

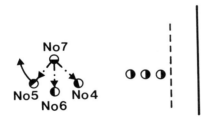

Fig. 49

Fig. 49 is an example of an umbrella if the 7 takes only 3 or 4 paces before jumping.

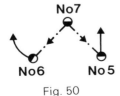

Fig. 50

Fig. 50 is an example of a mini-umbrella if the No. 7 runs far infield.

Drill 50 – 2 packs
One team throws in 8 consecutive times, but memorize beforehand that, say, 3 of the throws will be over the top of the lineout. They will know which throws will be over the top before the 8 consecutive throws are started – let us say the 2nd, 5th and 7th will be long. Through extra numbers at the breakdown they should secure the ball.

Peel around the front The peel around the front ideally needs the ball caught at No. 2 so that the No. 5 or 6 can drive in on this man with the shoulder nearest the touchline leading. If he leads with this shoulder he can 'roll off' towards the corridor between the touchline and 5-metre line, or present a pop-up pass to support to penetrate this corridor.

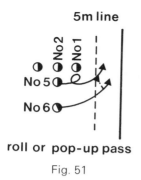

roll or pop-up pass

Fig. 51

lineout forwards should be confident to retain possession.

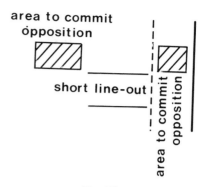

Fig. 52

Drill 51 – 2 packs
Peel either front or back with the opposition letting one pack get initial possession, then building up to active opposition.

Drill 52 – 2 packs or 4-a-side packs
Both teams have a fifty-fifty chance of securing the ball thrown over the top (this requires one unbiased thrower-in through-out). Vary the practice by throwing the ball short to secure and drive down the corridor near the touchline.

SHORT LINEOUTS

This does give a chance for a side to obtain possession, even if they feel that they are short of jumpers. It is also important to use them to break up the pattern of play and keep the mind alive.

Whether a team puts in 4, 3 or 2 men in the lineout, there will always be the prob-lem of the mid-field being cluttered up with extra players when initial possession has been gained. A team should expect to get possession from their own throw-in at short lineouts so it is important for them to plan further and use the non-participating for-wards to commit those extra opposition be-fore releasing the ball to the backs. The two logical areas to commit the opposition are shown on the diagram and, through close-knit formations, these non-participating

These are also areas not only to commit but to set up players coming from depth to penetrate.

Possession from short lineouts is obtained by:

1 Running back to collect the ball
2 Running forward into a gap
3 Late positional changes in the lineout
4 Outjumping the man opposite

The element of surprise and slickness in execution is so important for success.

For the second-phase possession the scrum-half would get the ball to the fly-half to set up penetrators from non-participating lineout forwards in mid-field. Or the scrum-half could set up support himself, running around extremes of the lineout front or back. Sometimes a forward taking the scrum-half position is more suited to this task. The scrum-half can also set up players down the corridor between the touchline and 5-metre line.

DEFENCE BY FORWARDS FROM LINEOUTS

As in the set scrums, it is again important to form a pincer movement on the scrum-half. Ideally, this should be done by the

49

thrower-in (usually the hooker) on the blind side and the No. 5 or 6 going through the back of the lineout. The No. 5 and 6 may have difficulty getting through the lineout so the scrum-half can be threatened by the No. 7. However, because the No. 7 is situated so much closer to the fly-half, it would be a shame to waste this opportunity of the No. 7 putting pressure on this man. This allows his own fly-half to drift across the field in defence. (This will be dealt with in detail in a later chapter.)

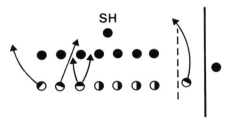

Fig. 53

Realizing that there is no variation on the tapped ball in the lineout, a pack should take full advantage of wayward tapping by the opposition.

Drill 53 – 2 packs
Allow the opposition to tap down to the touchline side of their scrum-half and put pressure on this man. If the ball is loose on the ground, secure and drive over it or drive over as the opposition secure.

Drill 54 – 2 packs
Allow the opposition to tap down to another forward and drive forward on the ensuing maul.

Drill 55 – 2 packs
Allow the opposition to tap down to the open side of the scrum-half and put pressure on the scrum-half and fly-half.

Defence by forwards for short lineouts

It is important to make sure there is a challenge when their jumper runs back. If the defence do not react quickly enough it gives the jumper a 'free' jump and an opportunity to set up attacks in mid-field. It is less important to mark the jumper that runs forward. It is easier to put a pincer movement on the scrum-half if the jumper runs forward and taps down to him.

LINEOUTS NEAR YOUR OWN LINE

The priority is to clear your own lines as simply as possible. This is usually done by kicking the ball to touch, so it is important to give the kicker as much time as possible. Much depends on which is the stronger kicking foot (or only kicking foot!) of the defenders. If it is accepted that most players are right-footed, a defensive lineout on the left-hand side of the field gives more options.

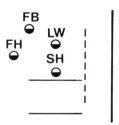

Fig. 54

The scrum-half, fly-half, left wing and full-back can all be used for kicking duties with the added advantage that the fly-half can side-step outside an advancing flanker and hook the ball to touch, being protected by the left-hand side of his own body.

The lineout on the right-hand side cuts down the kickers positioned nearer mid-field. The main kicker needs to stand directly behind the scrum-half.

The fly-half can always act as a pivot to set up the centres, or even the full-back, to take over the kicking duties, but the simple options have now been discounted and the final defensive kick may have to be directed to the opposite touchline. This is never a popular move with the forwards.

As a general rule, the lineout very close to the defensive try-line should determine a lobbed throw to the No. 2, 3 or 4 in the lineout. A short, flat ball can easily be knocked down by the opposition to an eager team-mate standing in the corridor. The lobbed ball also means that the defensive blind-side wing can be released to go mid-field because there is more time for the man throwing in to guard the corridor after he has thrown in.

Shortened lineouts can be used near a defensive try-line because the non-participating forwards can stand just behind the try-line and form a sort of 'double banking' and clean up any tapped ball. The ball thrown over the top to the fly-half or centre has the option of using these men as pivots to set another player up to kick or run, or for the catcher to kick, remembering again that the kick is easier for the right-footer if the lineout is on the left-hand side. It is also worth noting that some throwers-in need a

high trajectory to get the ball that distance. This is disaster for the catcher who can only wait while the ball takes time to come down, and has the opposition bearing down on him as well. So a flatter trajectory is needed, but making sure that the ball is not intercepted by lineout players en route.

POINTS FOR FORWARDS TO REMEMBER AT LINEOUTS

1 It is better for the thrower-in to over-throw than underthrow.
2 Know the lineout signals.
3 Know the personal signals of each jumper for his particular type of jump.
4 Concentrate on the one man opposite you.
5 Be prepared for the ball that is not collected by the nominated jumper.
6 All players in the lineout take a diagonal pace (forwards or backwards) to the gain line down the middle of the lineout.
7 Don't change stance in lineout when the ball is not being thrown to you.
8 Always aim to put the ball on the open side of the scrum-half.
9 Never end up empty-handed, grab something!
10 Challenge on their ball.

PART 3

Using Possession

5. Moving the Ball

Forwards get through an immense amount of hard work to obtain possession for their team. They are involved in physical contact both in set pieces and in the loose. Their object is to get the ball. When they get it they expect – and rightly – that the possession will be used constructively. Their job has not finished once they've obtained the ball – they then have to get to the next breakdown or be in support of any attacking move.

Possession must not be wasted. It is either used to extricate yourselves from a defensive situation or to set up an attacking move. It should never be used to give yourselves time to think, or to create a breathing space. Neither of these latter two options puts pressure on the opposition and it is pressure that leads to tries.

It is also vital to remember that as soon as you kick a ball you lose possession. To kick from five or six consecutive possessions is a criminal waste of the possession obtained. There is no variety in your distribution of the ball and in consequence your opponents have only to take limited countermeasures. There is also a fair chance you are handing them possession on a plate. That is bad rugby. Obtaining possession is hard and skilled work – don't waste it.

MAKING HANDLING INSTINCTIVE

As rugby football is a handling game it is essential that all players master the neces-sary skills to achieve a high degree of competency. The techniques will differ, ie backs from forwards. Backs will generally be moving in open spaces and will need to propel the ball further. Forwards are more likely to be moving in a more confined space and of paramount importance will be the catching of the ball and moving it at speed. This, of course, does not preclude either unit mastering the other but it does mean the emphasis to start with will be different.

Handling the ball is synonymous with running with the ball and players must realize that they possess the necessary ammunition to beat an opponent: swerve, sidestep and variation of pace. Kicking and passing are only two variations on the way a player may use the ball constructively. Handling means possession and possession should mean tries.

Players must be able to take a ball at speed and at varying heights. The ideal pass may not materialize under pressure and the side that handles everything instinctively will score many more tries.

Meet the ball and use of the wrists

The aim must be to transfer the ball as quickly as possible. This will mean receiving the ball early so the hands, and fingertips in particular, must be prepared to meet the ball. The player cannot wait for the ball to be cushioned by his body. Also the player must be prepared to adjust the ball that has arrived awkwardly while he is going through the action from receiving to giving. This means an emphasis on the use of the wrist.

Drill 56 – 5 or 6 players in a circle with arms outstretched towards the middle of the circle
Keeping the arms outstretched, keep the ball moving to any of the other players using wrist power only to transfer the ball.

Fig. 55

Drill 57 – in threes
Walking in a line (side by side) reach out for the ball which will be given, not passed, along the line. Emphasize reaching for the ball.

Drill 58 – in threes
Make the middle man run along a straight line still handing the ball, not passing it, to the player on either side of him. It will make the middle man 'detach' his lower body which will be running straight, from his upper body that will rotate naturally transferring the ball.

Drill 59 – in threes
Very gradually, change the handing of the ball to a pass, but make sure that the players do not spread too far.

Pass with sympathy

The passer must be sympathetic with the receiver and weight his passes accordingly. If the receiver is arriving in close support on the burst, he will need a 'pop-up' pass that he can accelerate onto. The further away the receiver is, the more direct and forceful the pass must be. It used to be said

that the ball should be given 'hip high and ahead'. This still holds true for the player in close support who wishes to shield the ball with a good body lean as he receives the ball, but for the receiver in open space he will want to look around him as he collects the ball. It makes more sense if that ball is given to him at eye level and ahead.

Drill 60 – in threes
Middle man passes each ball from below his knee onto which the receiver will accelerate. The wrist action is important. See the photo below.

Passing from below the knee

Drill 61 – in threes
Middle man will pass the ball as if avoiding a low tackle, ie one hand on top of the ball with the other hand underneath. Again, wrist action is important. See the photo below.

Passing as if avoiding a low tackle

Drill 62 – in threes
Middle man takes the ball early at eye level, but brings it down to hip level before transferring it on to the receiver. See the photos below.

Taking the ball early . . .

. . . and bringing it down . . .

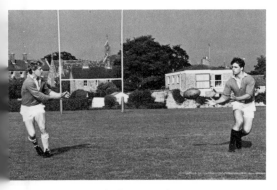

. . . before passing

Drill 63 – in sixes
Passing in a line, alternate between high and low passes, ie Drills 60 and 61.

Penetrate then spread

It is important for players to realize that, from broken play in particular, close passing to support players will initially penetrate. It will then be possible to bring in wider support. It is like besieging a castle – once a hole has been made in the wall, initially all go through that hole before spreading on the other side. Players have to recognize when to support 'on the shoulder' and when to look for lateral space. This is particularly important when a break has been made. For team-mates to react to the break and support closer.

Drill 64 – fours, fives or sixes
One man acts as opposition, but only initially. The ball is knocked out of his hand and snapped up by the others who immediately make progress with four on-the-shoulder passes. This is followed by four passes with the receivers spreading as they take their passes.

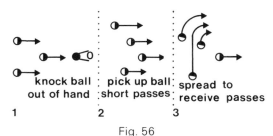

knock ball out of hand : pick up ball short passes : spread to receive passes

1   2   3

Fig. 56

Drill 65 – in fours, fives or sixes
Lateral passing. One of the group (or the coach) shouts 'ON THE SHOULDER' or 'SPREAD' every four or five passes and the group have to react.

Close support must come from behind

It is a common fault for the close support to be too lateral. The passer has probably committed a tackler if his timing of the pass has been good, so the receiver should go through the same gap and not be wide enough to interest another defender. The next drills should highlight the problem.

Drill 66 – in fives or sixes
To the on-the-shoulder passes make the players put the ball on the ground every four or five passes. If the players are not directly behind they will by-pass the ball and stand little chance of snapping up the ball on the ground.

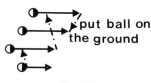

Fig. 57

Drill 67 – in fives or sixes
Combine drills 65 and 66, call 'SPREAD' and 'ON THE SHOULDER' but add 'BALL DOWN' when they have executed the latter.

Drill 68 – fives or sixes
Lateral passing. Call 'MAKE A BREAK'. The player with the ball in his hand at that moment breaks off at any angle with acceleration, the others react to support closely. He passes to support, so the theme can be continued.

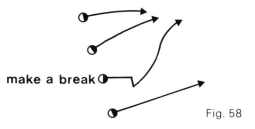

Fig. 58

Drill 69 – in sixes
Put the onus on one man to make a break. Every time the ball goes to a nominated man he always makes a break or runs off at an unexpected angle. The others have to support. He passes to support and runs off to a new position to eventually receive ball again. After a length of the field another man is nominated.

Drill 70 – in sixes
Lateral passing between 4 players, 2 players roam behind the 4 and enter the line when they feel it is right. One will enter on the burst and expect a pop-up pass. His acceleration onto the ball should take him clear of the four. He links with the four and then roams behind the four again. The other roamer will be in action while he is recovering and positioning himself again.

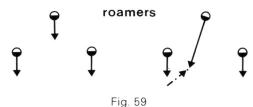

Fig. 59

LET THE BACKS PLAY NATURALLY

Cynically we nearly wrote – especially at international level. Whatever the level threequarters should be selected to create and score tries. They are the one unit that should vigorously resist being rigidly coached in predetermined attacking set pieces.

The ultimate aim of all threequarters is to find themselves in a two-to-one situation which should then proceed to a one-to-nought situation – and a try results.

Scissors and dummy scissors are useful ploys but not to the extent that the captain says: 'From this scrummage we are going to do the scissors.' Players then move into position and in consequence so do the defenders and soon a stalemate is reached. All threequarters *must* make their decisions in attack, at the time the situation develops.

Threequarters must have the ability to spot a gap or create one.

Spotting gaps is instinctive and cannot be coached easily. One way, however, is to run videos of matches where the coach can point out gaps that were not exploited and to emphasize when they were.

Creating gaps may be done by individuals or by groups of players. The ability to create gaps by an individual must be encouraged. This ability must not be *coached out* by the dogma of set moves. For any ploy that is set up there is a countermove and therefore creation of gaps made at the time according to the circumstances are far more likely to succeed. Not only that, but more importantly, in our view, they help a player's game to improve through experience.

Coaching is vital to a successful team but not at the expense of flair.

USING FOOTWORK – AS AN INDIVIDUAL

Every member of the team should have the ability to depress one leg by putting weight over it and driving off in a different direction. The word 'sidestep' has not been used because forwards tend to think that this is only a term and an action used by threequarters, and they feel they would probably be drummed out of 'the union' if they even talked about it.

If the ball-carrier can at least offput the angle of approach of the tackler, or force the tackler to mistime his tackle he will be in a much stronger position. The 'drive off' one leg can also give a wider base in close situations and make the ball-carrier a more difficult target to bring down. The sidestep

(for want of a better word) is usually determined by the angle of approach of the opposition.

Drill 71 – in pairs
The man with the ball runs diagonally across the field with his opponent doing the same (from the 22-metre line) to cut him off. The ball-carrier naturally depresses his left foot to cut inside the covering player. It is important for the ball-carrier to start also from the 22-metre line to practise depressing his right foot.

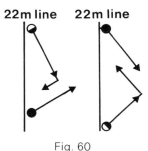

Fig. 60

The biggest fault will be that the ball-carrier tries to sidestep too close to the opposition.

Drill 72 – in pairs
Same as drill 71 but the covering defence player can choose whether to position himself to stop the cut back. This means that the attacking player has the option of cutting back or carrying on with his chosen path.

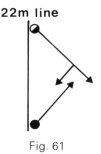

Fig. 61

Using Possession

Drill 73 – in sevens or eights
Men walk or jog continually across the field from the touchline to the 5-metre line and back again while players with the ball run between them, avoiding contact by the use of the sidestep. The opposition do not try and tackle the man with the ball.

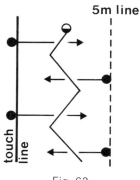

Fig. 62

Variation of pace

This is a very effective way to beat a tackler – and comparatively simple. The success of the move will depend upon timing and variation in pace. The aim is to deceive the tackler into thinking he has got himself into a position where he can launch into a successful tackle. By lengthening your stride or by shortening it and driving harder you are no longer in the position the tackler was expecting. You are running just below your top speed, for instance, and then move into overdrive as the tackler is about to launch himself.

The lengthening and shortening of stride is enough to make the tackler hesitate. This hesitation will put him off balance and the initiative passes to you the runner.

Drill 74 – in pairs
Using one of the lines crossing the field, run 15 metres at half speed, increase to just below top speed for 10 metres and then 10 metres at top speed. After two runs like this

(preferably with a ball in your hands) try and achieve two complete variations in every run across.

Now have both players about 5 metres apart. The runner has the ball and the other has to touch twice in rapid succession the runner in the run across the field. The players change round on the return run. The aim is for the runner with the ball to make the toucher miss the double touch as many times as possible. He can only use variation of pace and he must run in a straight line.

Running straight

The ball can travel through many pairs of hands on its journey to the open-side wing, but it is ineffective if the players are running across the field. This means that a defender can mark more than one person and the attackers are crowding themselves out on the touchline.

Receivers must have the confidence to run slightly towards the passer as he is in the process of catching the ball and be very aware of whether his shoulders are facing his opponents try-line. If his shoulders are facing the corner-flag, or worse the touchline, then he is running across the field.

This straightening-up gives the opportunity of 'interesting' his opposite number and forcing this defender back on his heels.

Drill 75 – in threes
Middle man runs along a straight line and tries to keep on this line as he receives and gives a pass.

Drill 76 – in fours or fives
Stand in line one behind the other, receive a pass by running into it.

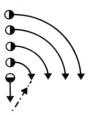

Fig. 63

60

Drill 77 – in fours
Run towards the opposition before releasing the ball.

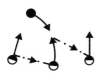

Fig. 64

The hand-off

The type of hand-off depends on the type of tackle. The high smothering tackle (aiming to make contact below shoulder height but above waist level) needs a hand-off which will attempt to stop or soak up the momentum of the tackler. The attacker straightens his arm, in a forceful manner with an open palm into the chest or head of the would-be tackler. This should make the drive of the tackler ineffective. The attacker must be prepared to be forced sideways himself with this vigorous action. In fact, this is desirable if there is room, because it puts more space between attacker and defender. It is important for the ball to be held securely in the far hand, high on the chest below the far shoulder, so that the hips are free to move outwards to add a lean into the vigorous arm action.

Countering the hand-off
The tackler does not want to be handed off. He must get under the fending-off arm of the player with the ball. The tackler's normal running position will be fairly high and therefore the fending-off arm of the attacker will also be in a high position. Just before contact, the tackler should 'swallow in' hard under this arm. This change of height should leave the tackler with the initiative.

Drill 78 – numbers of attackers with ball v stationary opposition

Fig. 65

The opposition are spaced as in the diagram, and remain stationary and upright. The attacker hands off each stationary player, using the time that it takes him to reach the next opponent to transfer the ball smoothly and effectively from one higher chest position to another on the other side with the other hand.

The second type of tackle is the low tackle (aiming to make contact below the waist). The tackler has much more drive from this position, so it is difficult for the attacker to stop this momentum with a hand-off. The attacker's aim should be to divert this tackler's drive downwards into the ground. The hand-off should be aimed at the top of the shoulders near the neck or the top of the head. A downward action is then required, as if the attacker was vaulting over a low gate. Obviously the feet do not leave the ground, but this action will again drive the hips, plus the knees, outwards. The aim of this hand-off is to protect the knees anyway, which is the object of most fending-off actions, as we shall see later in this section.

The swerve

This skill is probably more effective than the sidestep. While a slight slowing of pace is required to execute the sidestep, an acceleration is essential for the swerve to be effective. However, more room is required normally for the swerve.

61

Using Possession

The swerve can be divided into four parts:

1 A straight run-up is necessary. The opponent must be 'interested' in the run-up and perhaps forced back on his heels and slowed down. To run across the field and *then* swerve outside needs a lot of confidence in basic speed and change of pace.

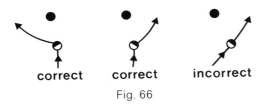

| correct | correct | incorrect |

Fig. 66

2 The movement is initiated by correct leading of the head. This will ensure a balanced run.
3 Vigorous footwork is required to map out the clear path of a swerve. If the feet are correctly placed the rest of the body should follow! A swerve to the left needs a vigorous cross-step by the right foot immediately after the left foot has initiated the swerve to the left. A full swerve will then be executed instead of a half swerve, or an apology for a swerve.

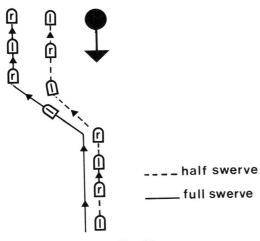

---- half swerve

—— full swerve

Fig. 67

4 Swing away of hips and knees will give space between the attacker and a despairing tackler. The attacker being prepared to use a hand-off will be extra security and will *naturally* swing the hips and knees away because the hand-off is used to protect them from the low tackle. By the time the attacker is clear of the tackler, he is travelling at top speed. That is why a break from a swerve is so deadly.

Drill 79 – number of players each with a ball v 2 stationary players
An attacker with the ball runs straight along the 15-metre line towards a stationary player also on the 15-metre line and then swerves out to the 5-metre line. He rejoins the 15-metre line and does the same again against the second stationary player. The stationary players must be well-spaced. When the group of attackers have completed this running drill, they turn around and repeat the drill swerving on the other side.

Drill 80 – number of players each with a ball v a smaller number of opposition
Same drill as before but the stationary players can move to tackle when the attacker starts his swerve. This should simulate keeping a defender on his heels and interesting this defender by running straight.

Drill 81 – players in pairs to get same number of defenders as attackers
Defenders are situated on the far 15-metre line between the 22-metre lines. The attackers are on the near 5-metre line or the try-line. The attacker veers in to interest and slow down the defender. He then swerves out again with vigorous footwork, acceleration and the threat of a hand-off. He repeats the veering-in and swerve-out for the second defender. The second defender must not leave too early.

The dummy

This is an extremely simple way of deceiving your opponent and is doubly effective against suspect tacklers. You have to persuade your opponent that you intend to release the ball, but at the last possible moment you hang on to it.

For a threequarter, who will be more likely to give the orthodox classical pass, his dummy pass should not be hurried. As he falls away he should naturally be into a sidestep or jink. This sidestep or jink should take him clear of his opponent, even if the opponent has realized that he has been set up for the dummy.

For a dummy to the right the passer's weight will be on his left foot as he starts to bring the ball back towards his body at the end of the passing swing. His right foot should then go in front of his left foot, or slightly to the left of it. It is this movement to the left that takes the runner with the ball further away from the prospective tackler. For a pass to the left the converse is true. If it is done properly, you can sell the dummy even when entirely on your own.

In more confined areas, for instance where a group of forwards are involved in a handling movement, the orthodox classical pass would be inappropriate. The dummy will be given with bent arms and at a quicker pace. Again the timing of the dummy will be vital and in all instances must be left as late as possible – one or two metres away from the prospective tackler. The more confident you become the closer you will be able to go towards the tackler. This ploy should lead to a complete break, and unless you have a clear run to the line the ball should be moved to another player as soon as possible – 'jink and link'. All too often promising threequarter moves break down because the player with the ball, having beaten one man, tries to take on the whole of the opposition.

Having completed a successful dummy, immediate acceleration is required.

Drill 82 – 2 against 1
The two have the ball, the one is the defender and a touch of the player with the ball constitutes a tackle. The two are allowed ten attempts and must use the dummy on at least five of them.

The defender changes after the tenth attempt.

A point is awarded if one attacker runs five metres when past the defender.

Drill 83 – in fives or sixes
Lateral passing and similar to Drill 68. One man dummies and makes a break. After the others have reacted, he links so the movement can start again.

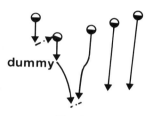

dummy

Fig. 68

Drill 84 – in sixes
One man is continually on the inside of the ball-carrier, who dummies this man and passes the ball out. The man who supported on the inside moves inside the new ball-carrier, he is dummied again. This keeps happening until the ball reaches the outside man who 'rewards' the support by giving him the ball. The ball is then passed back along the line, still dummying this man.

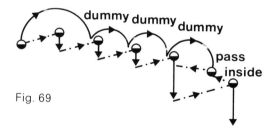

dummy dummy dummy

pass
inside

Fig. 69

USING FOOTWORK – AS A UNIT
Scissors and dummy scissors

The only difference between the scissors and dummy scissors is that the ball does not leave the hands in the dummy scissors. There is a great temptation to hurry the dummy scissors and not 'sell' the illusion to the opposition. The same ritual should be gone through as if the ball could be given. This is a healthier approach because the player then has options and can decide himself what will happen to the ball.

If the ball-carrier thinks of hiding the ball from the opposition in front of him, and also shows the ball all the time to the would-be receiver, he will never turn the wrong way to execute this movement.

The ball-carrier must make the initial path and the receivers adjust to this path.

... but not from the receiver

The biggest fault is the receiver taking too much of a lateral path when it is impossible to deviate from this chosen path.

This man is usually swallowed up by the covering opposition. He should take a path that gives him a choice of continuing running 'against the grain' or veering out again in the path of the original run. This means that he must come from a deeper position and run much straighter.

Ball hidden from the opposition ...

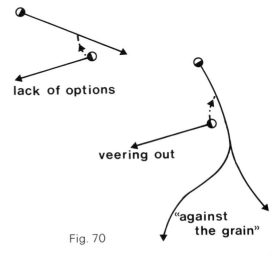

lack of options

veering out

"against the grain"

Fig. 70

Drill 85a – in fives

1 passes to 2, 2 passes to 3, 3 passes to 4. 4 runs across the field, 5 reacts and takes a scissor pass. See Fig. 71(a). 5 straightens and passes to 3, 3 passes to 2, 2 runs across the field, 1 reacts and takes a scissor pass – Fig. 71(b).

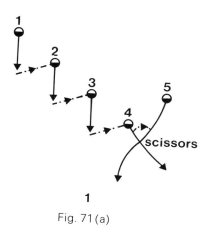

Fig. 71 (a)

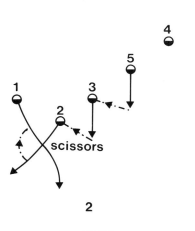

Fig. 71 (b)

Drill 85b – in fives or sixes

Lateral passing, one man runs across the field, the others react for the dummy scissors, the man with the ball then breaks

and links inside or outside. The movement continues with dummy scissors and breaks.

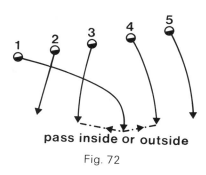

pass inside or outside

Fig. 72

Drill 86 – fives or sixes

Let the players continuously scissor and dummy scissor down the field. The players will weave patterns, but also only give the ball when the angles between passer and receiver are right.

Miss-a-man moves

The ball travels quicker than the man, so there is an advantage in missing men out so that the outside men get early ball with room to move. There is also the possibility, against man-to-man marking, of slightly shifting the marking channels and quite naturally putting a player through a gap.

The important factor for this to be successful is that the man who is going to be missed out must be in a position to be missed out. Again, there must be the option to give the ball to him if required. For the opposition, it is difficult for them to judge depth from their frontal position, so a player can threaten to take the pass but be missed out completely. There is no point in the decoy running in front of the pass.

Missing the middleman

In fives, 1 misses out 2 and passes to 3, 2 then loops 3 and receives a pop-up pass (as in groups of four). But 2 then misses out 4 and passes to 5, 4 loops around 5 and receives a pop-up pass.

In fives or sixes, the player missed out always loops outside so the passer must delay his pass to him.

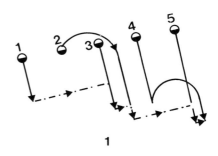

1

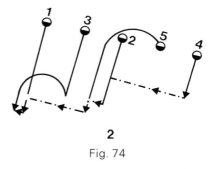

2

Fig. 74

Drill 87 – in fours, fives or sixes

1 misses out 2 and passes to 3, 2 then loops 3 and receives a pop-up pass. 2 passes to 4 who then misses out 2 again, 2 loops 3 and receives a pop-up pass. 2 will soon realize that he is doing all the work!

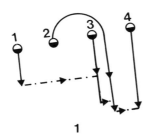

1

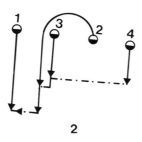

2

Fig. 73

Looping

With covering defences being so well organized, looping from players running across the field will be ineffective. If the passer can veer inwards and interest the cover, the loop will be effective. The most sophisticated method is for the outside man to veer into the tackler with his outside shoulder and side, giving the ball to the looper as contact is made, making the move look like a scissor move.

The tackler is committed

The support is clear

Drill 88 – in fours, fives or sixes
Lateral passing, but each man that passes runs to the other end of the line. He must run straight or he will be left behind, and each passer must veer in towards the pass before moving the ball on. Do not give them much width in which to run, make them straighten.

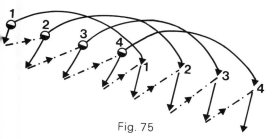

Fig. 75

Drill 89 – in fours, fives or sixes
Lateral passing, call tackled, the player will stay on his feet and others will loop the same way as the movement was going.

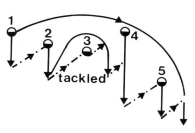

Fig. 76

Drill 90 – in fives or sixes
Lateral passing, call tackled, nearest man drives in to this standing man, takes the ball and gives the pass to the player looping the same way as the movement was going.

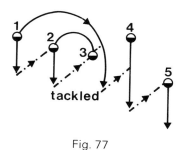

Fig. 77

Drill 91 – in fours or fives, two opposition
Lateral passing, the one opposition back-pedals to challenge the outside man, who veers towards the opposition in order to set up the looping player aiming outside the ball-carrier. The looping player initiates lateral passing the other way and the other opposition can then challenge the outside man on the other side, who will also veer in towards this opposition.

Using Possession

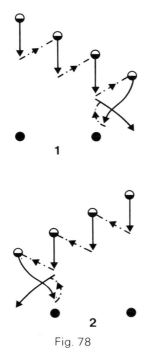

Fig. 78

Reacting to the ball-carrier

Hopefully, by this time players will have enough confidence in their handling to do things instinctively and react to broken play situations, running to support in various ways quite naturally. The following drills should test their reactions.

Drill 92 – in fours, fives or sixes
Whenever a nominated man in the group receives the ball, he calls 'SHORT BALL', 'SCISSORS', 'LOOP' or 'MISS'. The other players in the group react.

Drill 93 – in fours, fives or sixes
Lateral passing, shout to put the ball down, by-pass the ball completely. A different man picks the ball up and moves it immediately.

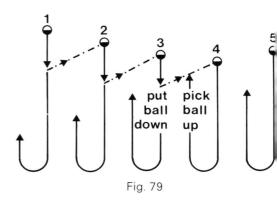

Fig. 79

Drill 94 – in fours, fives or sixes
Same as Drill 27, except when the ball is picked up again shout 'LEFT' or 'RIGHT'. Those that are not on the side of the passing side nominated will have to loop to that side.

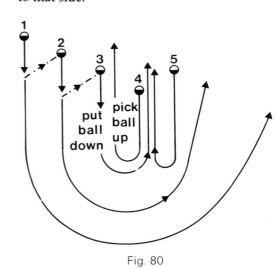

Fig. 80

6. Breaks – Spotting a Gap

Making a break

To score a try teams must endeavour to have a two-to-one situation in their favour. Only then is a try likely to ensue. As there are fifteen players a side marking each other, to reach this position someone has to beat a man or to make it possible for the next handling player to beat a man.

THE COMPLETE BREAK

The ability to spot a gap, or to create one, is a vital asset to any player. One can only be successful if a definite penetration is made. With the ability to spot an opening goes the ability to read a situation. There are two types of complete break: inside and outside.

The inside break is the one that many players favour. It is also the one that runs into the most trouble as it takes you back towards the covering defence. To be successful the move requires a sidestep or dummy, and fast acceleration once the break is made. It also incorporates one of the more difficult problems a defence has to cope with, which is change of direction. Good support is necessary as the player making the break must move the ball as soon as he is through the gap. That is unless he has a clear run to the line.

The outside break, whereby the player moves outside the defender, will rely for success upon the swerve and/or variation of pace. With both types of break the runner with the ball must consciously straighten up his run or else he will either run into the covering defence or crowd the rest of his support players towards the touchline. The 'breaker' must know when to pass if the movement is to be kept going – and at top speed. To achieve this, support must be at hand. In the threequarter line this requires the next player to be able to read the game. In other words, he will realize that a break is on and will react accordingly.

THE HALF-BREAK

This is probably the most telling break of all and the one which shows the class of the player. With the half-break you go for a gap and cause two players to converge towards you. When both are fully committed you give out your pass and the next player will accelerate through the gap created. The half-break has the advantage that the movement can continue at top speed and does not rely upon beating a man, which could slow down the pace of the attack.

Spot a potential gap, create it into a gap and accelerate through and out of it (complete break) or accelerate towards it and then pass (half-break).

Reaction to the break

More advantage should be taken from the clean break. The reason that progress from this break comes to an abrupt halt is that the reaction to the break from the support is slow. The initial thought of the player who has broken through must be: 'I have made a clean break, now I must give the ball to somebody in a better position than me.' He does not look for that man, the momentum would be lost, but he can expect the support to be in close support. His catch-phrase again is 'jink and link'.

This reaction by the support means running closer and deeper to the man who has broken, not fanning away into space. The hole has been made by the ball-carrier, the support goes through the same hole and can then fan.

Drill 95 – one set of backs
From handling, call 'MAKE A BREAK'. A break is made (without opposition) and after running 10 metres the ball is put on the ground. It is picked up by the support and ensures that the support is deep and close to pick up the stationary ball.

Drill 96 – one set of backs
Call 'MAKE A BREAK'. Then shout for the support inside or outside. There should be support on both sides unless it is the outside man that has broken.

Drill 97 – 2 sets of backs
Instruct one of the defence backs to run up ahead of the others or hang back. See if the attackers notice the gap.

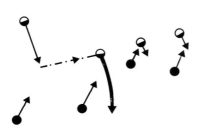

Fig. 81

Drill 98 – 2 sets of backs
Test drift defence by passing inside to support from depth, usually the blind-side wing or full-back from depth.

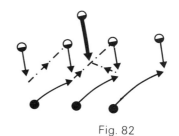

Fig. 82

Drill 99 – 2 sets of backs
Miss-a-man and pass back inside to the man that was missed out.

Drill 100 – 1 set of backs
Call 'MAKE A BREAK' then 'TACKLED'. The ball-carrier stops on his feet and a fellow threequarter takes the ball, not waiting for a pack member to do the job.

Drill 101 – 2 sets of backs
Nominate a player to give a dummy and break. If he fails to penetrate, his running should have been in control long enough for him to stay on his feet and hang on to the ball until support arrives.

Drill 102 – 2 sets of backs
Full-back (or blind-side wing) comes in between gaps (ie between the fly-half and centre, between the centres or between centre and wing). Token opposition to start with, becoming more active as the skills develop.

Drill 103 – 2 sets of backs
Full-back (or blind-side wing) comes in between gaps, wide out after dummy scissors

or miss-a-man. Token opposition until timing is right.

Drill 104 – 1 set of backs
On receiving the ball, the fly-half has a free rein to run in any direction that he wants. His fellow backs have to react to this run and link with him as support or a switch of direction.

Drill 105 – 1 set of backs
The fly-half takes the ball at any angle he wants from the scrum-half and immediately acts as a pivot. His fellow backs work off this pivot.

7. How to Let the Backs Play Naturally?

When it has been decided that passing and receiving in a variety of ways has reached a competent level, it can then be decided how many ways a threequarter line as a unit can beat the opposing threequarter line.

There is a great danger that there are missed opportunities of cutting through the opponent's line because a pre-determined move is religiously carried out, even if the circumstances are wrong for that particular move.

LET-OUT MOVES

The more complicated the move the more timing it takes, and if the source of possession is delayed or untidy the more difficult to perform. Also, the complicated move takes more time, and therefore gives a defence more time to make contact.

So it is important for every move to have a let-out move and every theme an alternative:

1 The switch has a dummy switch.
2 A loop has a dummy loop.
3 The quick distribution has a dummy pass.
4 The extra man in line has a miss-a-man situation.
5 The ball on the burst has a decoy run. Also angles of run can vary and length of passes can vary.

Drill 106 – 2 sets of backs
Token defence as the attacking side per-

forms a penetrating move. The defence then anticipates that move and the attacking side carries out the let-out or alternative move.

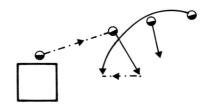

Fig. 83

Example: give the ball to the outside centre cutting back.

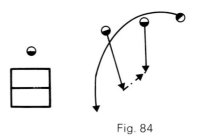

Fig. 84

Alternative: give it to the inside centre on the burst.
Another alternative: a long pass to the full-back or winger, missing out the inside centre.

Drill 107 – 2 sets of backs
Attacking side practises a particular move with its alternatives in any order. The

opposition touch the players' shorts with two hands in defence.

Drill 108 – 2 sets of backs, plus back rows
A defensive side can stop attackers by tackling. The attacking side practises a move with alternatives, but goes through the gap when it appears or hangs on if tackled on their feet, to link with the back row. If the attacker is grounded, he tries to leave the ball in a position for his back row to secure possession.

BACKS MUST RECOGNIZE WHEN THE BALL SHOULD BE PLAYED WIDE

It should be obvious to a back that the opposition has been swallowed up in a ruck, maul or tackling role and that a 5 against 4 or 4 against 3 situation can soon be made into a 2 against 1 situation with slick handling after the initial recognition. It is essential that the forwards' eyes – the scrum-half – gets the ball when he shouts for it to start off this producing of an overlap.

Drill 109 – 2 sets of backs
The coach holds the ball and wanders around the field so that the set of backs have to keep realigning. He then calls one or two of the opposing backs to try and get the ball off him. As they arrive he releases the ball to the other set of backs to see if they can take advantage of one or two of the opposition being out of position.

Drill 110 – 2 sets of backs
The blind-side wing or the full-back come into the line and the opposition are geared to take a channel each. The attacking side try to release the open-side wing.

Drill 111 – 2 sets of backs
The ball is released to a set of backs with the full-back included. They miss a man

naturally in order to get the ball to the open-side wing quickly. This wing will run on the outside of his man in order to widen the gap for the support on the inside.

Drill 112 – 2 sets of backs
The attacking side *naturally* performs a dummy scissors in order to check the defence. The attackers then move the ball out to the wing quickly.

Playing the ball wide from set play

Defences have the chance to be better organized from set play because the build-up of a set scrum or a lineout allows the backs to position themselves. Drift defences (when each defender takes one man further out) reap much benefit if the attackers run across the field. It is important to check the mid-field and back row before playing the ball wide or they will quite happily cover across the field, knocking down attackers on the way.

A curved run by the fly-half and a flat pass to the inside centre can interest the mid-field, but it needs slick handling to continue to play this ball wide because the ground in front of the attackers has been eaten up.

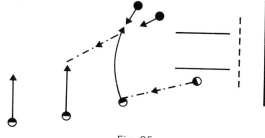

Fig. 85

Another way of straightening up and allowing the ball to be played wide is to give the fly-half a 'corridor' to run across if he wishes, but make sure that the centres

73

run straight when they receive the ball out-side that corridor.

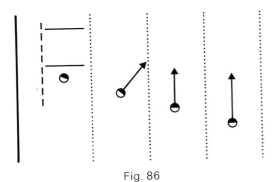

Fig. 86

This takes a lot of discipline from the centres on their lines of running and the timing of these runs. It also takes a sensitive pass from the fly-half because his angle of run is askew with the centres.

The defensive mid-field can also be in-terested by using the fly-half as a pivot with support running from depth to take the ball or act as a decoy.

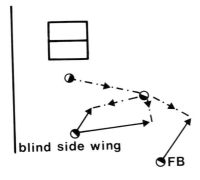

blind side wing

FB

Fig. 87

He would probably have to take the ball standing still for this ploy, and taking the ball standing still is also useful for using the fly-half as a second scrum-half.

For this to be successful, it is important for the inside centre not to move until the

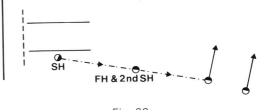

SH

FH & 2nd SH

Fig. 88

ball is in the fly-half's hands. In other words, treat him just as if he was the scrum-half and as if he was the fly-half.

Drill 113 – a set of backs plus 3 defence
Make the set of attacking backs play against a defence of fly-half and two centres. In-struct the three defenders to take defensive channels only to block off the initial paths of the attacking fly-half and two centres. See if the attackers can release men outside these channels.

Drill 114 – a set of backs plus 3 defence
An attacker does not have to *look* for a gap, the gap appears, he recognizes it and goes through it.

Let the 3 defenders drift in defence to cover the attack. When they overstretch, the attacker should take the gap.

Interest the defence by wrong-footing or contact

As every ploy introduced will have an alter-native ploy, it will be relatively simple to use a player as a decoy to wrong-foot a de-fence or to use the same player as a pene-trator. If this player is used as a decoy, he must convince the opposition that he may be given the ball. Sometimes a call for the ball can take the ear and the eye of the de-fender for that crucial second. The players that the ball is eventually given to should benefit from this lessening of pressure on them.

If the player is used as a penetrator, his priorities are:

1 To break through or create a gap.
2 To link with his forward support or to veer out immediately after the initial penetration to link with his fellow backs.
3 To stay in control on impact so that the support can move the ball quickly and take advantage of this initial penetration before the defence regroups. The contact is after all only another way of forcing the defence back on its heels.

Recognize and take advantage of the 2 v 1 situation

Whether the opposition has been wrong-footed, swallowed up or out-flanked, the ball-carrier still has to make sure that this last line of defence is forced to concentrate on one of the attackers only.

The timing of the pass is crucial. He need only study the heels of the defender; once he is flatfooted or committed to tackling the ball-carrier, the ball should be moved. If he is committed to the outside man, the dummy pass would seem appropriate. It is the same if the ball-carrier finds himself forced across the field by the cover. The outside man must react to this path by cutting across, anticipating a switch pass. The pass may well be given, but the important thing is that this run by the would-be receiver takes the opponent's eye and also the pressure off the ball-carrier. The ball-carrier can then make the choice of switching or dummy switching and continuing running.

Defences that try to eliminate a 2 v 1 situation

Many sides have a system of defence that instructs their outside man to stick to his opponent's outside man, even though he has not been given the ball. Again, the timing of the ball-carrier is crucial because the

idea of the defence is to allow the inside man to run and isolate him. The theory is that he will eventually be brought down because the cover has less distance to travel.

The timing of this pass depends on two factors. First, there is a time when this outside defender has to turn to stick with his man. If the attacking outside man can drift outside his defender at this time, the longer pass should put him away. If the outside defender is slow to turn, the ball-carrier should be through the gap inside this defender and ready to pass to the outside man before the defender recovers.

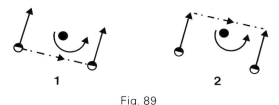

Fig. 89

Drill 115 – sets of 4
Each line interpasses through the line in front.

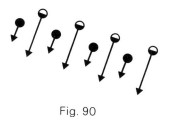

Fig. 90

BACK PLAY FROM SET SCRUMS

What the backs decide to do with the ball should be decided by five factors, which may be interlinked:

1 The position of the set scrum on the field.

75

Using Possession

2 Timing of the release of the ball from the set scrum.

3 The path of the ball from scrum-half to fly-half.

4 Noting the weak side of the scrum-half.

5 Any weakness of opposing backs.

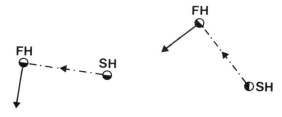

Fig. 92

Scrums on the left-hand side of the field

If a quick ball is wanted, this is the side to attempt to use it. The scrum-half is running his natural way with his opposing scrum-half chasing behind him. So although it is the weaker side for most scrum-halves to pass it is the easy side to dive pass, which can be the quickest pass to a fly-half. This quick pass can be wasted if the fly-half stands unnecessarily too far away.

There could also be less pressure on the fly-half by the flanker because he would have to watch the scrum-half first as it would be his natural running path.

The fly-half running perpendicular to the path of the ball has unlocked hips for passing, but he would have to run across the field to keep his hips unlocked with the deeper pass.

As the ball is quicker and the backs can run straighter, there is more time and the ball can be played wide. If the fly-half can interest his opposite number by running straighter, it should stop the defence drifting across. This man-to-man defence gives the opportunity for the attack to vary the lengths of passes and shift the alignment. Enough to run straight on the weak tackling side of the defender with a short pass, or a longer pass to get on the outside of the defender.

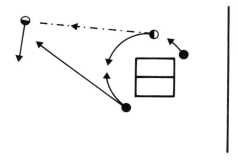

Fig. 91

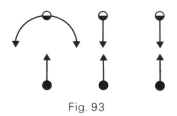

Fig. 93

However, this measure could be more effective using extra men. The obvious candidates are the left wing and the full-back.

The ball from scrum-half to fly-half can be a flatter ball, so the fly-half can run straighter, with unlocked hips, to distribute and he can run onto the ball if he wants to. To continue this straighter running a flatter alignment is wanted, coupled with slick handling.

The advantage of the left wing coming on the outside of any of the mid-field trio is that he is coming from depth on to a short ball, aiming to penetrate. If he delays moving until the ball is put into the scrum he may well shake off his opposite number. Backs tend to focus their eyes on the set scrum at that moment and not on their opposite number. The ball on the outside of the passer allows the penetrator to be shielded from view until the last seconds. The ball to the left wing on the inside really needs a decoy going wide to get the defence to drift across.

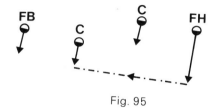

Fig. 95

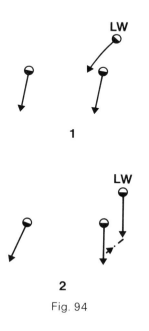

Fig. 94

The full-back can penetrate wide, but it must be remembered that from scrums the threequarter lines are fairly close together. Certainly closer than from lineouts because of the law demands. This means that the fewer hands the ball goes through, the quicker the ball can get into the full-back's hands. A deeper alignment gives more room but exaggerates running across the field, so the penetration by the full-back would be ineffective. Miss-a-man moves will certainly help get the ball into the full-back's hands quicker, but it must be remembered by coaches that the average threequarter has more difficulty passing from left to right. This should not stop him, but he should be aware of the problem.

Initially, threequarters have success in penetrating by bringing the ball back; they have more time, it is safer, and they can start with a deeper alignment. The ball is also being brought back to more support. There are many variations possible in performing this theme using either the centre, right wing or full-back. This can only be productive if the support is used properly when the penetrator is eventually stopped. This penetrator has done his job and if he keeps the ball available, a quick ball from the ruck or maul is essential to make it all worth while. If it is not a quick ball, all the team really has is a situation similar to the one as the ball was put into the original set scrum – probably in the same place! This quick ball can be used wide or for driving off again, but it must be quick.

If the left-hand side of the scrum is wide enough, a late call from the fly-half can carry the ball from right to left, linking with the full-back on the blind, or he can take the ball standing still and feed the full-back on the blind.

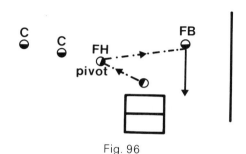

Fig. 96

Using Possession

The diagonal kick is widely used on this side of the field because most fly-halves are right-footed and the right leg is shielded by the body from potential initial contact. The kick back into the box is again widely used by right-footers on this side because the right leg is shielded and he can hook naturally his kick back. If the left wing can threaten to come into the line and tempt his opposite number over, the kick can be even more effective. The high kick under the posts is also easier to execute on this side because the kicker can hoist the ball with a hooked swinging action of the leg.

The sideways dive pass

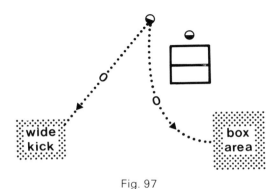

Fig. 97

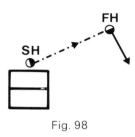

Fig. 98

Because of this initial pass, the fly-half runs on to the ball. To unlock hips he must run across the field and moves cutting back come quite naturally or at least dummy switches.

Scrums on the right-hand side of the field

The pass from scrum-half to fly-half is even more significant from this side of the field.

If a quick ball is wanted, the scrum-half will have to turn back on himself to deliver the pass. This turns into a sideways dive pass which also helps protect the ball from the opposing scrum-half. See the photo.

A twisting action is required for this pass, so the pass from scrum-half to fly-half cannot be expected to be as flat as the dive pass from left to right. See Fig. 98.

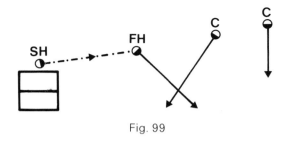

Fig. 99

If the threequarters want to play the ball wide, a conscious effort must be made by the centres to pick their own straight lines to meet up with the fly-half running across.

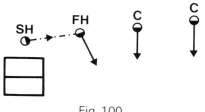

Fig. 100

The standing pass by the scrum-half is possible, but it requires control in the scrum and more time. This extra care is needed because the opposing scrum-half is between the scrum-half and fly-half. The advantage is that it is usually the easier way for the scrum-half to pass. He can stand directly behind the scrum and collect the ball from the No. 8 to give himself more room.

To play the ball wide, because it is usually the easier way for backs to pass as well, the fly-half may have to consider taking a standing pass, because time has been eaten up controlling the ball. The men outside the fly-half have to be disciplined enough to delay their run until it is in the fly-half's hands. More room has been made outside by giving the fly-half the role of scrum-half, and giving the inside centre the role of fly-half. The full-back can now be involved in this wide play.

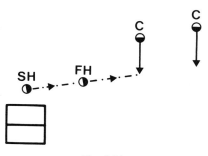

Fig. 101

This is the better side to bring the ball back as a general guide. The opposing right-hand flanker can unleash himself

easily from this side as seen in the defence systems, but he can overcommit himself on the fly-half and bringing the ball back could result in profitable penetration.

The right wing is difficult to bring into the open side of the field, but if used he can pick various angles to run on the blind side. As this is the natural running side of the scrum-half, there can be a direct linkage with the right wing with inside or outside passes, as long as this winger has the confidence to delay his run. As already mentioned, the right wing can be involved in back-row moves on this blind side. Once a set scrum has been earned on the right-hand side near their goal line, a try must be expected because of the variety of ways that a 2 v 1 situation can be created.

Kicks are not as easy for the right-footed kicker on this side of the field, and unless the fly-half stands behind the scrum or doubles back to face the right touchline, the box kick is not possible. However, the scrum-half can take over this role. The diagonal kick is possible but with an exposed leg to the tackle. A left-footed centre would help if the ball was transferred to him quickly, or the fly-half could become two-footed!

The high kick under the post is also difficult on this side unless the right-footer takes the ball standing still, and probably facing his own scrum-half so he can swing his kicking foot in a hooking action.

Scrums in the middle of the field

With a split defence facing the scrum, it is a simple matter to create a 4 against 3 situation. The 3 against 2 is more dangerous to the opposition, and ideally the most dangerous 2 against 1 will be created.

The defence is at its most stretched even before the ball is put into the scrum. The fly-half can stand directly behind his own scrum and run right or left. The weakness of course is that he will probably run across the field to collect the pass, but adjusting by using the men outside him should straighten the line and hopefully create an extra man.

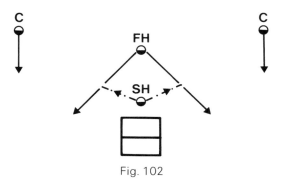

Fig. 102

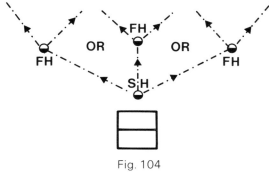

Fig. 104

To make middle-of-the-field situations really effective, the centres and the full-backs must be prepared to put themselves in the role of fly-half. The official fly-half can then use himself as a decoy, and a centre or the full-back can take the pass from the scrum-half.

of surprise plus the possible half wheel should allow the scrum-half or No. 8 to run to the left. Penetration should be simple and the opportunity should not be wasted.

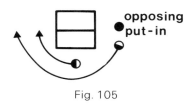

Fig. 105

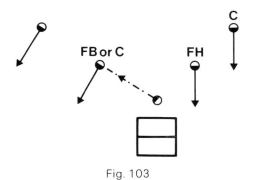

Fig. 103

The fly-half can also take a standing pass and use himself as a pivot to set off any of the backs as an 'extra' fly-half. See Fig. 104.

The ball against the head

This is one of the rare occasions for a scrum-half to run to the left. The element

Be positive from set scrums

The ball should be used in a positive way from set scrums because it is the only source of possession that a team should be able to depend on.

A team expects to get its own ball from a set scrum, so it must be used, positively and constructively.

BACK PLAY FROM LINEOUTS

From set scrums there were four inter-linked factors that determined what the backs could do when possession had been gained:

1 Position on field
2 Timing of release of ball

3 Path of ball from scrum-half to fly-half
4 Weak side of scrum-half.

None of these factors is as important from lineouts, which is quite ironic because the initial possession from the lineout is less assured and usually of an untidier nature. However, if a team can get possession from the lineout there should be more advantage from using this possession.

As the possession is usually near the touchline, there is always a great width of the field to use. If the ball is caught in the lineout and fed back after this possession, the opposition backs are still back 10 metres from the gain line. The path of the ball from scrum-half to fly-half can be flat from both sides of the field and the weak side of a scrum-half can be compensated with a pivot pass if the scrum-half is given the right protection.

Even if the fly-half wished to run diagonally across the field to set up a scissors or a dummy scissors he could still take a flat ball from the scrum-half because the nearest man from the opposition would be the flanker at the back of the lineout.

Of course the real advantage of ball from a lineout is the opportunity of playing the ball wider because of the gap between the attacking and defending backs.

With the flatter ball from scrum-half to fly-half and the space in front of the attackers, there is no excuse for the mid-field not to run straight and therefore leave many paths for the full-back to enter as a penetrator or a link. Also the winger has so much width that he can stretch a defence across the field. See Fig. 106.

The blind-side wing also has the opportunity to roam and he must bear in mind that the ideal time to move in field is when the lineout is in progress and all eyes are on that lineout. This may loosen his marking because the opposing blind-side wing will probably be stuck behind the lineout.

As the open-side wing has so much width

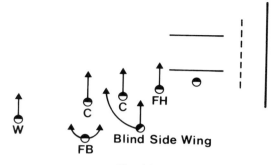

Fig. 106

and depth, his angles of run can be devastating. He can easily start on the outside of his opposite number or have the depth to run back to the centre to penetrate. A well-known ploy with options is as shown in Fig. 107.

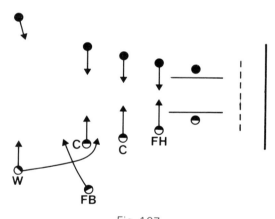

Fig. 107

The fly-half has the opportunity to straighten up before transferring.

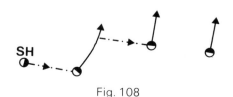

Fig. 108

81

But he also has the opportunity to take a standing pass and act as a second scrum-half. This alignment has been called *Whiplash* because the penetration suddenly comes wider out.

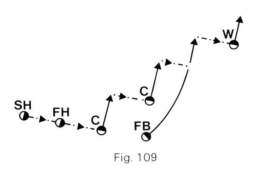

Fig. 109

It is so important that the centres do not move (or creep) before the ball is in the fly-half's hands. The full-back or blind-side wing can certainly inject pace to whiplash this movement.

ATTACKING KICKS FROM LINEOUTS

The advantage of the wide alignment is that an attacking winger can get outside his opposite wing before the ball is kicked to this wing. See Fig. 110.

It is natural to place this diagonal kick for the right wing because the fly-half shields his own kick if he is right-footed. It is just as effective for the left wing, probably due to the quicker and stronger pass of the scrum-half passing from right to left and the ability of the fly-half to interest the opposition by running and then hooking the ball to the left.

The box kick to the left over the lineout is also effective because the fly-half can first interest the defence by running right and perhaps lure the opposing right wing across before hooking the ball to the left touchline.

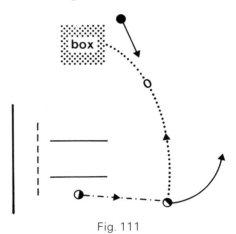

Fig. 111

The high kick under the posts is particularly effective because with the space in front of them and a flatter alignment, the

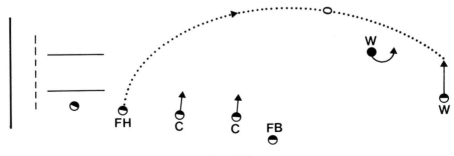

Fig. 110

centres can be adjacent to the fly-half kicking and cause problems to the catcher by chasing this high ball. They have been given the chance to build up a fair head of steam before the ball was kicked. It is important for these chasers to actually try and catch or knock back this hanging ball and they must realize that the defending catcher is flat-footed waiting for this ball to descend.

Scrum-halves can also be effective kickers into the box. The technique of taking a step back from the lineout before hoisting the kick to the box gives more time and an effective kick.

ALIGNMENT FROM RUCKS AND MAULS

The emphasis is on driving forward before the ball is released from the ruck and maul. This source of possession is an ever-moving base, and as possession is less certain, alignment can become 'lazy' or as a compromise never deep enough to run, never close enough to bring in opposition and then outflank them with slick handling, and never flat enough to be effective in defence. It is important to keep realigning on the man inside.

It is particularly important for the fly-half to be close to the scrum-half because possession could be untidy from rucks and mauls and a scrum-half does not have the time to look for his fly-half with a pass.

Drill 116 – 2 teams
The coach wanders between packs all over the field. The packs follow him and the backs constantly realign. He then gives the ball to one of the packs. The backs recognize whether they have won or lost the ball and align in an attacking or defending formation from the maul or ruck. Use the alignment to loop on the outside again.

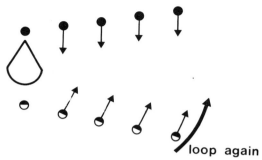

loop again

Fig. 112

How can the backs play naturally?

It is important for the backs to have the confidence to try things in the game and this confidence is boosted with the knowledge that if things go wrong it is easy to recover the situation. As long as 100 per cent decisions are made by players they should have the blessing of others to work out their own options. Confidence that a wrong decision or a thwarted attempt only *delays* progress or at least by hanging on to the ball will retain possession as support arrives, gives a fresh and positive approach to attack.

Drill 117 – 2 teams
One team practises attacking with only token opposition to start. The coach calls 'DROP THE BALL' when a movement is in full flow. This free ball will be dived on to secure possession, or the support will scoop it up to carry on the movement. This will certainly take away the tension that is felt when a team is uncertain that a movement can be successful. In this drill the team is practising breakdowns so they should react more quickly when one appears in a match.

Hang on

A threequarter must realize that when he is

83

tackled he is only being asked to 'hang on' for one to one-and-a-half seconds for the support to arrive. The support is certainly not expected to be more than five metres away, which is about one second away (assuming 100 metres in 20 seconds).

Drill 118 – 1 team
Before releasing the backs give one of these backs a number between 1 and 3. This player will make a break, simulate a tackle and give the ball to the support in order of the number given to him. For instance, if 3 was called he will dummy the ball to the first two that drive past him, but give it to the third man.

Using the blind side

There should always be an element of surprise about using the blind side – if there is not, the lack of space can easily be bottled up by the defending side. Set scrums on the right-hand side of the field are a natural way to create a 2 against 1 situation. The natural running side for the scrum-half has full support from the No. 8, blind-side flanker and right wing. A variety of movements on this side of the scrum are simple and direct and should develop 2 against 1 situations. Set scrums on the left can created blind-side ploys but they are more complicated and most of them depend on a slightly wheeled attacking scrum to start off the movement. This ensures that the defending back row is initially cut off from this blind side. Mauls and rucks provide the most opportunity to set up the blind side.

Drill 119 – 2 teams
From a set scrum or a lineout, create a ploy to penetrate. From the penetration demand a quick ball from the breakdown and probe the blind side immediately.

Increase the opposition and then allow the half-backs the option of using the blind side from quick possession, from breakdown or a continuation to the open.

Drill 120 – 1 team, limited opposition
The opposition are scattered around the field with a ball. The attacking pack goes for one of these men, turns him and takes the ball from him. The limited opposition are then hurriedly trying to regroup. The attacking fly-half calls 'BLIND' or 'OPEN' as he spots the weaker side. The other threequarters respond.

Drill 121 – 1 team or 1 threequarter line
During a passing movement, the coach calls 'TACKLED'. The ball-carrier stays on his feet and passes to any player looping outside him to carry on the movement the same way.

Let a man run

The deeper the position, the easier it is for a player to run because the marking is slacker. If this player is initially neglected by the defence, he has the opportunity to run, and if his own support reacts, this run will snowball as more players get into a position to support and continue a movement.

Drill 122 – 1 team and limited opposition
The opposition chip the ball to the opposition. The catcher uses his footwork to penetrate and either link or be 'picked up' by his forwards.

Drill 123 – 1 team and limited opposition
The 'One Man Road Show'. Nominate a back and he must be involved two or three times in a flowing movement from one end of the pitch to the other. The coach will call 'TACKLED', 'DOWN', 'RUCK' or 'MAUL', to set up breakdowns, but the nominated player must be involved after every breakdown. He will look for support or his team-mates will work the ball to him.

Drill 124 – 1 team and limited opposition
The coach will throw the ball to one of two nominated players. That player will attack immediately. Let the movement develop, then the team abandons that movement because the coach throws a second ball to the other nominated player to attack. By the time this movement has developed the coach has retrieved the original ball and is ready to set up the first nominated player again.

Have an attacking attitude from set play

There are players who think that it is very difficult to score from set play. This may be so, but tries must be scored from set play, and also many tries can be made possible by second-phase possession. A team tries to pierce the defence from first phase and this positive approach, plus a sophistication of keeping the ball available on contact, has made it possible for a score.

Drill 125 – 1 team and limited opposition
'Five lives.' Give a team an attacking position and let them initially have possession from a set scrum or lineout. If they score *direct* from the set play with limited opposition of say four threequarters plus a pack they get two points. If they score from the resulting ruck or maul from the original play, they get one point. Then a chart can be devised:

Opposition	Score from set play	Score from resultant ruck or maul
Pack + 4 threes (SH, FH, 2 centres)	2 pts	1 pt
Pack + 5 threes (SH, FH, 2 centres, blind-side wing)	3 pts	2 pts
Pack + 6 threes (SH, FH, 2 centres, 2 wings)	4 pts	3 pts
Full team	6 pts	4 pts

Drill 126 – 2 teams
In the opposition's 22-metre area, let the attacking team have an attacking three-quarter formation even when it is the opposition's throw-in. The lineout is such a lottery it seems a sensible thing to do. See if the attackers can react when the defence do get the ball. In the majority of cases the defending team will defend its lines by kicking anyway. If their kicks are directed to touch, the pack plus half-backs will put pressure on the kickers because they are in the vicinity. If the kick is put upfield, the attacking threequarters should be able to recover.

The backs need the confidence that they will get controlled possession

The backs certainly do not want the ball 'shovelled' out to them, together with an opposing back row and back division. A loose ball given to them by the pack is a liability. The possession must be quick, but above all it must come from a tight and driving forward combination that continues to drive forward until the ball is released to the scrum-half.

Drill 127 – 2 teams or 1 team and limited opposition to start with
The coach gives the ball to the attacking pack at various angles so they can gather, secure and drive. When the ball is in the scrum-half's hands, he immediately gives it to the coach so he can give the ball to the regrouping pack again. The coach does this three times. On the fourth possession, the scrum-half releases the ball to the backs.

Drill 128 – 2 teams or 1 team with limited opposition to start with
Similar to Drill 127 above, but this time the decision is with the scrum-half to 'snipe' or to set up a forward to snipe. Two snipings

85

Using Possession

by the scrum-half or forwards, then release the ball to the backs.

Get into a rhythm

Running lengths of the field with continual handling and different themes improves lines of running for the support. There is a danger that pack members will work on the theory that the shortest distance between two points is a straight line and be more concerned about getting to the breakdown quickly than about coming from an angle deep enough to support.

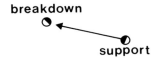

Wrong

Right

Fig. 113

The coach must be very conscious about the lines of running by the support.

Drill 129 – I team

The coach gives a theme to be carried out for the whole length of the field. For example:

1 Threequarters switch to penetrate, then the ball is picked up by the pack when 'TACKLED' is called; spin the ball to the wing, inside pass to the support, close interpassing by forwards, set up a ruck, or dummy scissors and spin out to score.

2 Run blind from set scrum, set up a maul, spin the ball to the open, full-back takes the ball on the burst, makes a break, call 'TACKLED', set up a ruck, use the blind side, set up a ruck, spin along the line to score.

The themes are announced before the ball is played and the team tries to complete each theme.

Drill 130 – I team

'Punch and Spin.' Let the team make their own decisions on how they penetrate (punch) or spin. The coach gives them the starting possession, scrum, lineout, ruck or maul and also the theme. Example: punch, punch, spin, spin.

The team then has to penetrate, penetrate from the breakdown position and close to the breakdown, then spin the ball wide, set up another breakdown, spin the ball wide again.

The theme can start with three instructions, for example spin, punch, spin. Then they will be ready to take four instructions.

PART 4

Retaining and Regaining Possession

8. The Ball Must Be Kept Available After Contact

Before the present tackle law came in, players were relatively competent in using the ball before contact and also dealing with the ball after they hit the ground. The tackle law now forbids players to touch the ball on hitting the ground, so techniques are required to use the time taken to fall down and present the ball to support. First of all, players must learn how to fall properly.

Drill 131 – individual practice
Players put their hands on their head and practise a 'parashooter's fall', where contact with the ground is done gradually up the side of the body from ankle upwards to armpit.

Drill 132 – individual practice
As in Drill 131, but running in between in a set direction.

USE THE TACKLER TO HELP YOU

Of course, there is a difference of wills here. The tackler is not only trying to bring his opponent down, but is also trying to stop the man passing.

The man who is being tackled has three priorities:

1 To stay on his feet.
2 To use the tackler to support him as he presents the ball.
3 To use the tackler to control his fall to

the ground, so that he can present the ball.

It is really a matter of the ball-carrier being completely in control of the pace that he is running when contact is inevitable. There is a great danger of going a metre too far, losing the ball and the opposition gaining 20 metres. It is not worth it for that extra metre.

When the ball-carrier is confronted with a tackler, he must think of one of four things:

1 Using footwork to beat or minimize the impact of the tackle.
2 Using the free arm to fend off or control the tackler.
3 Putting the ball beyond the tackler ready to distribute.
4 Putting his body in a position to shield the ball from the tackler.

Using footwork in the tackle

If the timing of the footwork is right, the ball-carrier can then force the tackler to take him to one side. This gives the ball-carrier more chance to take the impact on his terms and use the tackler as support.

When the impact is made, the ball will be held in two hands over the tackle. The ball-carrier will jack-knife and wrap his body around the tackler's head. By then, resting an elbow on the back of the tackler, the ball-carrier is in a strong position to distribute to support or control his fall and present the ball on the way down.

Use the tackler to help distribution

Drill 133 – in fours
3 players on the goal-line (middle man with the ball), 1 player 7 metres away. The player with the ball uses footwork to create a side tackle away from the fourth player. The other 2 players on the goal-line do not move until contact has been made, they then run to support, one on each side of the tackled man so that the tackled man has a choice of which side to pass. Normally, the pass will be on the same side as the tackle,

but the longer the delay the more the ball-carrier is twisted around until the support on the other side is the obvious man to give the ball to. See Fig. 114.

Drill 134 – 2 attackers, 2 defenders
One defender will be 3 metres away and an attacker with the ball will create a side tackle. He will try to make contact with the outside hip by turning in towards the tackle.

Outside hip on contact

This will give the ball-carrier the opportunity to spin out of the tackle or set up the support that is directly behind. If he spins out of the tackle, he carries on to meet the next defender who will be 7 metres away but coming from the same side as the first defender. If he is held, the support goes on

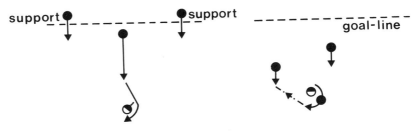

Fig. 114

to the next defender. Practise from both sides.

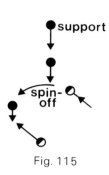

Fig. 115

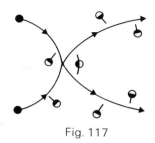

Fig. 117

Drill 137 – 4 attackers, 4 defenders

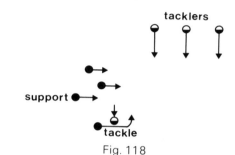

Fig. 118

Shielding the knee – use of the hand-off

Players have to get used to holding the ball in one hand and quickly transferring it to the other hand or both hands. The free hand can then be used to shield the knee from any low tackle. The hand-off is a useful weapon to protect the knee because it can be used as a lever to help sway the hips and knees from the tackler.

Drill 135 – 3 or 4 attackers, 6 or 7 defenders
The defenders kneel in one long line about 7 metres apart. The attackers weave between the defenders, handing off as the defenders try and tackle. The defenders must stay on their knees.

The defenders are 10 metres apart and the attacker with 3 men in support tries to hand off the defender. If he fails, he can still use the hand-off arm to steady himself as he leans on the back of the defender and presents the ball with one hand.

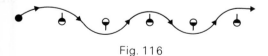

Fig. 116

Drill 136 – 3 attackers, 6 or 7 defenders
The defenders stand in a fairly confined space and the attackers weave between them, handing off to a defender's chest and therefore having to keep transferring the ball to the other arm.

Distribution after a failed hand-off

91

Shielding the knee – use of the arm with shoulder

It looks as if the player is dipping his shoulder into the opposition, but if a player emphasizes this there is a danger of him forcing the shoulder down, becoming un-stable and over-balancing. It is so much better for the player to think of protecting his knee with a bent arm, which will mean that the elbow is at the lowest point. This will naturally bring the shoulder down, but will have the advantage of making the player bend his knees.

Shielding the knee – use of the straight vertical arm

The difficulty created for the defender by this move is that he has to tackle three 'legs' instead of two. The attacker runs with his inside arm vertical. The defender has that extra width to tackle, and if the tackle is not broken the tackler usually can only grab the arm and one leg. Again, the attacker can lean into the tackler and present the ball to support with one hand.

Straight arm used to break a tackle

Body lean

Defences are very conscious about the tackled player being able to give the ball to support, so many tackles are higher in an attempt to 'smother' the man and the ball. The tackler is also aware of going for the ball in the tackle. This means that the more upright the attacker, the more vulnerable he is to contact and to losing the ball.

If the player with the ball has the attitude of mind that there should always be parts of or the whole of his arm plus shoulder between the ball and the would-be tackler, he will naturally develop body lean.

Drill 138 – 4 attackers, 8 defenders

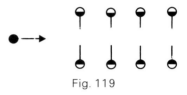

Fig. 119

This is called 'running the gauntlet'. The 8 defenders in pairs hold out an inside arm like the swing doors of a Wild West saloon. The attacker runs between these pairs, making sure that the ball is protected and that his upper body is first to make contact with the outstretched arms of the defenders.

CUTTING EDGE

The players should realize that one shoulder will tend to lead to produce a more forceful cutting edge – the difference between using the sharp edge of a knife to cut a cake and using the side of the knife.

Drill 139 – 4 attackers, 8 defenders
Same formation as Drill 138, but the attacker will progress from holding the ball in two hands to holding the ball in one hand. He will also fend off the outstretched arms with his forearm. The defenders will also progress to attempting to knock the ball from the attacker's grasp.

Drill 140 – 1 attacker, 2 distributors

Fig. 120

The 2 distributors hold the ball between them at different levels and the attacker accelerates between them to take the ball 'with the armpit'. Accelerating with the proper body lean will make sure that the ball sticks and is not dropped.

Drill 141 – 1 attacker, 3 or 4 passive defenders

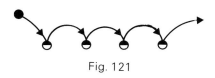

Fig. 121

The attacker drives into the passive defenders with the ball on the same side as contact. This means that the ball and the shoulder combined form a buffer and determine body lean. The attacker drives into each defender in turn.

Drill 142 – 3 attackers, 2 defenders

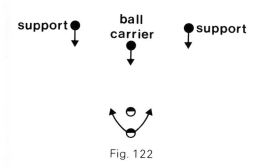

Fig. 122

Shield the ball with the shoulder and distribute. As the attacker approaches the static defender, the man behind the defender moves to the right or the left. Naturally, the ball-carrier will give the ball to the support on the opposite side to the one where the extra defender placed himself, after driving in with the shoulder to the static defender.

Drill 143 – 1 attacker, 2 defenders

Fig. 123

The ball-carrier sidesteps and aims at the gap between the two static defenders. The defenders should bring him down and the ball-carrier should continue driving as the ball is left behind him on the floor. The ball must be placed on the ground or 'persuaded' backwards as he is driving forward, not after he has hit the ground. (If the ball-carrier finds himself 'full-frontal' on his drive, the ball may well be persuaded backwards between his legs.)

Popeye

The strongest part of the body to fend off with is the forearm. In conjunction with the shoulder it is such a strong joint to lever away the would-be tackler, hence the name Popeye who is renowned for his strength in the forearm. It produces a much more aggressive approach by the attacker because he is able to force back the very man who initially wanted to force him back. The attacker is again full-frontal, but levering away with the forearm again produces a body lean and also allows the attacker to fall down on his own terms if he cannot get away from the defender.

93

Drill 144 – 1 attacker, 1 defender

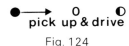

Fig. 124

The ball is placed one metre in front of a static defender. The attacker goes down on his knees to pick up the ball so that he can immediately drive upwards into the defender and lever away with his arm.

Drill 145 – 4 attackers, 8 defenders
Same formations as drills 138 and 139, except that the defenders are closer together (the gap is narrower) and the attacker has to be full-frontal. The defenders will still be passive, but the attacker must lever away with his forearm.

REACTING TO DIFFERENT TACKLES

The time has come for the ball-carrier to react to high and low tackles coming from different angles, so it is possible to build up a series of obstacles for the attacker to overcome. Tell the attacker what to expect on his path so that he can take evasive action or use support if he is stopped.

Give the attacker an easy obstacle to start him on his way.

Drill 146 – 1 attacker, 2 support, 5 defence
If ever the attacker is stopped at any of the 5 stations, the support players will carry on the role. See Fig. 125.

Obstacles can be changed or placed in a different order. See Figs. 126 and 127.

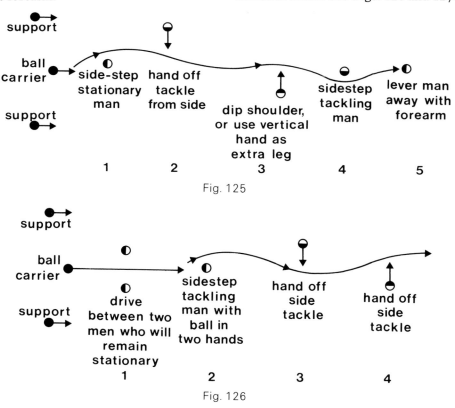

Fig. 125

Fig. 126

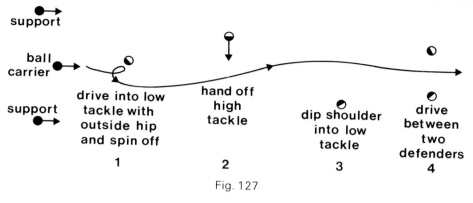

support

ball
carrier

support

drive into low
tackle with
outside hip
and spin off

1

hand off
high
tackle

2

dip shoulder
into low
tackle

3

drive
between
two
defenders

4

Fig. 127

9. Regaining Possession as a Unit

RECOGNIZING BROKEN PLAY SITUATIONS

Players must be made to recognize that they do not have to depend on the rub of the green to obtain possession from broken play. These situations can be recognized instantly and how to exploit them can be practised. Players must practise the unusual – which is what happens 80 per cent of the time!

The last chapter dealt with winning possession from ruck and maul, but it must be accepted that a team will have to regain possession not only if the opposition have the ball, but also if the opposition have stopped your initial flow of attack.

If these situations are practised, it should give a team more confidence to try attacking moves knowing that they have a chance to regain possession if they are stopped.

Rucking and mauling after going backwards

If a team is going backwards they have one aim, and that is to check the backward movement as quickly and efficiently as possible. If the ball is loose on the ground, it is not enough just to fall on the ball. The player must be prepared to drop and bounce up immediately into the oncoming opposition. If he succeeds in bouncing up towards the opposition it will certainly be a form of counterattack.

'Bouncing up' into opposition

If he succeeds in standing up, he can hang on and form a base for his support – a maul. If he gets halfway up, he can make sure that the ball is secure for the following ruck. If he stands up then there will be a priority towards mauling, and this makes sense because backsides would be facing the opposition and that is not recommended in rucking. As a general rule, if a player is going forward scoop the ball up, if going backwards drop on it.

Drill 147 – in sixes
The coach or person nominated in charge of the six stands in front of a semi-circle of players. See Fig. 128.

The coach rolls the ball in front of him and shouts a number. That player scoops the ball up and gives it to the coach, who

96

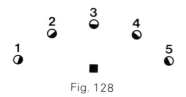

Fig. 128

rolls it straight away, calling another number. Meanwhile, the first player is getting back to his original position. There will soon be gaps in the semi-circle and the coach will throw the ball through the gap, one player will have to drop on it and bounce up and the others will be back in support to set up a maul.

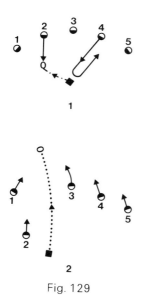

Fig. 129

The coach can have an ally by his side to chase the ball that goes behind the semi-circle and put pressure on the defenders.

Drill 148 – goalkeepers in groups of 4
The higher the level of play, the faster the game. To make a final point, the player may only have time to stop the ball bobbing about and that is all! So it is important that a player is prepared to get down on the

ground and stop any movement of the ball. This may mean just diving down and securing the ball with one hand as you would expect a goalkeeper in soccer to do.

One player rolls the ball along the ground and shouts the name of another player. This named player dives on this ball before it stops rolling of its own accord. He gets up right away and rolls the ball in a completely different direction, calling another name. It is important for all the group to follow the ball even though only one will dive on it. If not, the players will be too spread and the ball will not be able to be rolled *away* from the next player.

Drill 149 – the pack
Similar to Drill 23 on page 32 when one man jogged slightly in front of the others and braced himself when the command 'RUCK ON' was called. The instant body lean, binding and driving for 5 metres was looked for.

For this drill there is also a man behind. The commands are now 'RUCK ON' or 'RUCK BACK'. For the latter the pack have to race back in a tight circle parallel to the touchline to drive the back marker.

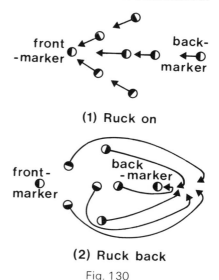

(1) Ruck on

(2) Ruck back

Fig. 130

97

Rob the opposition

If a player happens to catch a member of the opposition facing his way there is always a chance that he can rob him of the ball.

Drill 150 – in pairs
One upright player with the ball, the other gets his hands around the ball, he then slides his arm down to his armpit and continues applying his bodyweight and curling to the ground. He robs the opposition and then releases the ball as he reaches the ground.

Drill 151 – in pairs
In boxing they call it 'the old one two'. The robbing player exerts pressure downwards as in drill 150. The opposition responds with an upward resistance. If the first player goes with this upward movement, the ball will come loose. The timing of the initial downward exertion and the upward drive are very important.

Initial upward pressure followed by downward pressure is just as effective.

Drill 152 – 1 against 4, 5 or 6
The one 'volunteer' will try and find a way through the 4, 5 or 6 men. The only problem is that the area will be very restricted, and he will have to run upright with the ball!

The chances are that he will be swallowed up, but the practice is how quickly he can be robbed of the ball.

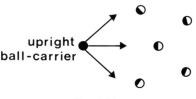

Fig. 131

Drill 153 – in fours
One man as opposition has the ball thrown behind him but high enough for him to get back and catch it. The first man will turn him and make sure that he remains open, ie he does not curl up to shield the ball. The following two men will organize themselves to rob the ball.

This is where confidence in each other is important. The robbing may be difficult, but the second man may only be able to lessen the grip by taking a hand or a finger away from the ball-carrier, but that makes it easier for the third man to rob.

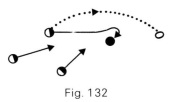

Fig. 132

If the first man is running at an angle, he can effortlessly grab the shoulder edges of the opposition and twist them around as he carries on at the same angle. The upper body then twists around quite easily – the rest of the body has got to follow!

If the opposition is pulled to the ground, the ball will still be exposed to your own team and the initial ball-carrier will have to release it.

Lazy alignment

Although players are quite sensitive to alignment from set play, they are not urgent about getting back to a position where they can run onto the ball from broken play, ruck and maul. Of course, the outside man cannot realign until his inside man has positioned himself. As a guide, the outside man should be able to read the number on the back of his inside man. The ball from broken play can be devastating if it is used well, but so many alignments are 'lazy', neither flat enough to defend nor deep enough to attack. In most cases, players should be able to see if they have a chance of winning or losing a ruck or maul, and as it develops have time to adjust their alignment.

Drill 154 – sixes, with a group (as wanted) to set up a mini ruck or maul

The coach has the ball and wanders up and down or sideways around the field, followed by his mini ruck or maul group. The backs continuously have to readjust to his position. The coach will also be shouting out if the team are about to lose or win the ball, and this will take a further adjustment by the backs. Every 5 or 6 shouts he will actually give the ball to his mini ruck or maul group or the opposition group and let them play from it.

Drill 155 – team with opposition as required

Same pattern as drill 154 but call in 1 or 2 threequarters with the forwards. Release these threequarters, giving them just enough time to realign before the forwards give the ball to the scrum-half.

Having a clatter

It is quite spectacular to see a pack of forwards interpassing in full flow. It has been called seeing the forwards 'having a clatter'. This interpassing unfortunately tends to peter out because the forwards do not use their strength of direct running and either spread out or pass across the field.

That is why forwards must be conscious of passing the ball back 'from whence it came'. Of course this does not happen every time, but forwards should be aware that if 2 or 3 passes have all gone to the left, play must be drifting that way and the defence is committed that way. The pass back should flat-foot and off-balance the defence. The support must be directly behind so

that they can adjust to the ball being passed either way.

Drill 156 – the pack
Interpassing up the field, continually passing the ball back from whence it came.

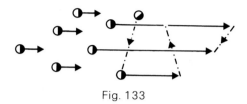

Fig. 133

Drill 157 – the team
Allow the backs to pass the ball from a ruck or maul, but somewhere along the line, call for an inside pass to a supporting forward. The forwards can then start interpassing. Allow the ball to go through 6 pairs of hands before setting up another maul or ruck for the backs.

Drill 158 – the team
The backs must get the ball to the outside man as quickly as possible. Depending on their alignment at the time, they will miss men out quite naturally to achieve this. The forward support will now be more spread than it was in drill 157 when the outside man passes inside to the nearest forward, but the forwards will still be able to interpass.

MAKING THE MOST OF BROKEN PLAY SITUATIONS

If a team has practised dealing with the ball going backwards, robbing the opposition of ball and realigning quickly, then a new attacking dimension should be added to their game. It will take the opposition by surprise if it is executed slickly because defences take time to organize against such play.

A quick ball from the loose

A pack in particular should be sensitive to previous situations. The opposition could be in disarray or some have been swallowed up at a breakdown point, or both. This would mean that the threequarters could profitably use a quick ball.

Most of this pack would probably have to be told that a quick ball is required. It must be remembered that most of this pack are 'donkeys', a bit blinkered but they have big ears for listening. Their eyes must be the scrum-half and he must shout commands all the time, especially when he wants the ball. The scrum-half can also help his pack by pointing out where the ball is. This sometimes helps the referee as well because there is nothing more infuriating than the referee blowing up for a set scrum just as the ball is emerging from the ruck or maul. The pack must get used to the scrum-half's ways of communication.

Drill 159 – the pack and scrum-half, plus opposition pack
The pack initially set up a maul and the scrum-half shouts 'UP, UP', 'DOWN, DOWN', or 'NOW'. 'Up, up' means that the ball is held off the ground in a maul and the pack shield the ball and penetrate through any weaknesses found.

'Now' means that the scrum-half wants the ball and he will run off the maul to link with his forwards to set up a maul or ruck again.

'Down, down' means that the ball is put on the ground and a ruck is formed. Again, the scrum-half will run off the ruck after picking up the ball and link with forwards to set up a maul or ruck again.

A quick ball and two quick passes to use open space

The ball will always move quicker than the man. If a pack manages to get a quick ball

and feed it quickly there is a chance that the opposition defence will be one man missing and in defensive disarray.

Two quick passes from an attacking threequarter line that has realigned quickly will drastically change the focal point and the man outside the two quick passes should be in open space ready to probe the gaps. Even if the two quick passes are standing passes, it still gives the outside men more time. In fact in some situations it is better, especially if the opposition have been committed in numbers to the original breakdown.

Drill 160 – the team with 6 opposition
The 6 opposition are spread around the field, each with a ball. The pack follow the coach around and he points to one of the opposition shouting 'FRIEND' or 'FOE'.

If he calls 'Friend', the pack will drive into this man, taking the ball and presenting it to the scrum-half as a ruck or a maul – but quickly. By this time the backs have aligned ready for 2 quick passes and space to use.

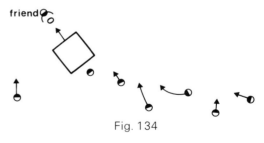

Fig. 134

If the coach calls 'Foe', the opposition will turn his back to the oncoming forwards. He will be turned, opened up and robbed of the ball. By this time he will probably be quite willing to part with the ball! From the quick ruck and maul the backs will again use 2 quick passes to find space. See Fig. 135.

The coach will also call on Friends and Foes that are behind the pack, but the team must continue to play the same way.

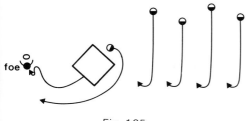

Fig. 135

A quick ball and probe early

With some defences the opposition could be involved in the breakdown and other opposition could quickly realize that the ball has been lost and cover accordingly. The situation could also be such that the breakdown has just left men from both sides scattered around the field.

In both cases an early probe should be advantageous. In the first case to penetrate early and effectively, and in the second case to commit more of the opposition before unleashing your own backs.

Drill 161 – the team with 6 opposition
The 6 opposition are spread around the field holding a ball on their shoulder. The pack follow the coach as in drill 160 and when he points at one of the opposition the pack go in to tackle him. The opponent can use both hands to fend off the tackle, so the ball on the shoulder will be spilt in an unpredictable way. The pack will be expected to react to this ball and the first man flicks it up for support to drive forward. Alternatively, that first man can set up a ruck or a maul and the backs can move the ball to open space as in drill 160 or probe early themselves.

Drill 162 – the team, with limited opposition
Set up ruck and maul, but the ball presented to the scrum-half is then handed to the coach who will roll it backwards or sideways for the pack to secure again. This will happen for three rucks and mauls and then the scrum-half will use his backs.

This can be extended by the backs having a theme of moving it wide and passing inside to support, or bringing the ball back to be 'picked up' by the forwards to set up a ruck or maul again.

It can be further extended by the coach on the first three rucks or mauls not only rolling the ball backwards or sideways for the forwards but also throwing it high backwards or rolling it far backwards and sideways for the backs to secure. The backs will try, through elusive running, to get in front of their pack again before setting up a ruck or maul.

Once the backs set up the next set of rucks or mauls, the coach will be ready to manufacture three more sideways and backwards situations.

Rolling mauls and rolling rucks

The idea of the game of rugby football is to go forward, so a variety of ways have to be found to penetrate.

If penetration is wanted from the backs, the team may have to be patient and make sure that the opposition is soaked up close to the source of possession, thus stopping the opposition flying out to knock down their backs. This is a long-term policy and may be necessary for a limited time so that when the backs are finally unleashed they are at their most dangerous.

It may be necessary to create a rhythm of commit, commit, then spin, in the early stage of a game. This will depend on second and third phase possession, to sustain the pressure. The 'commit' stage would interest the opposing back row and half-backs in such a way that when the ball is released to the backs, the defensive picture should be more clear-cut with more chance of a one to one situation confronting the backs.

It must be remembered that this first commitment around the base of the rucks and mauls may find out an obvious weakness in the opposition. It would be a waste not to try the opposition out. Attacking ploys from mauls and rucks must be developed.

Rolling maul – narrow
For this to be successful, it is important to emphasize that the basic technique must be sound. The ball must be taken with the armpit so that the drive can be given with the right body lean. The drive has to be from the legs and one shoulder should be in a pushing position to 'feel' the weakness of the opposition around the flanks or through the middle. The rolling maul is not possible if the weakness is through the middle. But with the drive through the middle the rolling maul would not be necessary.

If the weakness is around the flanks, the pack will feel the axis shift and a natural path to penetrate will be evident.

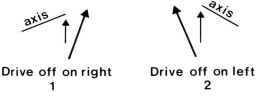

Drive off on right
1   Drive off on left
2

Fig. 136

Apart from recognizing which way the axis has swung, the players must go in with the correct shoulder to shield the ball when they detach from the maul. Basically, go in with the right shoulder if the player is rolling off right, and go in with the left shoulder if he is rolling off left.

Drill 163 – in fours

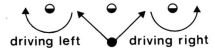

driving left   driving right

Fig. 137

The 3 opposition are in a line, with linked arms. The ball-carrier is told by the middle man to go left or right, or the middle man just points left or right (he can still do this with linked arms). The ball-carrier will be no more than 3 metres away, so an instant reaction is wanted. If he drives right, he aims at the gap between the middle man and right-hand man. He hits the gap with right shoulder and, keeping contact, rolls off his back until he is in open space. If he drives left, he aims at the gap on the other side and rolls off to open space there.

Drill 164 – in fives

Fig. 138

Same formation as in drill 163, but the ball-carrier drives between the gap and waits until the second man drives into him. As a pair, they drive off into open space and this is the beginning of a rolling maul. What forwards must realize is when they are in open space and break off to run straight.

Rolling maul – wide
The problem with the narrow rolling maul is that the security of shielding the ball in pairs is offset by the ball-carriers having to be upright when they progress forward. If a side is expecting the rolling maul they can counter this comparatively easily if the opposition's transfer of the ball is not slick.

This is why it is important to develop a technique that can release men running straight with correct body lean. There are three important factors to be understood if this is to succeed:

1 The axis must swing to the right or the left, and the initial ball-carrier must be driving with the correct shoulder.

2 When the maul is initially static there must be communication between the pack members so that the right person can be fed with the ball.

3 The scrum-half must be prepared to act as a ninth forward because he may be in the ideal position to be fed.

Once the axis has been forced around one side, the ball-carrier can call off the support and flick a pop-up pass to him.

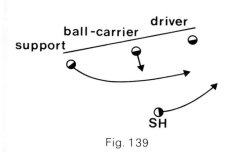

Fig. 139

The ball-carrier has the option of giving the ball to a support forward or to the scrum-half. Ideally, he would prefer to give the ball to the support forward so that he has men on the inside and outside. Also it cuts down the possibility of the scrum-half being caught up in a following ruck or maul.

Unravelling a carpet

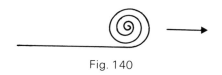

Fig. 140

The above technique depends on the drivers on the flank forcing the opposition away from the ball, coupled with the natural axis swing.

This will give more space to penetrate. It will also give the ball-carriers a chance to drive with the outside hip against the tack-

lers, setting up the support and eventually bringing their backs into play – like unravelling a carpet.

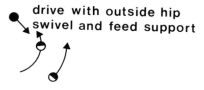

Fig. 141

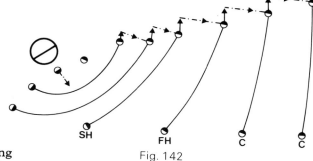

Fig. 142

Rolling rucks – narrow

It used to be said that you could put a blanket over the whole of the All Blacks pack when they rucked. This is a bit of a fallacy because although this was probably possible before they produced the ball, they in fact continued driving until the whole of the pack was there.

Again the scrum-half must count himself as one of the participants in the rolling ruck. He can be devastating because he is picking up the ball from the ground, coming from depth and accelerating forward to get in front of his future support.

The rolling ruck is simply picking up (or scooping up) the ball that has been left behind by the support and driving again. The reason why the man picking up the ball seems to have so much success is because the path in front of him has been cleared by the initial wave of players that drove, leaving the ball behind them on the ground and continuing to drive. If the ball is left behind in good time, the scooping up can happen two or three times consecutively. This should ensure that the opposition is soaked up before releasing the backs again.

Rolling rucks – wide
Certain forwards should have the role of hanging off a ruck so that they can be used to penetrate again. It is important to pick these two or three forwards carefully. They should be forwards with judgment who know when it is important to secure the ball in the ruck or when to hang off. Never fall into the trap of saying 'last two men hang off the ruck' or you will probably find eight forwards negotiating who were the last two, while the opposition pack are busily getting the ball. There are certain forwards who you would never want in the wide open spaces. So don't mention to them that there is the possibility – they will probably never notice this dimension of attack anyway!

It is also important to sort out the starting positions of the forwards who are hanging off. It would be ideal if the forwards could run on to the ball from depth, but they must remember that from the ruck it is a quicker ball than from the maul. The scrum-half must have the option of passing out to his fly-half or running himself and then linking with the hanging-off forward. There are three basic positions for the forward support.

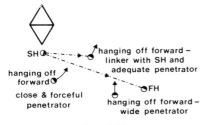

Fig. 143

Forwards can also hang off mauls, but as the maul is usually more static the best role for these forwards is as a pivot for inside or outside support.

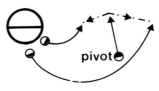

Fig. 144

Ruck from maul

Basically, if a quick ball is wanted, especially just after committing the opposition, a ruck should be created. Two situations in particular require this:

1 Ball stuck in a maul – make a ruck.
2 Narrow rolling mauls tend to end in a ruck.

Drill 165 – team with opposition pack
Set up a maul, force a ruck and drive over using the ball for the backs or rolling rucks, narrow and wide.

Drill 166 – team with opposition pack
Set up a maul. Make it a narrow rolling maul and end up with a ruck. Quick ball from this situation to be used by the backs.

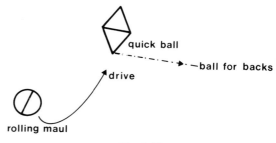

Fig. 145

10. Regaining Possession as a Team

KICK-OFFS

Their kick-off

There has to be a well-organized drill for receiving their kick-off.

This is the time when concentration can be at its lowest if you have just scored. Still thinking about the score as the opposition are preparing to advance back into your half is bad preparation for the next session. So receiving kick-offs properly is vital if you are making sure that the opposition's advance into your half is only temporary.

If possible, the receiver must try and catch the ball on the run. He does not want to receive a kick-off standing still.

The receiving players leave a space in front of them for two reasons:

1 It is easier to run onto a ball than back-pedal to catch it.
2 It may make the opposition kick too far for his own forwards to make contact with the ball.

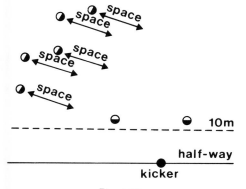

Fig. 146

The player on the 10-metre line is simply a deterrent to dissuade the kicker from kicking a short ball, because this ball would be difficult for the main catchers to reach.

Pick a beam

The main catchers have to 'pick a beam' and if anybody else is in their beam they must move out. This beam is an imaginary spotlight's path of the direction of the kick.

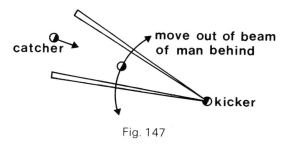

Fig. 147

The catcher can run forward and catch the ball, meeting the path of the ball. This is easier than trying to catch the ball coming on an angled line.

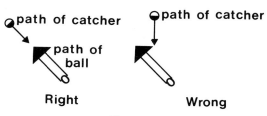

Fig. 148

Retaining and Regaining Possession

Each catcher can have a beam and collect the ball while he is in motion. The run is not parallel to the touchline but he can adjust after he has caught the ball. This running back at the opposition certainly puts them back on their heels and the catcher's support is beginning to drive forward already.

With the good high kick-off, the catcher must try and delay his run so that he takes the catch on the run, but he must make sure that the opposition chasers do not intercept the ball before it reaches him.

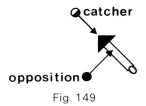

Fig. 149

Of course, a good deep kick-off will leave the catcher static. It is then important for the support to be in position *as* he catches the ball, not *when* he's caught it.

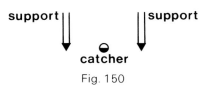

Fig. 150

The scrum-half then must have the option of playing the ball open or using the blind side to get back into the opponent's half.

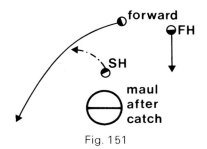

Fig. 151

The dummy jump

Pressure can be taken off the catcher by the first 'catcher' leaping and allowing the ball to go through his hands, it is then collected by the second man who is in the same beam.

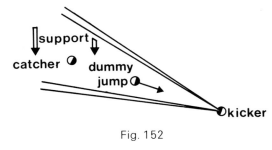

Fig. 152

The long kick-off

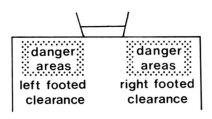

Fig. 153

The idea of the long kick-off is to force a clearance kick so that the opposition carry on with a lineout deep in your half with their throw-in. The danger areas must be covered by competent kickers or runners, runners because the catching side has the whole field in which to operate. The catcher can spot where the defence looks thinnest and he can either spin out a long pass to that side or run in that direction. There will be support there for him as the defending side will have covered for the kick going the wrong way. This support can also switch direction again by executing a scissors. It can also be just as effective being in a position for a dummy scissors. This takes the pressure off the runner because it makes the opposition uncertain.

OUR KICK-OFF

The attacking kick-off

This is the kick-off that the kicking side expect to gain possession through. It requires: a good high accurate kick; and chasing players who reach the ball first.

For the chasers to stand a chance of reaching this ball that has to travel at least ten metres forward, they have to be travelling quite fast as they pass the halfway line.

To do this, the chasers start on the halfway line with the kicker, whether it is a place kick or a drop-kick. The kicker then takes the number of paces back that he will need as a run-up before he kicks the ball. The chasing forwards take the same paces back as the kicker and when he stops the chasers take two more paces. They will then be ready to build up speed as the kicker runs up and the chasers will *hit* the halfway line as the ball is kicked.

It is also important for the chasing forwards to team up in pairs, one attempted catcher and one supporter. The attempted catcher will try to knock the ball down to his supporting player.

The catcher must be on the touchline side when the pairs run up so that he can face the ball and knock it down *inside* to the support.

The attacking long kick-off
The ball is kicked to the danger areas and although it is chased, the middle of the field deep in their half must be filled to isolate the catcher and force him to kick to touch. Blocking the middle of the field will cut down the catcher's options of running the ball out of defence by using deep-lying support.

22-METRE DROP-OUTS

Their drop-out

It is easier to take a 'beam' each because more depth has to be covered as the ball does not have to travel ten metres.

Your 'heavies' are needed as catchers so a smaller man can stand on the 22-metre line guarding the kicker and making sure that the kicker does not take a short kick to retrieve the ball himself. Another man, usually the open-side flanker, is guarding the opposite side from where the forwards are positioned in case the kicker is tempted to take a short kick to himself away from his forwards.

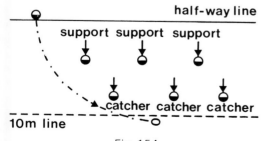

Fig. 154

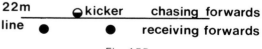

Fig. 155

It is even more important for the catcher to travel along his beam and for the support to be in position *as* he catches the ball rather than *when* he has caught the ball.

The backs should be guarding the deep touchlines, giving themselves space in front to run onto the ball. This is an ideal counterattack situation because the kicker cannot kick the ball directly to touch.

The attacking 22-metre drop-out

Again the chasing forwards are in pairs, with the support on the inside of the attempted catcher of the chasing group.

The kick must be high and long enough for the chasing group to attempt to take the ball on the run. If the chasing group has to stop and wait for the ball, the advantage swings back to the receiving team. The support runner on the inside of the attempted catcher is there in case the ball is not caught properly, but it is important that the chasing group do not run with the intention of tapping back to the support, as they would at a kick-off, because this would mean loose play in their own half. The chasing group must attempt to catch the kick. A set scrum from a knock-on is a better alternative than a loose tap near your own 22-metre line.

The long or quick 22-metre drop-out

The kicker must always have the ball quickly so that he has the option of:

1 Taking a quick drop-out to himself.
2 Kicking the ball to wide open spaces for chasing back in their half.
3 Settling down and waiting for the forwards to reassemble.

The quick ball to the kicker depends on:

1 The kicker going to his kicking position quickly and waiting for the ball.
2 *Two* quick passes to get the ball to this kicker. One lobbed pass takes too much time.

The long kick to space is usually effective rolling towards the touchline because it is easier to isolate the receiver from his support by blocking off the middle of the field when chasing as others chase to put pressure on the receiver.

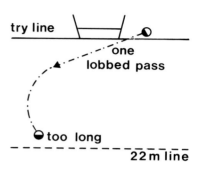

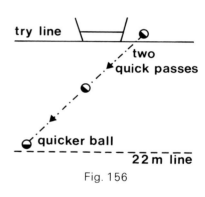

Fig. 156

COUNTERATTACKS

Three full-backs

The full-back and the two wingers must realize that they are classed as three full-backs with an imaginary length of rope linking them together.

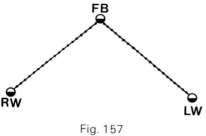

Fig. 157

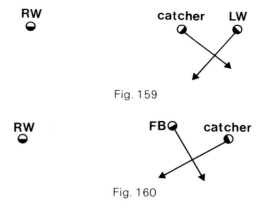

Fig. 159

Fig. 160

If the full-back is brought into the attack, the winger on the opposite side of the attack is pulled back to the full-back's former area by this imaginary rope.

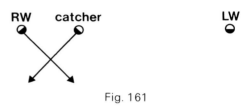

Fig. 161

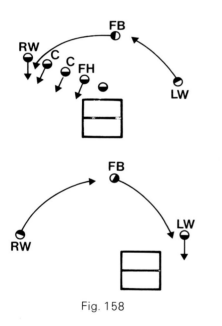

Fig. 158

The run of the would-be receiver is also useful as a dummy switch because it takes the pressure off the ball-carrier. The would-be receiver takes at least the eye of the opposition with him.

COUNTERATTACK FROM KICKS

The switch or dummy switch

The catcher can run direct and switch or dummy switch with one of the other full-backs. The run must be on a definite path so that the player planning to switch can base the angle of his own run on the cateher.

The loop or dummy loop

If the catcher only has time to secure the ball but not to run, it is important for one of the other full-backs to loop around him to receive the ball or act as a dummy loop to take the pressure off the catcher.

The looper is determined by the angle the kick comes from and the way that he is facing as he catches the ball.

It is important for the catcher to lead with one shoulder and pivot his upperbody towards his own goal-line. Then, if the ball is not taken cleanly it is knocked back and not knocked on. The way the catcher faces as he catches the ball should determine from which side the looper comes. See Fig. 162.

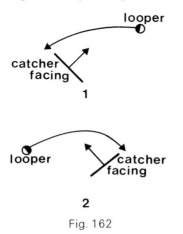

Fig. 162

It is hoped that the mid-field trio and the scrum-half can make an effort to be back with the catcher – perhaps not all four of these players, but at least one. These players can link from the switch or dummy switch. They can also link from the loop or dummy loop.

Let the ball do the work

If the support has worked hard to get into a position to help the catcher, they can assist in *changing the focal point* and completely wrong-footing the chasing opposition.

Working again on the principle that the ball travels faster than the man, two standing passes can release runners from a completely new area on the field. This is particularly effective when the ball is caught near the touchline.

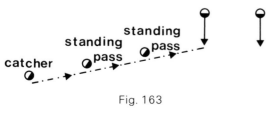

Fig. 163

Drill 167 – 1 team, pack v threes
Pack in formation on their knees against the backs who are positioned in normal defensive alignment.

The ball is kicked to the backs, who immediately try to change the focal point by: switching and linking; dummy switching and linking; looping and linking; dummy looping and linking; or two standing passes, then run and link.

The forwards are released when the coach gives the order and they try to cover the counterattack by the backs and stop their progress.

If the man is caught, the pack rob him of the ball and interpass among themselves. The forwards will drive forward with short pop-up passes. They will *not* spread out. The backs try to stop this progress.

COUNTERATTACK FROM TACKLES

Drill 168 – 1 team, limited number of opposition backs
Allow each member of the opposition to run freely but upright into the team. This man is tackled and robbed quickly by the pack. The backs realign to move the ball quickly as a counterattack.

Drill 169 – 1 team, pack v threes
Let the backs handle and call 'TACKLED' as the pack are defending against them. The tackled man immediately turns his back to the opposing pack. The pack turn this man by turning his shoulders. He is robbed and the pack simulate quick possession from this robbing. The turning must be in the same direction as the run.

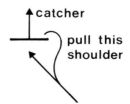

Fig. 164

Drill 170 – 1 team, opposition threequarter line

Allow the opposition to have the ball, tackle them and snap up loose ball to immediately flick it up to support. Two close passes to get to open space, then use the space to spread the passes.

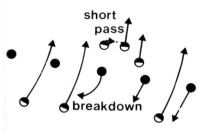

Fig. 165

Drill 171 – 1 team, opposition threequarter line

Allow the opposition to have the ball, tackle them and *secure* loose ball on the ground for a quick ruck, or on feet for a quick maul. Move this possession quickly. Reaction and understanding between half-backs will also be strengthened.

Drill 172 – 1 team, opposition threequarter line

Allow a player from the opposition three-quarter line to cut back. Immediately this player will be swallowed up by support inside, would-be tackler, who would have to tackle on weak-tackling side.

Fig. 166

The tackler should always have a man on his inside to assist him with the cut-back of the opposition: the fly-half has the flankers; the inside centre has the fly-half; the outside centre has the inside centre; and the open-side wing has the outside centre.

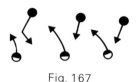

Fig. 167

When the ball-carrier who has cut back has been swallowed up, he is then robbed and the ball is counterattacked from the ruck or maul by moving it quickly, or by the scrum-half running through any gap that has developed.

Drill 173 – 1 team, 1 opposition pack plus half-backs

Let the opposition have possession and their half-backs probe for openings. The team should be able to contain these half-backs by developing a pincer system to cover scrums, lineouts, rucks or mauls.

Scrums

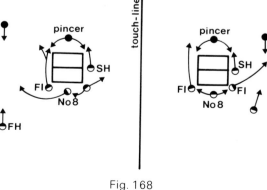

Fig. 168

Retaining and Regaining Possession

Lineouts

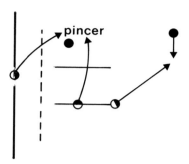

Fig. 169

Rucks and Mauls

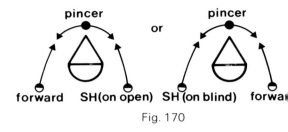

Fig. 170

The defence dispossess the half-backs and counterattack from ruck or maul by moving the ball quickly or by penetrating at the point of breakdown.

Drill 174 – 1 team, opposition full-back and two wingers
Chase a variety of kicks to the opposition full-back and two wingers. When they catch the ball they can only jink. If the chasing group are at least in pairs and do not hang off, the catcher should only be able to beat one man with a *sideways* movement. He should then be tackled by the supporting chaser.

PART 5

Essential Backups

11. Fitness

A rugby player must be fit if he is to play the game to the best of his ability and enjoy it. According to the position he plays, he will also need to develop and strengthen certain muscles.

Keeping fit, let alone getting fit, can be a chore – but remember that usually, as far as attitude is concerned, the hardest part of training is getting changed! It is hoped that this section will offer enough variety to make this department of the complete rugby player both more interesting and more effective. It also tells you which areas for your position you need to concentrate upon.

THE MAIN COMPONENTS OF FITNESS

These are generally grouped as the four Ss:
1. Speed
2. Suppleness
3. Stamina
   (a) heart and lungs (cardiovascular)
   (b) local muscular endurance (dynamic strength used continually)
4. Strength
   (a) dynamic strength (ability to move, lift or support a body)
   (b) static strength (maximum force against a relatively immovable object)
   (c) explosive strength (power – maximum force in shortest possible time).

The following demands of the game of rugby are shown to highlight the components of fitness that are most needed in order to be efficient and able to cope with these demands.

1. Running at different speeds, with the ability to vary that speed during a particular stretch of running.
   SPEED, SUPPLENESS, CARDIOVASCULAR, EXPLOSIVE STRENGTH.
2. Running for varying distances.
   SPEED, SUPPLENESS, CARDIOVASCULAR.
3. Changing direction and twisting.
   SPEED, SUPPLENESS, EXPLOSIVE STRENGTH.
4. Securing ball or distributing ball.
   SPEED, SUPPLENESS, LOCAL MUSCULAR ENDURANCE, DYNAMIC STRENGTH.
5. Supporting play.
   SPEED, SUPPLENESS, CARDIOVASCULAR, LOCAL MUSCULAR ENDURANCE, EXPLOSIVE STRENGTH.
6. Tackling and being tackled.
   SPEED, SUPPLENESS, LOCAL MUSCULAR ENDURANCE, DYNAMIC STRENGTH, EXPLOSIVE STRENGTH.
7. Rucking.
   SPEED, SUPPLENESS, CARDIOVASCULAR, EXPLOSIVE STRENGTH.
8. Mauling
   SUPPLENESS, LOCAL MUSCULAR ENDURANCE, DYNAMIC STRENGTH, STATIC STRENGTH.
9. Scrummaging
   SUPPLENESS, LOCAL MUSCULAR ENDURANCE, DYNAMIC STRENGTH, STATIC STRENGTH.

10 Lineout

SUPPLENESS, LOCAL MUSCULAR ENDUR-
ANCE, DYNAMIC STRENGTH, STATIC
STRENGTH, EXPLOSIVE STRENGTH.

HOW SHOULD WE TRAIN?

Mobility exercises

From the above lists of demands of the game it will be noticed that SUPPLENESS is required for all activities. SPEED can definitely be improved by improving stride length, by stretching the muscles of the legs and having hip flexibility. It will then be found that a corresponding range of movement will be wanted from the shoulders and arms. One has only got to try and run fast with arms clasped behind the back to realize how much the arms are needed for sprinting.

The manoeuvrability needed in general play and the unnatural positions that players find themselves in in ball-getting situations will add trunk and back mobility to the list.

The exercises should isolate muscle blocks with the aim of improving the range of movement within a joint or joint complex. There should be no wrenching of muscles but a gentle squeeze to a full-stretch position. That position should then be held for 2 to 8 seconds. Other training can tighten up muscles, so it is important to regularly do a series of mobility exercises.

Sprint training

It is important to improve quickness off the mark as over half the action in a game lasts for less than 10 seconds. A threequarter will do about 50 sprints in a game lasting an average 3.5 seconds and covering an average of 25 metres. A forward will have 60 to 80 rucks and mauls in the game and will be expected to accelerate into all the rucks and some of the mauls.

Drill 175
Sprint from different starting positions, e.g. sitting, lying, etc.

Drill 176
Shuttle running with variety. Examples:
(a) Picking up and putting down ball.

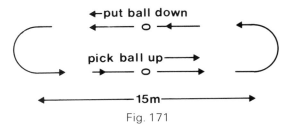

Fig. 171

(b) Pick up ball one at a time and bring back.

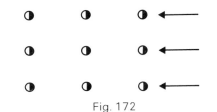

Fig. 172

Next man puts them out again one at a time. As we are dealing with quickness off the mark, the distances can be quite short.

Drill 177
Running backwards to strengthen hamstrings.

Drill 178
Running downhill with controlled stop at the end.

Drill 179
Variety in running. Examples: high knee lift, light running on toes, kicking backside with heels, striding, hopping and bounding.

Drill 180
Harness runner in inner tube or towel and

give resistance enough for him to continue with natural driving action.

Fartlek

A player can cover anything from 4000 to 7000 metres in a game. Usually one third of this is at full speed, the rest from jogging up to threequarter speed. It is easy to prepare for this demand of the game by using *Fartlek* running. This is simply alternate jogging and sprinting over a distance of 2, 3 or 4 miles and can be done almost anywhere.

Time each run, improving the time and increasing the number and length of the sprints. Landmarks en route are important to indicate where sprints start and finish.

Interval training

The game consists of approximately 50–60 lineouts, 40 scrums, 15 penalties, 10 kick-offs and 10 drop-outs. So a forward can expect about 125 stopping points or lulls in a match before his exertion. With about 60 more rucks or mauls, a threequarter can expect about 185 lulls before exertion. Actual play in a match adds up to approximately 27 minutes, so it is important to use this with quality running and power in the various facets of play that confront a player.

There is certainly no point in a player pacing himself through a game because he cannot plan how the pattern of play will emerge or when the lulls will appear. Therefore it is important for a player to use a fitness programme that aids his recovery rate. His exertion should push up his pulse rate to 140 to 180 beats per minute. The heart must be able to cope with these demands and use his recovery times to quickly allow this pulse rate to come down to between 100 and 140 beats per minute.

Interval training can certainly help the running demands that tend to push up the pulse rate, and as most rugby action lasts less than 20 seconds it makes sense to cover distances from 10 metres to 100 metres.

Drill 181 – pyramids
Pyramids mean more repetitions with shorter distances, less repetitions with longer distances. An example: using the markings on a pitch, 7 sprints to near the 22-metre line, 6 sprints to near the 10-metre line, 5 sprints to the halfway line, 4 sprints to the far 10-metre line, 3 sprints to the far 22-metre line, 2 sprints to the far try-line, 1 sprints to the dead ball line. Rest periods vary, but try to get players jogging slowly to recover, and out of that nasty habit of walking.

Drill 182 – shuttle runs
Similar to those for speed but over longer distances.

Drill 183 – *Paarlauf* running (paired running)

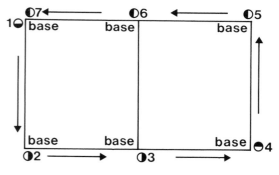

Fig. 173

This can be competitive and can last as long as the coach requires because when 1 has run and given the ball to 2, 1 stays at 2's base. 2 of course stays at 3's base when he has given him the ball. This continues until 6 gives the ball to 7, who then starts the run again, by running to the base where 1 is now standing and giving him the ball.

Any number from 3 to 10 can make up a

team as long as the bases are well-defined and there is one less base than team members.

Drill 184 – box running

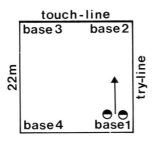

Fig. 174

Players work in pairs. From base 1 the pair sprints one leg, then jogs 3 legs, sprints 2 legs and jogs 2 legs, sprints 3 legs, jogs 1 leg, and finally sprints the complete circuit.

The players will then be sprinting varying distances, recovering in different times, but they can also give all their effort because they know when it will end.

Drill 185

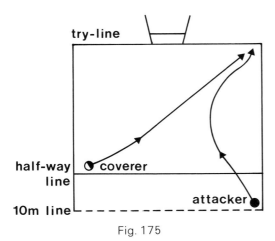

Fig. 175

The attacker with the ball must cut in towards the coverer then swing out again towards the corner flag. If the coverer catches

the attacker, by touching him on the shoulder, he must not touch the attacker until he is nearly at the corner-flag so that the pair get a full 65-metre sprint.

Circuit training

Interval training deals effectively with the cardiovascular heart and lungs training that is required for running at various speeds and differing distances. Another type of training is required for the local muscular endurance that is required when players are in contact trying to gain or regain possession.

Circuit training prepares various muscle blocks to offset fatigue and builds up endurance in the muscles. A basic circuit training programme does not need sophisticated equipment and can be done in the home. 9 exercises should be done in order, legs, shoulders, trunk, legs etc, and the 9 exercises should be done 3 times in succession, ie Exercises 1 to 9, back to 1, through to 9, back to 1, through to 9. To calculate the number of repetitions for each exercise, do a maximum in one minute for each exercise and halve that number.

Circuit training for the home schedule
1 STEP-UPS Use a chair or a bench.
2 PRESS-UPS Front support position, feet up on a chair, or hands suspended on a chair each as well as the feet.
3 TRUNK CURLS Lie on back, bend knees. Hands behind neck. Raise shoulders and back off the ground and look up to help keep back straight.
4 SQUAT JUMPS Squat with one foot behind the other. Fingers touching the ground on each side of legs. Jump up in the air and change position of feet on landing, ie the other foot in front. Keep back straight throughout and look ahead.
5 DIPS 'Suspended-sitting' position supported by hands on a chair on each side of the body. Legs stretched out in front

with heels resting on another chair. Bend the arms until the backside touches the ground, then return to the original position.

6 BACK CONTRACTORS Lie chest down, clasp hands behind back and raise chest off the ground. Then return to lying.

7 STAR JUMPS Start in crouch position with hands on the ground. Jump up with arms and legs extended outwards. Go back to crouch position.

8 PULL-UPS Find a bar to pull up on, with an under-grasp position. If this is not possible, put a bar across two chairs, hang on the bar with body supported by heels stretched out in front as far as possible. Then pull up to the bar and back to the hang position.

9 BURPEES or SQUAT THRUSTS From the upright position go down to crouch position with hands flat on the floor in front. Shoot legs backwards to front support position. Return to crouch position, then stand upright.

If a gym is available the following exercises can be added or substituted:

SQUAT and PRESS with bench hooked into wall-bar or beam at one end. Person squats to lift end resting on the floor and pushes it up until he is at full extension. He then brings bench down until he is squatting again.

DOUBLE-FOOTED JUMPS over a bench.

ASTRIDE JUMPS onto a bench.

TRUNK CURLS on inclined bench.

USING BARBELLS, light weights for repetitions in shoulder press, upright rowing, arm curls, tricep press, press behind neck.

USING DUMB-BELLS for alternate arm press, lateral raise.

Obstacle circuit

The gym is useful for setting up an obstacle circuit using the equipment available for players to continually use their own bodyweight by going over or under the equipment. The player will negotiate each obstacle on the circuit for one minute (this could mean 2 or 3 circuits each time) when his partner will continue for the next minute while the first player rests and recovers. The number of one-minute circuits will be determined by the coach, and the course can be rearranged for variety before each session. Also the times can be varied from 30 seconds to 3 minutes each run.

BEAMS can be used for gate vaults, through-vaults or scrambling under low beam.

BOXES can be tiered for striding up to highest box and jumping down to safety mat. They can also be vaulted over.

MATS used for forward rolls before continuing running.

SAFETY MATS used for diving on before continuing running.

If there is a lack of equipment to take the bodyweight over or under an obstacle, exercises can be introduced along the obstacle course such as pull-ups, trunk curls, tuck jumps, star jumps. These are not desirable if there is plenty of equipment because the competitive atmosphere of the circuit tempts the player to rush through the repetitions of the exercises, sacrificing quality.

Weight training

Dynamic, static and explosive strength will definitely be improved with a weight training programme. There are enough weight training exercises using barbells, dumbbells and pulley machines to deal with the different demands of each position in a rugby team.

Obviously a front-row forward or a lock will need more static strength than others in the team. However, basic strength is needed by all and off-season is the ideal time to deal with this aspect of preparation. As the season approaches, the programme can be modified to maintain strength but bring in endurance. There will also be times

Essential Backups

Strength – Pyramid system

1st set	75%	of maximum weight able to lift	10–12 repetitions
2nd set	80%	of maximum weight able to lift	8–10 repetitions
3rd set	85%	of maximum weight able to lift	6–8 repetitions
4th set	90%	of maximum weight able to lift	4–5 repetitions
5th set	95%	of maximum weight able to lift	3–4 repetitions
6th set	100%	of maximum weight able to lift	1–2 repetitions

during the season when the local muscular endurance can be improved with the use of weights.

A typical programme can deal with these three categories as seen above.

An inverse pyramid can be performed with maximum lift first. Another variation is to aim at 16 repetitions with a particular weight continually taking off 20 kg from a maximum lift until the 16 repetitions can be completed.

Strength with endurance
The weight trainer always aims at 3 × 10 repetitions in a particular exercise. This may mean varying the weights used in one set but the three sets must be completed.

Local muscular endurance
The weights are lighter and the repetitions increased to 15–20. A group of three or four exercises to deal with one muscle group would be performed in rotation. This group of exercises should be repeated two or three times before another group of exercises for another muscle group is introduced.

Weight training at home

Players should realize that it is not essential to have conventional weight equipment to develop strength. Dynamic and explosive strength in particular can be developed at home.

Shoulders
Use an iron bar with buckets of sand at each end, or pillowcases filled with sand or any other bags. For lighter weights a broom handle can be used instead of an iron bar.
1 SHOULDER SHRUG The bar is held in both hands. Shrug or lift shoulders towards the ears, press back as far as possible and return to starting position.

Shoulder shrug

2 UPRIGHT ROWING The bar is held shoulder width apart. The bar is raised to the chin by lifting the elbows high and keeping bar near the body. Lower weight to starting position.

Lateral arm raise

Upright rowing

Lateral raise on bench or table

3 PRESS-UPS Feet on chair. Weighted pillowcases (filled with sand) around neck.

4 PULL-UPS Overgrasp. Weighted pillowcases around neck.

5 LATERAL ARM RAISE Weighted pillowcases or plastic bottles filled with sand. Arms down by sides, grip bottle or pillowcase in each hand. The weights are lifted sidewards as high as possible. The weights are held momentarily and slowly lowered to the starting position. Keep arms straight throughout the exercise.

6 LATERAL RAISE ON BENCH Weights are held in each hand, palms facing in, at arm's length above the chest. Slowly the weights are lowered outwards towards the floor to the maximum range of motion and then returned to the starting position.

7 FORWARD RAISE Arms down by side, hands gripping weights. The weights are raised directly in front of the body to straight above the head, with straight arms. From overhead, the weights are lowered to the start position.

Forward raise

121

Essential Backups

Neck

It is very important to develop the neck muscles, not only to guard against impact but also to offset fatigue. Athletes can often be seen rolling the head or the head sinking back to the shoulders when they are tired. Obviously, pack members need to use their neck muscles in scrummaging and rucking. Tackling needs firm, strong neck muscles plus the trapezius muscles covering the top of the shoulders and leading to the neck.

1 HEAD HARNESS RAISE   A weight (bucket of sand) is attached to a head harness or scrum cap. The harness is put around the head with the player bending down with hands on knees. He then lifts his head, holds, then back to starting position.

Head harness raise

2 SUPPORT NECK ON EDGE OF CHAIR   Sit on floor with legs slightly bent, feet flat on floor. Raise trunk area off the ground so body is supported by neck and feet only. This position is held for 15 to 20 seconds

at a time. A weight can be held on stomach while body is supported.

3 PRESS BEHIND NECK   On sitting position, raise weighted bar behind neck and bring back to starting position behind neck.

Press behind neck

Wrists and forearms

This is a very much neglected area when there is so much emphasis on shoulders. The limbs below the elbow are so much in demand for scrummaging, grappling, wrestling, wrenching, mauling, tackling, holding on, protecting and fending-off. Rugby players are fairly similar with their shoulder strength, so the wrists and forearms can make a marked difference between opposing players.

1 WRIST CURL   Forearms resting on table, hands hanging over edge holding weights with fingers. Raise hands and wrist as high as possible keeping forearms on the table. Weights can be on a bar or again pillowcases or bags filled with sand.

2 ARM CURL   There are three types of arm curl. The grips for the first two are the same: the bar is held in two hands, shoulder width apart with palms facing away from the body. Curl the bar up to the shoulder, but if the biceps are to be

Wrist curl

Curl for forearm: palms upwards

emphasized let the elbow be free to move from the body and the bar remain close to the body throughout curl.

For the forearm to be emphasized keep the elbows close to the sides of the body or lean against a wall to restrict the movement of the elbow.

To emphasize the forearm again, grip the bar with palms facing towards the body, then curl. The biceps are then deactivated and the forearms do the work to raise the weight.

Curl for forearm: palms downwards

Curl for bicep

3 ONE-ARM CURL Rest upper arm and triceps in particular on a table (better if the table can be inclined). Lift weight by curling one arm at a time. See p. 124.

4 WRIST ROLLING Hold bar which has weights tied to it on a thin rope. Keep elbows close to the sides of the body, forearms horizontal and grip on bar with palms upwards. Twist bar until weight has been wound up on bar, then unwind in a controlled twisting action the other way. Keep shoulders still throughout. See photo on p. 124.

Essential Backups

One-arm curl

Wrist rolling

Backs

Back strength must be coupled with mobility, so it is important for the strengthening work to go through a full range of movement.

1 BACK RAISING   Hips supported on bench or bed, partner sitting on legs or holding down feet. Starting position has head and upper body hanging at the waist towards the floor. Hands are behind head or holding weight behind neck. The body is raised horizontal to the floor and slowly lowered.

Back raising

2 GOOD MORNING EXERCISE   The feet are placed shoulder width apart with the barbell resting across the shoulders behind the neck. Bend forward keeping the legs straight until the body is parallel to the floor. Raise the trunk back to an upright position. Keep chin up throughout the movement to flex neck.

Good morning exercise

3 BACK TWISTING Forwards scrummaging, rucking and mauling have to drive with their backs at different angles. Threequarters have to tackle and drive through with their backs also at different angles.

A player can strengthen his back muscles for rotation by 'scrummaging' against a partner. This partner will bind in a way so that his elbows are outside the working player. The working player will then raise an elbow and twist in that direction with enough resistance from his partner for the working player to push through a full range with a smooth action. The working player will then raise the other elbow and twist in that direction.

Trunk

Strong stomach muscles are a vital part of any driving action – crucial for dynamic strength and manoeuvrability and essential for soaking up impact if a player wishes to distribute the ball on contact. Strong stomach muscles help cardiovascular fitness through aiding the respiratory system and so offset fatigue.

1 SIT-UPS Arms are placed across the forehead, knees bent, and feet flat on the floor. Beginning with the head, the upper body is curled up to a sitting position and slowly lowered. The feet should not be anchored because the hip flexors are then activated. A limited range is desirable to keep the tension in the abdominals.

Sit-ups

2 LEG RAISE Lie on back, put hands under bottom and raise heels off ground (8 cm only). Hold this position for 15 to 20 seconds.

Lower body

Explosive strength is needed by the legs and the formula for power must be uppermost in the mind: $power = \dfrac{force \times distance}{time}$.

So a player is trying to aim as much force as possible through the furthest distance in the least possible time for many physical demands in rugby. This shows up in such actions as lineout jumping, rucking, driving, penetrating running and quickness off the mark.

Power from the lower body must affect acceleration and speed.

1 DEPTH JUMPING This involves a player standing on a platform 60 cm to 1 metre off the ground. He jumps off the platform onto the floor, absorbing the force by flexing the knees. As soon as the shock is absorbed the player immediately jumps back on the platform.

Aim at a certain number of consecutive jumps and try to add to that number as time goes on. Also raise the height of the platform for further improvement.

2 POWER JUMPS A mixture of power jumps can be mixed and measured. The power jumps include hops, double-footed jumps and bounding steps. Repetitions of any combination of the above can be measured. Maintaining a constant distance for each repetition can be motivation as can improving the distance.

A player could start with a simple combination of 3 double-footed jumps. A combination could build up: 2 hops on left leg followed by 2 hops on right leg, followed by 3 bounding steps, followed by 2 double-footed jumps. The total distance would be noted and the combination repeated as many times as required.

3 HIGH KNEE SKIPPING   This is an exaggerated skip in which the force is directed upwards. The time in the air is more important than the distance travelled or the time taken to cover a certain distance.

4 HIGH KNEE RUNNING   Maximum speed lifting the knees as high as possible is required. Distance travelled is not important.

5 HALF-SQUATS   From a half-squat position lift a heavy bag with each hand until standing upright. Speed from half-squat to standing is essential.

weight or weights and raise heels off the ground. This develops calf muscles.

Heel raise

Half-squats

6 HEEL RAISE   Balls of feet on block of wood with heels on the floor. Hold

7 LEG EXTENSION   Sit on a table, drape weighted pillowcases over front of foot. Flex legs and lift weight with feet until legs horizontal. Isolates quadriceps for working. See p. 127.

MEASURING OUR FITNESS AT HOME

Upper body strength (mainly for local muscular endurance and dynamic strength)

Different body builds are an important factor when measuring the upper body

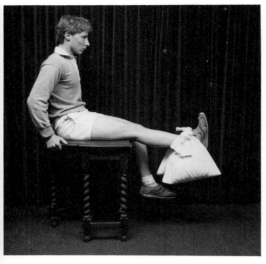

Leg extension

strength, and although a bulky forward could be quite strong he would be at a disadvantage lifting his own weight compared with a lighter player. A formula has been devised to even out these problems:

$$(\text{pull-ups} + \text{dips}) \times \frac{\text{weight (lbs)} + \text{height (ins)} - 60}{10}$$

The pull-ups are performed by the player hanging from a bar with an overgrasp grip (ie palms facing forwards). The player pulls himself up until his chin is level with the top of the bar and then lowers himself until his arms are straight. One point for a complete action, incomplete action can secure half points up to a maximum of four half points. No rest or pause of more than two seconds is allowed, and the player does as many as he can.

The dips are performed between three chairs as previously described with each arm supported on a chair and feet supported on the third chair. The player is in a suspended-sitting position. The body is lowered until the elbows form a right angle. The player then pushes to a straight-arm support again. This scores 1 point. An incomplete dip scores half a point with a maximum of four half points. No rest or pause of more than two seconds is allowed and, again, the player does as many as he can.

Vertical jump (for explosive strength)

Only a wall or suspended board is required. The player stands facing the board with both arms raised. The tester notes the height reached by the fingertips. Then the player wets his fingers or dips them in powdered chalk, depending on the texture of the wall or board. He then stands sideways to the wall or board and performs a standing jump to make a mark as high as possible on the wall or board with the fingertips that are nearest the wall or board. The difference between the two marks is his score. As a guide, a score over 65 cm would be regarded as excellent.

61 to 65 cm – very good
57 to 61 cm – good
53 to 57 cm – average
51 to 53 cm – fair
49 to 51 cm – poor
42 to 49 cm – very poor

Harvard step test (cardiovascular fitness)

Endurance and recovery rate are tested in this activity.

A bench 50 cm high is needed and the player steps up and down on the bench. The rhythm up (right leg), up (left leg) – on bench, down (right leg) down (left leg) – on floor, is done every two seconds. This is continued for a total of five minutes, making a total of 150 step-ups.

After the step-ups, the player sits down and his pulse is taken after one minute for half a minute, after two minutes for half a minute, after three minutes for half a minute. The sum of the three pulse counts is totalled and the following formula is used:

$$Index = \frac{30,000}{2 \times \text{sum of pulse counts}}$$

The index can be rated:

excellent	100+
very good	90−99
good	80−89
average	65−79
below average	55−64
poor	below 55

THE POSITIVE EFFECTS OF FITNESS ON RUGBY PLAYERS

1 Increased lean body mass – the muscle tissue will increase in proportion to fat tissue. The fat can only hinder the power and contraction of the muscle fitness and reduce muscle efficiency.

2 Greater muscle girth – the size of a muscle will increase. A player can be heavier without hindering his speed or mobility. Muscle is heavier than fat and that extra power with increased weight can only help an athletic performance.

3 Increased speed, quickness off the mark and explosive strength will also quicken reactions and improve ball-getting ability.

4 Strength will aid confidence. If a player knows that he is stronger than his opponent, he will know that this gap will widen as the game goes on because of the exertions needed by his opponent just to try and obtain par.

5 Improved muscular endurance. Again if a player knows that he can outlast his opponent, that gap will widen as the game goes on. Also concentration can be maintained longer and a high skill level can be prolonged. The skill factor breaks down as fatigue sets in. Support play is not possible without being able to sustain play for long periods, so endurance has to be in evidence.

6 Team spirit is built up by physical exertion with a group suffering together. A person's character is exposed and the determination, competitive urge, honesty and unselfish attitude are brought to the fore.

7 Pride. Fitness is a personal thing and the more a player can train by himself or in small groups to attain higher fitness levels, the more self-pride that player will have. This self-pride will make the player strive for higher standards from himself and those around him.

8 Injury. Players should be less prone to injury. Muscles and connective tissue will have been prepared to withstand more stress because they are also more supple. This, coupled with confidence and concentration being at a higher level, should certainly help to prevent certain injuries. Also, if a player is injured with sprains, muscle tears or bruising, he can expect to recover more quickly if he is fit.

12. Schedules for Coaches Dealing with Beginners

INTRODUCTION

The schedules for coaches are aimed at providing a planned progression programme and can be adapted to cover teaching the game from beginners to those already in a team. Individual, unit and team skills are incorporated to provide a framework for a coach to build on. The time factor is only for guidance as the time available and learning ability of the players will vary considerably.

The schedules are so designed that the drills in the book can be interspersed into any schedule to cover all ranges of ability and some suggestions are given. The drills are cross-referenced and although players at School 1st XV and also at Club level may raise their eyebrows at some of the drills, it is *vital* to emphasize that breakdowns at all levels, including or especially at International level can always be traced back to the essential basic skills – be they individual or unit.

The essential requirement of the game is to score tries and that, with the exception of the pushover try, is dependent on **a break**. All skills and ploys are aimed to achieve just that.

It is essential to give all players a feel for the game – and this especially applies to beginners. It is more likely to be achieved by variety and constant participation, whether in pairs or groups, rather than by playing a game in ignorance of what is trying to be achieved, and also lacking the basic techniques. Nothing is more likely to dampen enthusiasm than a practice game where players may only touch the ball once or twice during the session.

Match practice

We would emphasize that little will be achieved by using a games period entirely for a practice game. Although competition is essential, unless a player can improve upon his own performance – a unit becoming more effective in their combined skills – there is little incentive for players to give their all. Be they beginners or more experienced players, they will respond to the satisfaction that their game is improving. All playing sessions **must** start with a planned schedule and match practice should be limited to 15 or 20 minutes only. If the coach is dealing with beginners then there will be at least 5 sessions completed before the players should take part in a game.

Encouragement is the keyword – and even the more timid players will get satisfaction from being able to kick or catch the ball correctly. Although bodily contact is an integral part of rugby football, the percentage of participants who relish this may not be as high as is generally imagined!

To avoid boredom in practice sessions 15 balls are needed; 30 are a luxury, but very nearly a necessary one. It is possible to obtain balls cheaply and a gradual build-up of stock should be aimed for. Plastic balls can be used and will provide a more than adequate substitute.

Variety is the keynote for success: try and cover 3 or 4 different skills per session. Passing – taking a pass – kicking – catching – picking up and falling on the ball are the first essential ingredients to a successful player, and team. Tackling obviously cannot be ignored but confidence is of the essence. Give the players a base upon which to build and the contact side of the game will improve considerably.

Always use a logical progression: players working individually, then in pairs, then groups. The groups can consist of a mixture of threequarters and forwards. All players when learning the game should have experience of all positions. They will then appreciate the difficulties that are inherent to playing in certain positions. The coach will also discover each player's aptitudes, which may not have been immediately apparent from their physique or mobility.

Progression is an important keyword in all coaching sessions and you have to establish a system that will give every player the chance of fulfilling their potential. In order to achieve this both the interest and the ambition of the player must be kept uppermost in the coach's mind.

We repeat – a training schedule must be used. The following schedules are devised so that their flexibility allows the coach to devise how best to use his sessions. For beginners he may work through the sessions given. There will be enough variety there to keep a player's interest and to encourage him to develop both his stronger and also his weaker points without overemphasizing the latter.

To become a good coach you do not need an International or County background, although the more experience you have the better.

The main requirements are:

(a) Knowledge of the game

(b) To be able to read the game

(c) An immense enthusiasm

Possess those requisites and you will produce a successful side because the players will be dedicated to both enjoyment and success.

The schedules do not require special markings. They are able to be used on an ordinary rugby pitch. We have worked on the basis that each session will consist of around 50 minutes. Do your own timings but try to, and we reiterate, cover several aspects of the game in each schedule.

Players will enjoy the contact aspect of the sport more if they have confidence. 'Cold blood' tackling practice will achieve nothing but an even firmer dislike for this skill. Progress slowly and logically, ie walk, jog, run (but not sprint) and at this stage give the advantage to the tackler (limited room in which the runner can move). Once they have achieved several good tackles players will have the confidence to cope with hand-offs, swerves etc.

It is essential that before each session starts there is a warming up period. Whatever their age, players must have loosened up and their muscles supple. If players can have a ball in their hands during this period so much the better.

SCHEDULE 1

1 Warming up. This should be varied and most coaches will have their own ideas as to what is effective. As long as players are told not to just jog up and down the field you are on the right lines. The more experienced player will know how best to warm up as far as he is concerned. The younger player will need guidance.

Guideline: Start the players off as they arrive on the pitch. From one set of goal posts to jog around the goal and touchlines to the other goal posts. Then run to the 22-metre line, jog to the halfway line, sprint to the 22-metre line and then jog to the starting point. Then five squat thrusts, five press-ups and running on the spot to a count of fifteen.

As the season progresses, so it may be necessary to increase the warming up session. Remember not to bore players by too much repetition. Also, a ball in the hands is twice the value in these sessions to performing without one.

At the end of the initial session give the players a ball and tell them to dribble it. If they can do the sprint session successfully with a ball at their feet, you have a very successful player in the making!

2 To kick a ball is the natural desire of most players. It is popular therefore to encourage it, but to do it successfully it has to be coached.

Drill 186

Split the players into pairs with a rugby ball apiece. Station them on the respective 10-metre lines, let them kick the ball towards their partners. Their partner should attempt to catch the ball or field it. For the first few minutes the coach should observe rather than correct. Now call the players together and suggest how they may improve their techniques.

POINTS TO EMPHASIZE

Kicking (punt)

a) Hold the ball with the right hand on top of the ball at the near end and the left hand on the side at the far end of the ball (converse for left-footed kickers).
b) Push the ball *down* towards foot.
c) Kicking foot straight upon contact.
d) Head down.
e) Toe pointed towards direction of kick.
f) Kicking leg straight on full follow through.

If the players are experienced then have them kicking with their other foot for the last few minutes.

3 Another essential basic skill which will fit

naturally into this session is catching the ball. The vital point to get over to the players is that they must be *under* the ball as it comes down. Judging the flight of the ball is an art in itself and here the players will learn from experience.

POINTS TO EMPHASIZE

a) Eyes on the ball.
b) One foot slightly forward.
c) Arms bent and hands at head level.
d) Guide ball to chest.
e) Elbows close to body.

When under pressure from an opponent, on taking the catch swivel your body around so that any prospective tackler meets your side. Grasp the ball tightly, so that upon impact the ball does not go loose.

In this pairs kicking practice the ball will not always arrive as a straight catch – as in match situations! The miskick or bad kick also has to be dealt with.

4 Fielding the ball. The points to emphasize are:

a) Get behind the ball.
b) Eyes on the ball.
c) Use two hands.
d) One foot slightly forward.
e) Guide ball to chest.

These guidelines apply to the rolling ball as well as to the bouncing one. As the kickers improve then the distance between them will increase.

5 Passing and receiving of pass. Although it is essential to be able to pass quickly – and this ideally means taking and giving a pass in one stride – the coach must not ignore the orthodox one where there is a falling away with straight arms on the follow-through. For close passing, getting the ball from player to player quickly is of the essence and in consequence the orthodox pass will not apply. In open play this pass is essential as it opens up options, eg dummy and sidestep which in turn leads to the break or half-break. Passing sessions should be of the two types: distant passing and close passing.

Orthodox Pass (initially to be practised in twos or threes)

If the ball is moving to the right then the receiver of the pass should aim to take the ball before it has reached his left shoulder and then in a flowing movement give it to the next player.

POINTS TO EMPHASIZE

For pass to right:

a) Arms should be straight.
b) Swing your arms to left and turn the ball to right.
c) Swing straightened across body and this means the body will automatically start turning towards the receiver.
d) Release the ball just before the end of the swing with final thrust from fingers and wrists.

6 Final session. This will give more practice in the skills already covered and also trying to create a match situation.

Drill 187

Have players in groups of 5 or 6, two groups facing each other 22 metres apart.

One kicker in the first group punts the ball towards the other group where it is caught or fielded. Then immediately a passing movement is set up. The aim is to get as many passes in as possible before the kicker's group touches (not tackles) the next passer. The last player to receive the pass then allows the kicker's team to sprint back to their places and he then puts in a punt towards them. As their kicking skill improves increase the distance between the groups.

SCHEDULE 2

1 Warming up. As the final session in Schedule 1.

2 Dribbling is an essential art for all players. We can all remember instances in matches where a dribble would have been far more effective than a pick-up, or even worse an attempted pick-up.

Drill 188

Have two teams of 5 standing behind each other 22 metres apart (use 22 metre line and goal-line). The first player dribbles the ball to his opponent who takes over the ball and dribbles back to the first team. Continue until all players have had a turn.

POINTS TO EMPHASIZE

a) Legs should be apart and slightly bent.
b) Knees are bent outwards.
c) Body leaning forward.
d) Eyes on ball.

Start at a gentle pace so that:

e) The ball is always kept within a metre of the dribbling foot.

3 As catching and fielding the ball is complementary to the punt then 'falling on the ball' is complementary to dribbling. This will be the first element of physical contact to the beginner in the schedules, so a gradual build-up is essential. This is one skill where coaching must be given before the players participate.

Most falling on the ball will be either to stop a dribble or to bring a kick ahead under control. It is the latter type of ball we will deal with first.

Drill 189

Have the players in groups of 3, one pair standing side-by-side and the third standing some 15 metres back. One of the pairs kicks or bowls the ball along the ground and the other one runs after it to fall on it. (Emphasize that you are not interested in seeing how far the kicker can kick the ball.) After falling, the player immediately gets up and passes it to the third player. The player who has fallen on the ball then bowls or kicks the ball back towards the other player.

POINTS TO EMPHASIZE

a) Go in hard.

b) Try to go over the ball and pull it into the body.

c) Get up *immediately* with back towards the opposition.

After several sessions of this type of fall you can progress to falling to stop the dribble. Put players in pairs, about 3 metres apart. One player dribbles towards the other who is standing 1 or 2 metres to the side.

POINTS TO EMPHASIZE

a) Go in hard.

b) *Back* to dribbler.

c) Pull ball into chest.

d) Get up *immediately*.

For beginners we suggest that the dribbler moves at just above walking pace and then increases the speed as both confidence and ability to do this skill build up.

4 Final session. Split the players into groups of 6, 2 on the goal-line and the others on the 22-metre line. One of the pair on the goal-line bowls the ball for one of the other to fall. After the fall the faller immediately gets up and starts a passing movement into the group in front of him. The last two players to receive the pass then become the pair on the goal-line. Proceed until all players have fallen on the ball.

SCHEDULE 3

Unit skills are brought in – but in easy stages.

1 Warming up – close passing. Players, in groups of 4 or 5, to stay not more than a metre apart. Insistence upon speed of pass – this will come from wrist and fingers. The arms will bend. Emphasizing passing the ball just in front of the player. To keep the flow, players will have to accelerate into position.

2 Basic principles of scrummaging.

Drill 190

Have the players in pairs, scrummaging against each other. Use the 5-metre line and touchline with the pairs midway between. This will provide the necessary element of competition. After this, move to groups of 4 and then finally 6. You will now have two front rows – the base of any set scrum.

POINTS TO EMPHASIZE

One against one:

a) Heads up.

b) Hollow backs.

c) Low knees – which means low buttocks.

Two against two:

a) Heads up and hollow backs.

b) Low knees and low buttocks.

c) Position of feet.

d) Strong binding.

Three against three:

The points are exactly the same as two against two.

3 The lineout. Of all the set pieces forwards will find scrummaging and lineout occupying a lot of their time. It is a good idea to bring in both unit skills within the same session. The lineout should be dealt with in developing stages as for the scrummage.

Drill 191

Split the players into groups of 6, one thrower-in, 3 in lineout and two halves. After three throws all the players move around one place in an anticlockwise direction, ie front of lineout becomes the thrower-in, the thrower-in moves to scrum-half, etc.

4 Throwing in

POINTS TO EMPHASIZE (for a right-handed thrower – converse for left)

a) Left leg slightly forward.

b) Ball resting in palm of hand.

c) Non-throwing hand steadies the ball.

d) Bring hand back above head so that player's eyes are in line with it.

e) Little finger touches lace on ball.

133

f) In the follow-through throwing hand follows the ball.

5 Catching the ball. Not only can the technique of catching be covered, but equally important binding in and delivery to the scrum-half.

POINTS TO EMPHASIZE

a) Don't jump until the ball is sighted.

b) Jump off *two* legs.

c) On the catch turn 90 degrees towards your scrum-half.

d) On the catch bring the ball down to the waist and feed to scrum-half.

6 Scrum-half pass. To coordinate the backs with the forwards the most usual link will be the scrum-half. But if you include breakdown situations then any member of the team may well be required to perform this very vital service. Every player should be able to give a base pass.

Drill 192

Split the players into pairs, standing along the touchlines with their opposite numbers on the 5-metre line. Put the ball on the ground and get the passer to send it as far as he can, emphasizing that it must be a pass his partner can take. Some players will opt for the dive pass and others the stand-up one. Although the latter is to be encouraged because of its flexibility and speed of pass from giver to receiver, do not ban the beginner from the dive pass. The natural scrum-half will be adaptable. The fly-half or backing up player is primarily concerned with a speedy takable pass.

You cannot over-emphasize speed of pass, and the direction of it. There are times when the fly-half may take the ball stationary and leaving himself the option as to which side of the field he launches his threequarters' attack. Other than that pass, all passes to be given in front of the receiver so that he is running on to the ball.

POINTS TO EMPHASIZE

Stand up pass (to right):

a) Left foot positioned near the ball, right foot a metre or so to right with toe pointing towards receiver of pass.

b) Pick-up is off back foot.

c) Knees well bent.

d) Pick-up and pass to be completed in one movement.

Dive pass:

a) From pick-up to dive pass as near as possible one movement.

b) Alignment – the scrum-half *must* pass along a given line. It is up to the receiver (fly-half) to know that line. This is the only way to initiate real thrust. This also applies to the stand-up or pivot pass.

After several passes get each player to attempt the other type of pass. As coach you will soon see which players have potential for the scrum-half position.

7 Final session

Drill 193

Have players in groups of 10, give a front row and a pair of half-backs a side. You will now give the scrum-half his first taste of getting and passing under pressure. His aim is a clean collect and swift pass to his outside half. If there is time, do a similar drill using the three forwards in a lineout situation.

Although these schedules may seem to contain a lot of material, especially for beginners, we cannot over-emphasize that success is built upon variation rather than constant repetition. Repetition is necessary, but over a period of sessions rather than half an hour on one drill in an afternoon.

If players lose interest they lose enjoyment.

If they lose enjoyment they lose incentive.

At this stage the coach will have some idea as to which positions the players may well finally end up in. Resist telling a 9-, 10- or 11-year-old after three or four sessions: 'Ah, you are obviously a budding fly-half.' He may well be but he needs the all-round experience of all basic and unit skills for a platform upon which to launch his rugby career.

SCHEDULE 4

1 Warming up. Send the players off in groups of three with a ball. On jogs and runs practise close passing, when sprinting orthodox passing.
2 By now the players should be able to punt to reasonable effect. They can now progress to **place kicking**.

Drill 194
This should be done in pairs. Align the players along the touchline with their partners some 20 metres away. The value of this exercise is that it again incorporates catching and fielding the ball. Place kicking techniques vary, and the players will have their own ideas as to whether the head-on approach or the round-the-corner method suits them better. Let the players have a couple of minutes kicking and then call them together.
POINTS TO EMPHASIZE
a) Teeing up. The ball should be teed up as high as possible. This requires two heel marks back to back but some players may prefer to manage with just one heel mark. Look at the posts for the last time just prior to the run-up.
b) Run-up. Players again will work out what suits them, but emphasize that distance of run-up does not proportionally increase the distance of the kick. In fact the longer the run-up the greater the scope for inaccuracy.
c) At the point of contact the non-kicking foot ends up slightly behind and to the side of the ball.
d) The kicking leg must be straight upon impact at the bottom of the swing – and at the bottom of the ball.
e) The body will be leaning forward on the point of impact.

f) Head kept down until finish of the follow-through – keeping that kicking leg straight.

Drill 195
Take these stages one by one and the first essential is to get the ball off the ground.
Make the non-kicker take his kick from the spot at which he catches or fields the ball. This will bring an element of competition into the practice. After a little while change players until they are with someone of comparable ability. This will ensure that the weaker kicker does not become too discouraged.
3 The next stage is *pack building*. Have players in groups of ten so that you can start the build-up of the second row.
POINTS TO EMPHASIZE
a) Binding: front row. The hooker's binding is over and above the prop's binding. Grip tightly as far round the shirt as possible. Hooker grips under the armpit, prop grips at chest level. Binding: second row. The right lock binds over left lock. Strong grip under armpit of fellow lock before binding on prop.
b) Position of feet: front row. Loose-head prop – outside foot forward. Hooker – feet in line placed slightly towards loose-head. Tight-head prop – outside foot forward.
Second row. Both legs back so that right angle is formed between upper leg and lower leg.
Get the mini-scrums to pack down against each other.
POINTS TO EMPHASIZE
a) Heads up – hollow backs.
b) Correct positioning of feet.
c) Correct binding and tight grip.
d) Head above hips.
e) Bend at knees.

Drill 196
Now get packs to shove against each other, holding a straight line on the drive. Bring

in half-backs and then extra threequarters. When there is a breakdown, then at speed a new scrummage is set up. (By breakdown we mean a dropped or forward pass – tackling should not be allowed at this stage.)

4 This is now the point when tackling should be introduced. At last the players are introduced to real physical contact. However, their confidence should have been built up in previous schedules, as they become more proficient in various skills.

Start with the side tackle as the tackler should have a cushion, ie the tackled player. Perhaps more importantly, from the tackler's point of view that is, if he has manœuvred the runner so that he can make a side tackle the runner has far less scope in which to escape the tackle. In a head-on or rear tackle the advantage must lie with the runner.

Tackling takes courage. Courage requires confidence. If the tackling process is taken gradually then both courage and confidence will gather momentum.

POINTS TO EMPHASIZE

a) It is the tackler's shoulder that does the initial damage.

b) The tackler's head must always be 'behind' his opponent. We use the word advisedly.

c) The arms must be clasped just above the runner's knees. Beware of 'tackle low', although it is a near impossibility to aim the tackle just above the runner's ankles. Just as important is to eradicate any form of tackling that might be called a smother tackle. All too often this is an excuse to cover up the soft option of high tackling. High tackling is the easiest form of tackling to counter and the coach should aim to discourage this tackle from the earliest age.

d) The tackler must 'drive off'. The momentum will come from the right foot of the tackler if he is approaching from the left (and conversely if he is approaching from the right).

Drill 197

Have the players in pairs. The tackler is stationed not more than one metre from the point of the tackle. The player with the ball *walks* along a given line. After the tackle, roles are immediately changed.

After 3 or 4 tackles by each player, the player with the ball then jogs gently. It is essential at this stage not to destroy the tackler's confidence, because if this is done it may well never return and you will have another potential member of the High Tacklers' Union. If it is possible, always have the runner (or walker) with a ball in his hands, so that from the earliest stage he learns how to make the ball available to his own team (rather than the opposition).

5 Final session. Split the players into groups of 6. One player has the ball and runs in front of the others. On the whistle he puts the ball down, the next player picks it up, turns and short passes to the support runners. Each of the support runners receives a pass, in the quickest possible time. The last player receiving the pass then goes to the front and the sequence is repeated.

SCHEDULE 5

1 Warming up. As for the final session of Schedule 4.

2 Continue with the side tackle: (a) 3 or 4 walking tackles; (b) 2 or 3 jogging tackles; (c) Now bring in the running tackle.

It is essential to have the player (with ball) being tackled running along a straight line – at the most a metre away from the tackler. The coach's task is still to instil confidence into both players. All too often we have seen players getting rid of the ball because they did not fancy being tackled. The tackler and the tackled player must be encouraged to accept tackling as a natural part of the game, which it is.

3 Rucking: more physical contact – and a natural sequence to tackling.

Drill 198

Have players in groups of 5. One player will run two metres in front of the others and on the whistle he will place the ball on the ground. The other four will bind in, go over and ruck the ball back.

POINTS TO EMPHASIZE

a) No daylight between players – so bind in tight.
b) Stay on feet.
c) Wide shoulders.
d) Drive over the ball.

Drill 199

After 3 or 4 minutes put two groups in opposition: five players on each side, 3 in front, 2 behind; one group on the touchline, one on the 5-metre line. Put the ball in between. On the whistle the touchline group drive over the ball in a good rucking position. At the same time the 5-metre group advance in an *upright* position. Now have a player holding the ball between the two teams – this time a metre apart. On the whistle he drops the ball – and retreats quickly as both groups repeat the previous manœuvre.

The coach should be looking for quality of binding, not only by each side but in to each other.

4 Split players into groups of 7 or 8.

Drill 200

The groups of 7 are likely to be threequarters and the groups of 8 forwards. The 7 do orthodox passing at speed, using one player as scrum-half who is also the roamer. His job is to set up each passing session from any position. The threequarters will use orthodox passing. This should be done in 30-second periods and counting the number of passes received. Get each player to shout out the number taken as they receive it.

The group of 8 (forwards) will undertake a similar routine, but with short passes. The forwards will be given the task of exceeding the threequarters' target by 50 per cent. The scrum-half, or forward initiating the movement, should start it by dropping the ball on the ground so that all movements originate from a rolling ball – pressure again.

5 Final session. Simply reverse the roles: threequarters doing the short passes and forwards the orthodox ones. It will be interesting to compare the results.

SCHEDULE 6

1 Warming up. A mixture of 5 and 6 of Schedule 5. Start with the players jogging before proceeding to running.

2 Mauling. In open play both rucking and mauling will occupy players in matches for rather more time than set pieces. It is a good idea to deal with these unit skills in successive schedules.

Drill 201

Split players into groups of 10–5 a side. Position them either side of the goal-line in a 2–3 formation. Throw the ball to one player and see if his side can work it back.

POINTS TO EMPHASIZE

a) The ball-carrier turns towards his own side.
b) Narrow shoulders – burrowing in.
c) Keep on feet.
d) Opposition must try to *rip* ball away. Rip is the correct word. It signifies aggression. Introduce a pair of half-backs behind each pack to initiate movement.

The coach may now turn to alternate ruck and maul and, according to whether he passes or drops the ball, one or other of the unit skills is set up. After some minutes introduce two or three threequarters and see which group can get the ball to the end of their threequarter line first. Emphasis on speed.

3 The drop kick.

Drill 202

Have the players in pairs, around 20 metres apart.

POINTS TO EMPHASIZE

a) Push the ball, leaning slightly towards you, down to the ground.
b) The ball should bounce just opposite and slightly in front of the non-kicking foot.
c) Ball is kicked immediately on rebound.
d) Keep head down as weight is transferred to non-kicking foot.
e) Follow through with straight leg.

Again, this practice will incorporate both catching and fielding the ball. For the first few kicks suggest that these practices are done from a standing position. All too often beginners lose all co-ordination when trying this on the run.

4 Scrummaging. Bring in a No. 8. 2 groups of six packing 3–2–1.

POINTS TO EMPHASIZE

a) Check binding.
b) Check feet positions.

Bring in halves.

5 Lineout practice. Have 6 players in line, one thrower-in and 3 threequarters (no opposition).

The thrower-in will either throw long or flat on the scrum-half's command. If there is not a clean catch the forwards will practise support in lineout. Bring two lineouts against each other and add threequarters. After 5 or 6 practices let play flow for a little while. At any breakdown shout 'RUCK' or 'MAUL'. Keep the players moving at speed. After two consecutive breakdowns take players back to a lineout.

6 Final session. In groups of 6, dribbling as a pack. On the whistle pick up and close passing – whistle, then back to dribbling. Variations including unopposed ruck and maul can be introduced.

SCHEDULE 7

1 Warming up. As 5 in Schedule 6. The coach may now decide to warm up as three-quarters and packs. However, we think at this stage it may be more beneficial to make no distinction. Threequarters in match situations are often involved in a maul and may well find themselves in a rucking position.

2 The rear tackle. Have the players in pairs and go through the side tackle routine. Using the gradual build-up of walk, jog, run. Make sure that the runner with the ball does not slow down or collapse for the tackler. Once this fault is allowed to go unchecked it will start a knock-on reaction: the tackler will become used to players who 'give themselves up' and the runner with the ball surrenders at the slightest touch. Runners with ball must be encouraged to make life as difficult as possible for the tackler. The coach must also realize that cold-blooded tackling is not easy for the participant and in practice they should not be expected to tackle sprinting players at this stage. However, the rear tackle will require the tackler to be moving slightly faster than the player with the ball. It may well be that the faster player in the team will have to perform this tackle – but it is a try saver.

Drill 203

Have the players in pairs, immediately behind each other on the touchline facing across the pitch. The front player kneels down with both hands and one knee on the ground. On the whistle the rear player launches into the tackle.

POINTS TO EMPHASIZE

a) Tackler's head is put to the side of the runner's hips.
b) The *drive* shoulder is aimed at the upper posterior which will off balance the runner.

c) Arms lock around the thighs.

In the first instance the tackler should have little in the way of problems at performing the tackle. If the runner does have the edge then get him to have both knees on the ground as well. Immediately after the tackle players should change around quickly so that pressure is built up.

Progression: now let the runner jog gently with the tackler about a metre behind the runner. Gradually the speed of the runner can be increased but never to a sprint. This session should not last more than five or six minutes.

3 Scrummaging: the full pack. Flankers are now brought in for the first time. Concentrate on binding – position of feet and developing a shove.

POINTS TO EMPHASIZE

a) Hollow backs and chins up.
b) Low knees so low buttocks.
c) Strong binding.
d) Firm and correct feet positions.

Now bring in the halves. The scrum-half should start building up an understanding with the hooker. Whether the ball comes in on a verbal command or a signal will depend on which method the pack prefers. Emphasize the straight drive shove. Correct any tendency to wheel. A wheel to the left has to be stopped by the effort of the right-side prop and conversely for a wheel to the right. It is essential to have the halves with the packs for all forward practices.

While the full pack practice is proceeding the threequarters will be developing their skills of both orthodox and close passing.
4 Final session. In groups of 6, the middle player of the group does a high punt ahead. The group fields the ball and then each player must handle, the first punt close passing, the second orthodox and finally a combination of the two. The coach will instruct the kicker how far ahead he wants the kick to bounce. This should assist in kicking accuracy. Again emphasize the number of dangerous situations or the failure to cap-

italize on an attacking situation because of a misplaced kick.

SCHEDULE 8

1 Warming up. As for final session of Schedule 7.
2 The lineout in its entirety (7 man). The more players participating in a lineout the more difficult to control the ball. Accuracy of throwing is an essential ingredient of the successful lineout. Practise short–long–flat throws. At this stage concentrate on catching the ball. (The deflection or knockdown have their places but are difficult to control. Unfortunately they are often used because the lineout jumper is not good enough to make the catch.) Tidying up and lineout support will automatically fit into this session.
3 Head-on tackle. This is one of the most difficult of tackles to achieve as the advantage will always be with the ball runner. To suggest to beginners that they will ideally knock the runner backwards is likely to achieve a negative effect. That is really a crash tackle and very few tacklers at whatever level relish performing this tackle.

Ideally the tackler should have manoeuvred the runner with the ball to one side, but in a midfield movement it may well be that the prospective tackler will have little room in which to do this.

Drill 204
Have the players in pairs and start the tackling drill at a slow jog. The tackler should aim to get his body and legs to one side of the runner, and his head also. Grasp the opponent round the thighs and if necessary allow him to come over the top, but *not* on top. Many of the practices at this stage are to build up confidence – do not overdo cold-blooded tackling practices.

Smother tackling should *not* be coached because all too often this type of tackle becomes an excuse for a high tackle. A high tackle is a half tackle and usually leads to a break through. When a tackle is needed it must be low; never encourage players to opt for the high tackle as an easy way out.

4 Punting (2). To be able to punt is essential, but not so essential as being able to punt accurately. Think positive. Take the attacking kick first: the cross and diagonal kicks.

Drill 205
In groups of 6, one kicker and five followers-up.

The kicker runs up the centre of the field and puts in diagonal kicks some 20 metres ahead. The followers-up have to gather the ball and continue the movement. Close passing preferably and encourage the passers to change direction.

5 The cross kick. This is done in similar fashion with the kicker being rather off centre (according to the strength of his kick).

Give all players in the group the opportunity of kicking. The cross kick should land into the arms of one of the followers-up. They will have practice at catching the ball on the run and no doubt gathering the rolling ball and setting up attacks. Alternate close and orthodox passing and also change of direction. The coach should shout what he requires.

6 The final session. Using the same groups practise following up high up-and-unders. As a variation the coach can shout 'RUCK' or 'MAUL'.

SCHEDULE 9

1 Warming up. As the final session of Schedule 8.

Drill 206
2 Punting (3) – in pairs. As follow-up to the accuracy sessions, development of the length of kick should now be brought in.

Have corner-flags or markers 10 metres apart along the touchlines. The kicker should be stationed on the 5-metre lines. For distance the torpedo kick is likely to be the most successful.

POINTS TO EMPHASIZE
a) The kicker will aim to strike the inside edge of the ball with the outside edge of his kicking foot.
b) On the swing of the leg the foot will cut under the ball at a slight angle. The ball should then travel nose first and rotating. For a right-footed kick the ball will rotate in a clockwise direction. This means that the ball will, at the end of its flight, dip in towards the left-hand touchline.

Remind the players that a 15-metre touch is better than a 30-metre kick still in play. For, all too often, it gives the opposition an opportunity to launch a counterattack.

Get the kicker to do some kicks facing the other way so that he has the opportunity of kicking with his weaker foot. This ability to kick with either foot is essential for three-quarters and desirable for all players. Under pressure the player will not always be able to dictate how and when he kicks. Use the whole pitch and all line markings so that the whole squad gets the opportunity to improve this basic but vital skill.

Drill 207
3 Split the squad into groups of three-quarters and forwards. Let the three-quarters continue with this form of punting and get the forwards to concentrate upon lineout support and introduce the peel. The success of the peel will again depend on the accuracy of the thrower-in and on the catcher to guide the ball accurately to the peeler.
Use the drills under the heading:
(i) Accuracy of throw and timing of back jumper. (Thrower-in may come closer to front of lineout to start off.)
(ii) Order of 3 men running round to col-

lect deflection. Umbrella formation by 3 runners to give jumper more of a target to aim at.

(iii) The deflection must be 'sensitive' enough for the collectors to run on to.

Always start these drills in an unopposed situation. The players will find them difficult enough to perform on their own without opposition forwards creating their problems. Only when a degree of confidence is obtained should opposition be introduced.

In all skills, be they individual or unit, pressure must be brought in. It is conducive to good play to bring in this pressure until the individual or unit can at least perform the skill satisfactorily.

Drill 208

4 Final session. Have the players in groups of six, each group with a ball. On the whistle dribble is begun and then the coach shouts out a series of commands, to include close passing, maul, orthodox passing, ruck, up-and-under, etc. There should be no pause between one movement and the next.

SUMMARY OF SCHEDULES

Schedule 1

Warming Up
Kicking: The Punt
Catching the Ball
Fielding the Ball
Passing
Taking a Pass
Final Session

Schedule 2

Warming Up
Dribbling
Falling on the Ball
Final Session

Schedule 3

Warming Up – Close passing
Start of scrummaging
The Lineout
Throwing in
Catching ball in lineout
Scrum-half pass
Final Session

Schedule 4

Warming Up
Place kicking
Scrummaging – 5 players
Tackling – Side tackle
Final Session

Schedule 5

Warming Up
Side Tackle
Rucking (5 players)
Short Passing – Forwards
Final Session

Schedule 6

Warming Up
The Maul
The Drop Kick
Using a No. 8 in Pack
Lineout
Final Session

Schedule 7

Warming Up
Scrummaging – Full Pack
Rear Tackle
Final Session

Schedule 8

Warming Up
Lineout in full
Head-on Tackle
Diagonal and
Cross kicking
Final Session

Schedule 9

Punting
Lineout support
Peeling

13. Training Games

INTRODUCTION

To have any real value a training game must incorporate skills training together with pressure. It is preferable to have team games in direct contact with each other than to be playing against the clock.

Although the participants must enjoy these games they should never be looked upon as being just light relief in the training session. They must form an integral part of training and preparation and should bring into practice basic skills under pressure. It is suggested that they are limited to 10 per cent of the time available. However, when practice out of doors is limited this ratio can be increased.

Rugby is a handling game under pressure, therefore any games which encourage this skill should be given full rein. As seen from the text on threequarter and forward play, the handling skills of both these units may be somewhat different in execution but both require the ball to be taken surely and at speed – to transfer the ball from one player to another as quickly and accurately as possible. The number of occasions a player receives the ball exactly as other textbooks may recommend are few and far between – pressure and circumstances will dictate this. The classical pass given by any one of a group of forwards in a confined space is more likely to lead to a breakdown than anything else. All players must be able to take a ball at speed and with confidence. The wayward pass must be taken as well as the one easy to hand if the initiative is to be kept by the handling side. Players must be given the opportunity to practise taking passes at all angles without making players deliberately give bad passes.

The following games will help achieve a proficiency in handling and have the advantage that they may be played indoors if necessary.

RUGBY NEWCOMBE

The pitch you require is ideally the size of a badminton or volleyball pitch. Indoors this may be marked out, on the field use the area between the 5-metre line and the touchline, the length of the pitch being limited by the halfway line and the 10-metre line. There are obviously other permutations. A net or rope somewhere between the height of a tennis net and badminton net should be put on the halfway line. Teams should consist of 4 to 8 players according to the size of the playing area.

Rules

1 The aim is to make the rugby ball hit the ground on your opponents side.
2 The ball must be propelled by two hands.
3 The ball must be released below head height.
4 On receiving the ball it must be passed immediately, either to a member of his own side or across the net.

5 If the ball is not passed immediately it is given to the other side, who start the game from the base line.

6 The ball is passed alternately until a point is scored. When a point has been scored the ball is returned to the scoring side who restart the game from their base line with a pass.

7 The game is always started from the base line.

8 The first team to reach 11 points wins the set. A match is the best of three sets.

This is an excellent game for forwards. As they are primarily going to be concerned with transferring the ball quickly and accurately at close quarters during a rugby game, play half the game allowing the players to pass the ball with either one or two hands. How they do it is of less importance than that it is done quickly and accurately.

Being able to take the ball – one- or two-handed – at all heights is of course necessarily complementary to this. All too often in practices lines of players are seen running up and down the field receiving stereotyped passes at roughly the right height and under no pressure – a very different thing from what they may well receive in a match.

RUGBY TOUCH

This is an ideal game – if played constructively. The rules must be adhered to and the game strictly refereed.

Not only is it excellent practice for the giving and taking of passes but it also gives plenty of opportunities for players to learn the value of the half-break. Players also have to move into open spaces for support and it helps speed up their reactions in such situations.

To be effective at rugby touch – and rugby football – a player must know when to pass. As a move is negated if a player is touched twice the ball must be released at the correct time. If this can be achieved at rugby touch then this knowledge becomes far more devastating in an actual game of rugby. It is a game that the coach can easily control and if necessary can set up the situations he requires. Teams should consist of forwards and backs equally rather than forwards playing forwards or backs playing backs. A game between a team of forwards and one of backs is good training and the result may surprise the coach.

The pitch

So as to keep the game moving with plenty of opportunities for all players to be involved, play across the pitch: either between the 10-metre lines; or between the 22-metre line and the try-line.

This way you can occupy thirty players at a time, if playing 5-a-side. The coach can vary the number of players in each side according to their ability or on what points he is trying to emphasize.

Laws

1 No kicking.

2 No scrums, lineouts, rucks, mauls.

3 At any breakdown, knock on, forward pass, touch, the ball is given immediately to the opposition and the offender must retire five metres.

4 A tackle (therefore the *immediate* passing of the ball) is achieved by touching the player twice in close succession.

5 Kicks at goal after a try may or may not be taken. This may well depend on how much practice the coach thinks the goal-kicker needs.

Handling skills are of paramount importance and any games that foster this are to be encouraged. Another game which can be adapted is basketball. Excluding dribbling, the game can be played with a few variations. Allow the catcher 4 paces before he must pass. When shooting at the net the same sort of accuracy as for throwing in is called for. Interception and cleaning up after a net shot are useful lineout training.

Although handling the ball is of paramount importance in the game of rugby football, kicking skills should not be neglected. These games have the added advantage that besides developing kicking skills they provide valuable practice at catching and fielding the ball.

RUGBY PUNTABOUT

Each team defends half the playing pitch.

Rules

1 Start by allowing each team to have two balls.
2 A point is scored if the catching side allows the ball to hit the ground in the field of play.
3 The area between the 10-metre lines is a dead ball area and no points are allowed for a ball bouncing in this area.
4 When the ball is kicked directly into touch the ball is brought back into play at the point it went into touch.
5 Players must kick as soon as they have fielded the ball and may not run more than 3 paces before kicking the ball.

According to the ability and ages of the players, the pitch can be contracted by only playing to the 22-metre lines and by increasing or decreasing the number of balls used. Each side may well need their own scorer!

BETWEEN THE POSTS

Encouraging accuracy should always be uppermost in the coach's mind – accuracy is nearly always more important than the length of kick. A simple game to encourage this is Between the Posts.

Rules

1 Teams 5-a-side.
2 Stationed opposite each other with a set of rugby posts in between.
3 Only one player is allowed directly in front of the posts.
4 Each team has a ball.
5 A point is scored every time the ball is 'converted' by a punt. (As a variation teams may only drop-kick.)
6 No players allowed within 15 metres of the try-line (22 metres in the case of more experienced players).

DRIBBLE BALL

A much neglected art today on the rugby field is dribbling. This is a game which provides invaluable practice.

Rules

1 Teams 6-a-side.
2 Rules basically as for soccer but using a rugby ball.
3 Play across the rugby pitch between the 22-metre line and the try-line. Size of pitch can be varied to suit players concerned.
4 Goals 5 to 7 metres apart.
5 Have one period in the game when each side has one player, preferably in a different jersey, who is allowed to fall upon the ball. He is a rover. If he falls successfully his side obtains possession and the opposition must immediately retire 5 metres. The faller can only fall on the ball in his own half; when in the attacking half he must play as the rest of the team. This rover should be changed frequently so that all players have the opportunity of acting as the rover.

SOCBY

This is a game which not only gives plenty of practice in the basic individual skills but also creates situations where both orthodox and unorthodox attacking and defending ploys can be used to the full.

Rules

1 Kicking is only allowed outside the 22-metre line.
2 Handling is only allowed inside the 22-metre line.
3 No limit on the number of balls allowed in play at any one time. Start with two and increase gradually.
4 No scrums or lineouts. Where these would have taken place the ball is given to the non-offending team.

This is an ideal game for beginners as laws can be introduced gradually. There is physical contact, handling and kicking skills, pressure and non-stop action. (No shivering players waiting for the ball and the coach is able to dictate how the game progresses.)

SPEEDBALL (6 to 8 a side)

An indoor area like a sports hall is ideal here and a soccer ball is used.

In this game players have to be aware of where their team-mates are and also where the opposition is. Anticipation and resulting interceptions are an integral part of the game.

The aim is to score a 'try' (1 point) by

touching the ball on a wall defended by the opposition, or to score a 'goal' (2 points) by kicking the ball against a bench which would be on the floor in the centre of this wall. Your team obviously has to defend a similar set-up at the far end.

Rules

1 The ball can be handled at the start of play, caught if thrown or kicked or if it rebounds off any wall as long as it does not bounce on the ground more than once. That means it can be caught directly as well as after one bounce.
2 The player with the ball in his hand can take one pace only and he cannot hold the ball for more than three seconds. The referee will start counting the seconds aloud if there is a delay.
3 The player can *place* the ball on the ground and make progress with a soccer dribble or kicking pass. He cannot drop-kick or punt the ball.
4 If the ball is *rolling* on the ground it cannot be handled but it can be flicked up with the foot into the air and then caught, or kicked against any wall and the rebound caught.
5 A player with the ball in his hand cannot be tackled.
6 Normal soccer tackles are allowed if the ball is at the feet.

It is a game where instant decisions are required and reactions are sharpened. A player has to use a mixture of handling and footwork to spread the defence away from the bench where a kicked goal would be worth two points. His supporting team members would be eager to collect the ball near the wall, no matter how wide they position themselves, in order to score a try. These same team members will then be quickly repositioning themselves to defend their own wall after the opposition gain possession.

GAMES IN SMALL AREAS
(approximately 10m × 10m)

PASS WITH CHASE
(4 v 1) (4 v 2) (3 v 3)
Object

The players see how many consecutive passes they can obtain while the chaser (or chasers) try to intercept.

Rules

1 Pass the ball in any direction to your team.
2 Ball must be caught cleanly.
3 No running with the ball.
4 No stepping out of the area.
5 Ball must be passed immediately.
6 No tackling or touch allowed.
7 All passes below shoulder height.

Progressions

1 Aim at 10 consecutive passes.
2 First team to 21 passes – not necessarily consecutive.
3 A player should be allowed to dummy.
4 If there is one or two chasers, they are allowed to tackle.
5 Aim at the same number of chasers as catchers and more than four-a-side (bigger area required).

END BALL (4 v 4)
Object

3 players to pass the ball to a catcher at an end standing outside the area.

Rules

1 A player can pass in any direction.
2 No running with the ball.

3 All passes below shoulder height.
4 Catcher must catch ball cleanly.
5 No tackling.

CORNER BALL (4 v 4)

Object

To touch the opposition with the ball while it is held in both hands. See how long it takes to touch all four opposition. When an opposition is touched he retires from the area.

Rules

1 Only one step can be taken with the ball.
2 All participating players must stay within the area.

The ball-carriers try to manoeuvre the opposition into a corner where they can touch him with the ball. The ball-carriers must be aware where the opposition are but keep their eye on the ball as they receive it.

BRITISH BULLDOG

Object

To improve tackling, with one tackler attempting to bring down one player as any number of players try and run past him to a 'safety' line.

The area boundaries are determined by the number of players and/or their age and experience. The less experience they have, the smaller the area.

Rules

1 When a player has been tackled he becomes a tackler himself to help the original tackler.
2 The remaining players then try to get back to their original line past the two tacklers.

3 Every player that is caught becomes a tackler.

4 The last player left trying to avoid being tackled is the winner.

RATS AND RABBITS (in pairs)

Object

To improve tackling and quickness off the mark.

Rules

1 Players lie down in pairs on their backs, head to head.

2 Coach calls out 'RATS' or 'RABBITS'. Each pair of players has to be one or the other.

3 The Rat or the Rabbit must run back to a safety line about 5 to 10 metres away while the other player in the pair tries to stop him by tackling him.

Progression

The player who is trying to get back to his safety line must pick up a stationary rugby ball off the ground on his way back to his safety line.

14. Selection

INTRODUCTION

Whatever a coach hopes to achieve will be limited by the natural abilities of the players with whom he has to work. This section is so important that perhaps it should come first in any book on rugby coaching.

At school level the coach is the chief selector, if not the only one. The standards achieved by many school XVs with their limited field of choice is often higher than by teams who can draw from a far wider field.

If the best results are to be achieved from any group of players, then the coach must have a say in the composition of that group. The selection committee should be kept to the smallest number possible, ideally 3. However, selecting some sides may involve a great deal of travelling and this would prove extremely difficult, even so 5 is very likely the maximum number desirable.

With the 'squad' system so much in evidence these days, for the final team a selection committee of 3 is feasible, one of whose members must be the coach. At whatever level, the performance of the team will be judged critically and the person responsible for that performance must therefore have a say in the composition of it. Coaching sessions often reveal strengths and weaknesses of players that are not so apparent in matches. Very likely the coach is the only person who possesses the overall picture of players both as individuals and as a team.

Honesty is the most important factor between selector and player. The selector must be recognized as being someone of the highest integrity and he will expect an honest approach from the player.

The player should expect reasons to be given for decisions by selectors and in return selectors can expect performances well up to the player's ability. A selector has the right for the player's wholehearted physical commitment and should be able to make forthright decisions.

WHAT MAKES A GOOD SELECTOR?

Knowledge

He knows the basic requirements of each position and the importance of combinations to blend these requirements together. He also knows how each position depends on the skill and standards of team-mates, e.g. the lineout player depends on the thrower-in; the hooker depends on his scrum-half's service in the set scrum; the space available for a threequarter depends on the distribution of his fellow backs. He must be able to visualize how a person's play would fit into a certain style of play. Or, probably more important, how to use a player's assets to determine a certain style of play. He must be able to 'read' a game and understand the tactics employed by a team.

Watching off the ball

Selectors must be able to watch a player and not the ball. It is ludicrous to watch a ball 30 metres in the air when you know that the ball will come down eventually. Better to watch the individual players at ground level.

Vary places of observation

Most spectators watch from the touchline to see the game. This is a good viewing place for selectors also, especially for set play. However, lines of running in attack and defence can best be seen from behind the goal-posts.

WHAT QUALITIES IS THE SELECTOR LOOKING FOR?

Self-pride

This self-pride will show itself in a variety of ways:

a) *Fitness* A player should not want to play this demanding game unless he has reached a certain level of fitness. He must realize that the skill factor will be seriously undermined if fatigue sets in and a player will not be able to demonstrate his talents. Time that could be used for individual, unit or team preparation should not be wasted on basic fitness training. Self-pride should motivate the individual to reach a level of fitness before a team practice so that he can cope with the demands of the session.

A high work-rate will enable a player to support his colleagues and perhaps inspire them to new levels of fitness and concentration.

(b) *Basic skills* A player with pride will be continually brushing up and expanding the basic skills of the game. As a player will revert to type as the game becomes faster and more intense, it is important that the player would have practised enough to make these skills instinctive. This is very much like the instinctive reactions that are required when driving a car and facing a situation that is unusual.

(c) *Specialists* A player takes pride that he is a specialist in his own position and knows the requirements that his position demands. In a game like rugby these specialist skills are so varied. The power, strength and techniques of the forwards vary widely from the running skills and ability to read a game that is required from a back.

Pace

The main difference that is experienced by a player as the level of rugby gets higher is the greater pace of the game. A player must be able to cope with the pace physically and mentally.

The physical pace includes the ability to change direction quickly and the ability to get down on the ground and get up instantly. Physically the player must have mobility and flexibility.

The mental pace is a test of a player's reactions and if a player is found wanting, the pace will pressurize him into mistakes. Continual play and practice at this higher pace will of course help the reactions of the player and make his play more instinctive, but a player's limitations will be evident as the level of play and pace improve.

Some players are misunderstood as being casual when in fact they are so talented they seem to have so much time to perform. When a player has that much time he is in more control of the situation and is not hurried into errors.

Mental hardness

It is a hard physical game and however talented a player is he must not be put off his game by the physical contact or the hustling of the opposition.

To a certain extent, the degree of competitive element, ruthlessness, determination and powers of concentration is inbred in a person and he will react accordingly – not only on the field but in the way that he prepares. Rugby does not depend on skill alone so these other attributes are so important to the player and the team.

The right mental approach will certainly help to cut down mistakes, offset fatigue, improve concentration and help a player make positive decisions. To certain players it comes more naturally than others.

Judgment

Every position on the field has its own specialist role concerning judgment. The main decision-makers are the half-backs and the No. 8 in overall strategy, but all players should have positional awareness, whether it is a back receiving the ball from a kick or a forward filling gaps in a lineout.

Players should also have the judgment of when to release a ball, whether it be a back on a 2 to 1 situation, or a forward with control of the ball in a maul.

Peripheral vision in a break is particularly important if he is to make good judgments. It is equally important for a forward to know where and what is around him if he finds himself in the middle of a ruck or maul with control of the ball.

To be able to make these judgments correctly really determines the class of the players involved.

Size

The expression still holds true that 'a good big 'un is better than a good little 'un' but other factors must be taken into account:

a) Pace and mobility
b) Pace of thought

c) Aggressive approach
d) Skill and technique
e) Balanced running

To expand on the last two factors. Certain positions could find size a liability: a front row forward with size but little technique could be a disruptive influence to his own team. A large pack without players that can secure the ball on the ground before the opposition would be found lacking.

Certain players who are big and fast can be exposed in attack and defence by players that are better balanced runners with a lower centre of gravity. This could make the player with the lower centre of gravity more elusive in attack, and the ability to adjust position quicker in defence.

Arrogance

It is important for a player to have confidence in his own ability. This will give a player a more positive approach in decision-making, testing his own skills and ability against the opposition and out-lasting opponents through greater fitness and superior technique.

The good player will come to the fore if he has arrogance.

WHAT TEAM QUALITIES IS A SELECTOR LOOKING FOR?

Style

There should be enough dominant players in a team to determine a style of play. The strengths and qualities of the players should be highlighted and used in the preparation of tactics and strategy. It is no use adopting a style of play if it does not suit the players; the players must be confident that they are allowed to play their natural game and a pattern of play will emerge from this.

151

Ball players and ball handlers

Being realistic, a team will have a sprinkling of good ball players to a greater or lesser degree. These are the natural ball players that seem to be able to adapt to most ball games because they have natural eyeball co-ordination. These are the players that are always competent at games like soccer, cricket, hockey and tennis, so they easily adapt to the use of space and control of a rugby ball in handling and kicking.

Fortunately, the lesser mortals in the team are still an essential part of the rugby team which is a game that does not depend on ball skills alone. However, those who are not natural ball players can develop into good *ball handlers*. There is no excuse for a player not to be a good ball handler and this handling should become instinctive. Basketball and waterpolo would certainly help this development.

Combinations

Rugby is a team game in the true sense of the word because no player can perform properly without the co-operation of others. By experience it has been found that certain smaller units in a team need a balance to play well as a group, so the combination of these smaller groups is important. These combinations can be split up thus:

1 *The front row* The priority of the front row is scrummaging. So it is important that they have confidence in each other to bind together in a solid unit because their physiques are compatible to take the pressure from the opposition in front, and the rest of their pack behind. It is particularly important that the hooker can fit into this scrummaging unit as props can be of varying sizes.

Another important consideration is the expertise of each prop at the lineout. The techniques required at the front of the lineout are different to those standing at No. 3. Usually the bigger prop is more useful at No. 3 where there are larger gaps to cover.

2 *The locks* Scrummaging is again a priority, but a pack must have the inspiration of a middle-line jumper who can jump high as opposed to a front jumper who must have the ability to jump across. The style of play of a team may need this high jumper nearer the front of the lineout, so the other lock must accept the role of support jumper and more general grafting forward.

A selector must check which side of the scrum each lock prefers to pack and where each likes to position himself in the lineout.

3 *The back row* One of the back row, usually a flanker, must have exceptional pace to the point of breakdown and a freer running role in attack and defence. Another of the back row – this must be a flanker – should have the capability to seal the short side from a scrum, a good mauling technique and an effective lineout presence either as a support for a middle jumper or a jumper in his own right depending on the lineout strengths of the No. 8.

The No. 8 must possess awareness and control at the base of the scrum, being an important decision-maker in the timing of releasing of this ball. This control is also required at the back of the lineout. Whilst the No. 8 does not have to be the tallest man in the back row, it is essential that at least one back row player has lineout ability.

4 *The half-backs* It is important that they have complementary skills because both are main decision-makers. Both must have the ability to read the game. Both dictate the style of play, so both have their periods of domination and must be able to communicate with each other instantly so that the role of responsibility can be smoothly passed from one to the other.

5 *Centres* It is particularly important to get the balance right with the centres for fluency and penetration in attack, and understanding in defence. A steadier all-round player would probably bring out the best from an attacking runner and would take over the role of setting up this potential attacker and creating space for him by his own running and/or distribution of the ball. This steadier player should be able to harness the defence of his co-centre. Communication and teamwork are essential in defence for the two centres.

A selector should be able to advise on whether inside or outside centre or left and right centre would suit the personalities involved. It depends on the qualities of the centres and the style of play. A closer understanding between centre and wing may determine that left and right centre would suit a team more than inside and outside centre.

6 *Wings and full-back* These players must be classed as three full-backs in defensive kicking situations and three differing attackers when in possession of the ball.

Covering and sweeping for each other to receive kicks is the ideal way to instantly counterattack. If their attacking styles differ there is a variety of options open when an attacking team is in possession. A bustling wing can offer different problems to the opposition than the smoother runner who enjoys outflanking the opposition. The full-back can add that extra dimension by entering the line in the style that suits his running skills. The ultimate aim will be to take advantage of a 2 v 1 situation and this often involves the full-back and wing, or the two wings.

Selectors must note the different qualities needed playing on the left wing or the right wing. Basically, the left wing is the more defensive wing in fielding kicks and tackling and this must be taken into account when selecting.

Qualities looked for in individual positions

Loose-head prop

Technique and strength in scrummaging. Feet positioned so that he can transmit, shove and also channel the ball and remain steady. Flat back with head driving under the tight head's right breast and sternum. Tight binding, especially with his own hooker. The ability to use legs, hips and back to drive upwards and leave a clear path and view for the hooker. He cannot afford to take an easy scrummaging position outside his opposite number because it forces his own hooker away from the ball in the set scrum and causes disruption to those scrummaging behind the front row. So a sustained aggressive attitude is required.

Hooker

He must have the technique and flexibility to scrummage and win his own ball in the set scrum. Accurate lineout throwing in of the ball is the next important priority. He must have the qualities of a flank forward at lineout, rucks and mauls.

Tight-head prop

He must be built to be able to withstand the compression that he will experience in the set scrum. He should be able to persecute with scrummaging power without disrupting his own scrum, who need him as a solid base to scrummage themselves. He must be able to slow down or stop attempted wheels by the opposition and be able to assist his own hooker on the opposition ball.

He will probably be the support man to the front and middle jumpers and must know his lineout duties for both. He is expected to be a good wrestler and mauler in all phases of support play.

Locks

The first priority must be scrummaging,

but it is accepted that one of these locks may be selected because of his lineout jumping talents or support play around the field. However, the scrummaging cannot be neglected and certain standards are required. A flat back, feet back, binding and raised chin are essential for scrummaging.

The ability to win ball in the lineout is necessary, but also the ability to deny or spoil the opposition lineout ball.

Locks are usually large in physique and their role in set play, rucks, mauls and support play makes great demands on their strength and stamina. Even though they are larger and heavier than most of the team, they are expected to reach breakdowns quickly and be effective on arrival. The locks and back row should be more interchangeable these days.

Flankers

Aggressive tackling and the ability to gain and/or regain the ball in contact and distribute the ball. To have pace off the mark to get to the breakdown or to support a team-mate.

At least one of the flankers must have the ability to instinctively secure the ball on the ground. Also at least one of the flankers must have a good mauling technique for his support play. There must be a tight defensive role on the short side for one of the flankers so it is essential that one of the flankers has the ability and physique to deal with this. The other flanker must be able to cover vast distances across the field, at pace, in order to get to breakdowns quickly.

Help out with the defensive role of the backs, and support his own backs in attack. There are many flankers that fly around the field but they must be effective when they are involved in breakdowns, tackling and support. Both flankers must have awareness in the lineout. One of the flankers usually stands at No. 5 in the lineout and must have a lineout presence. The other flanker is usually at the tail of the lineout, he develops

his own technique for lineout ball-getting by timing his jump or using his pace.

The ability to read a game is a great advantage because this determines the flanker's lines of running.

No. 8

Control at the base of the scrum is the most important job of the No. 8. He must have tactical sense, knowing when to release the ball quickly, when to hold the ball, and when to call on a variety of back-row moves, always being in communication with his scrum-half. He can be branded as a 'scavenger', being usually second in a defensive role to his flankers and scrum-half around the set scrum, so quite often he can secure the loose ball if a flanker or scrum-half has already disrupted the scrum-half. He is also a scavenger in attack, hoping to carry on movements that started because the flankers secured the ball in a breakdown originally.

The back of the lineout tends to get loose with gaps appearing because the lineout is not as compressed. The No. 8 must control this loose situation and again know how quickly to distribute this ball. As the No. 8 is usually one of the main lineout players it is easier for him to make these decisions.

Scrum-half

A quick pass either way from all facets of possession is a scrum-half's main asset.

This player must be aggressive, courageous and resilient with a great tactical awareness. He is the communication and link between forwards and backs and he will decide how the ball will be used. There must be a balance between his passing, running and kicking. He should not be able to be branded as a running scrum-half, a kicking scrum-half or a scrum-half that can only pass.

The length of his pass is not as important as the quickness, but he must be able to vary the length, decide on a diving or standing pass, and when to put the ball in front of his scrum-half or directly to him.

As he is the 'eyes' for the forwards, it is important that the scrum-half is a dominant character and tells the pack exactly what he wants.

Outside-half

He is the pivot of a team's attack and defence. He must have good hands and be able to move the ball quickly and accurately both ways. He must be an accurate kicker with either foot, with a variety of attacking kicks. He must also give his team confidence and inspiration by his ability to kick defensively in an effective manner.

Speed off the mark with a change of pace and direction is required but it must be realized that lateral runners are difficult to adjust to.

As well as being a pivot the fly-half must aim to penetrate the opposition three-quarter line. If he just acts as a pivot this reduces the defensive options the opposition have to cover. The fly-half may go for the complete break – or just as telling, the half-break. He must never allow the opposition to set up defensive routines by his only kicking or passing.

Tackling must be one of his duties, especially as he has to bring up the threequarter line as a unit. Even if his physique is not ideal for tackling it is still important for him to realize that the centres need him to orientate their efforts and their timing in defence. Above all, the main qualification of an outside-half is the ability to read the game. The outside-half can dominate a game.

Centres

Again, good hands are essential with the ability to take and give a pass both ways. As the ball has already gone through other hands, there is extra pressure on the handling of the centres because defences are closer.

A centre's build is probably more robust because he is still expected to distribute after a half-tackle. Centres are also engineering 3 v 2 and 2 v 1 situations, so timing the giving of the pass is important. Centres usually release other players to run, so it is essential that they run straight themselves so as not to crowd their support towards the touchline. They must also interest the opposition and stop them drifting across to mark the receiver of the pass.

Centres must be aware of correct alignment in attack and defence and be able to adjust this alignment depending on the situation. Speed of reaction is necessary, especially in realignment and support play.

Aggressive tackling is required with the mentality and style of flankers retaining and gaining possession in contact situations. This attitude makes a centre prepared to go in and obtain the ball. Much of the flankers role is done by the centres, they are just starting from a different position, that is in the middle of the field, not flanking a scrum or standing near the end of a lineout.

In attack, it is expected that the centre has balanced running with control and a change in direction and pace. In other words, his running skills should be expert enough to beat a man. He should be creative, with the ability to make a half-break, or break, to set up his fellow players. He will be needed to kick tactically and as a pair they will be expected to chase kicks. It is a most athletic and demanding position.

Wing

The main requirements are speed, elusiveness and power. It is very difficult for the opposition to counter pace, so an overlap situation must be taken full advantage of. The elusiveness and power have to be weapons at the ready when a winger is cramped for room but is still expected to make something from the situation. Good handling is wanted in all situations because the winger can often find himself a long way from his support and a loose ball can be taken advantage of, if they are in the vicinity first. Also, a winger may find himself as a 'finisher-off' of a movement that took good work and time to develop. He would be expected to complete the task.

A winger will definitely be called upon to field kicks, and to cover for the full-back when he fields a kick or decides to join the line. So good positional sense is required by the wing who must realize that he is, in fact, one of three full-backs.

This positional sense will help the wing to look for work in attack. He is not expected to stay on his wing waiting for the ball. He must support a variety of players because he has the speed to cover vast distances, so he can pop up in many places at different running angles. To maintain the attack, the wing should be able to execute a variety of kicks, keeping the ball in play and keeping the ball alive. He must also be able to give the team confidence with his tackling and ability to cope with contact. If he is found lacking, he is in such an exposed position that the opposition will soon detect a weakness.

Full-back
Like a goalkeeper in soccer, the full-back can instil so much confidence in the rest of the team by being dependable in the basic skills that are required in his position. The most important requirement is he must be able to field a ball and kick well with either foot. Again, he is in such an exposed position that the tactics of the opposition would be determined if there was a weakness in this basic priority.

The full-back can make the game much easier to control if he has sound positional sense. He can then cover and tackle any break. He must show courage in keeping his eye on the ball if he has to collect an opposition kick, no matter how much pressure from the chasers. He must try and wait for the support if he is caught as the last line of defence. He must show courage in the tackle which is usually in the wide open spaces and inevitably the last line of defence.

A full-back is also expected to enter the line in attack, either as a link or a penetrator. So his handling must be sure and his timing of entry precise. His ability to read the game should determine when and where he enters the line. His judgment of when to counterattack is crucial because if he fails he is so short of cover that the opposition can take advantage enough to score.

Key members

A captain
The captain must be a good enough player to give his team confidence. He must be tactically aware with clear-cut ideas on how a certain game should be approached, and he should be able to pass these strategies on to his team. The preparations and instructions should be geared to that particular game but, once on the field, he must be able to adjust to certain circumstances and adjust his strategy and tactics accordingly. This adjustment and communication is the important part of a captain's role. The captain must know his men and know how to get the best out of them. He can inspire his team by his own example on the field.

The pack leader
As the pack leader is also a member of the pack it is difficult for him to view the pack with a detached view so he must be careful not to be too emotional. However, as a member of the pack he can sense the mood and state of the eight men as a unit.

His instructions must be clear and have conviction. We emphasize that it is better for eight men in a pack to be doing the wrong thing together than for four to do it right and four to do it wrong.

As fatigue sets in, the basic and unit skills standards fall, so a continual reminder of these is necessary, usually at times of reforming of scrums and lineouts when there is a slight lull in the game and a pack leader can get the attention of his pack. A continual nagging and shouting tends to go over the heads of the pack and is a waste of time. A forward in this high pitch of emotion is particularly susceptible to praise. A pack leader who recognizes achievements by a player usually gets a maintaining of this standard or inspires the player to even better achievements. On the other hand, a player who has made a mistake does not want a reminder of that mistake. The pack must bear the brunt of any individual's weakness or mistake as a group, so it should always be remembered by a pack leader 'Collective criticism, individual praise'.

A kicker

A kicker is essential. Many penalties have been earned by continual pressure forcing the opposition into mistakes, or a breaking of the law to stop a team scoring a try. This attacking effort must be converted into points, so a quality and consistent kicker has to be included in a team.

15. Conclusion

Rugby football is very likely the most complete team game to be found on the sports fields of the world.

It is a game to be enjoyed – and enjoyment comes from attainment, or a player realizing his potential. To do this he needs coaching, but a style of coaching that does not stifle individuality or flair.

Have faith in your players – this will give them confidence and if given the opportunity to express themselves they may well surprise *you*, and themselves.

Index

Index

DRILLS INDEX

FACTS of
the MATTER
CHRISTIAN CLASSICS SERIES

What Christians believe

by
Ian Barclay

Inter-Varsity Press

INTER-VARSITY PRESS
38 De Montfort Street, Leicester LE1 7GP, England

Unless otherwise stated, quotations from the Bible are from
the Revised Standard Version, copyrighted 1946, 1952.

First published by Church Pastoral Aid Society in 1971
First published in Christian Classics by Inter-Varsity Press in 1997

British Library Cataloguing in Publication Data
A catalogue record for this book is available from the British Library.

ISBN 0-85111-244-7

Printed and bound in Great Britain by Cox & Wyman Ltd, Reading,
Berkshire.

*Inter-Varsity Press is the book-publishing division of the Universities and
Colleges Christian Fellowship (formerly the Inter-Varsity Fellowship), a
student movement linking Christian Unions in universities and colleges
throughout the United Kingdom and the Republic of Ireland, and a member
movement of the International Fellowship of Evangelical Students. For
information about local and national activities write to UCCF, 38 De Montfort
Street, Leicester LE1 7GP.*

Contents

Foreword

'No Faith without Facts' is how the apostles and early leaders of the Christian church saw it. Bluntly, Paul said on one occasion that if Christ did not rise from the dead, not only is the Christian faith not worth talking about, but any experience of God's forgiveness men may claim, and any hopes of eternal life they may cherish, are quite illusory. Or to put it another way, if we pay little attention to the facts concerning Jesus of Nazareth – what he taught, and did, and what happened to him – belief and unbelief are just different forms of wishful thinking.

So any book about these important 'facts of the matter' is welcome, and not least this one. Ian Barclay has a deserved reputation for preaching sermons people come to hear, and writing books that people read. He has successfully introduced the splendid truths of the Christian story to many for the first time in a way that 'got through'. If you, who have picked this book up, have got as far as reading this Preface, read on and you will not be disappointed, either in the author or in the good things of which he tells.

London   **Dick Lucas**

Introduction

Because of a bad transport connection when I was on a preaching tour, I decided to spend a night in the comfort of a hotel. Next morning, going down to breakfast I amused myself by reading the advertisements that covered every available space on the inside of the lift. The advertisement that caught my eye simply said *'Why not visit the minister? He keeps office hours in Suite 512'*. Having breakfasted, I set out to find Room 512. We introduced ourselves. Almost immediately the telephone rang, and I politely turned to examine the books that usually line the walls of a minister's office. There were books on psychology, clinical theology, sociology, anthropology and ecology; it almost became a game trying to find a handful of books that dealt with real spiritual issues, but eventually I found them tucked away in a corner. Do not misunderstand me. I think that that list of subjects should concern every minister; but the greater proportion of his reading should be on the great biblical truths with which he seeks to feed his congregation each week. Certainly, ministers must learn much more about man – but only to be better equipped to tell him about God.

The telephone call finished and I found that I was talking to a man who had all the trappings of Christianity but who had lost his own faith. I left Room 512 feeling very sad, but determined that when I got home I would try to set down *the facts of the matter* concerning Jesus Christ.

George Terryl in a letter to Baron Frederick von Hügel, a great Christian man who lived at the turn of the century, said 'What a relief it would be if one could conscientiously wash one's hands of the whole business of religion! But then there is that strange man on his cross who drives one back again and again.' I think that exactly sums up the situation for many people today. They would like to wash their hands of religion, but the thought of that man on the cross constantly returns to their minds. People are understandably disenchanted with the Church, but at the back of their minds is the nagging thought that perhaps Jesus of Nazareth is after all the answer to the problems of life. And that is what this book is about. It is about Jesus Christ, his death, his resurrection. It tries to give the facts about the pardon he offers, his Spirit, his Church and his heaven.

Perhaps I ought to say something about the style of this book. As a minister I find it very difficult to give books to people about the great themes of Christianity because so often they are too heavy for the average man, and the 'currants' are few and far between. I have tried to make *the facts of the matter* solid fruit cake and as readable as possible. If that sounds pretentious, I do not mean it to be so, because in a hundred years I could not write a scholarly book about Jesus of Nazareth.

So in the limited way that I see them, these are *the facts of the matter*.

Brighton   **Ian Barclay**

God's only forgotten Son

In the first place it was, of course, a schoolboy howler.
When his form master had questioned him he had meant
to say that Jesus was God's only begotten son. But his slip
contained much more truth than some theologians would
care to admit. Using the term 'the fatherhood of God' in
its most general sense, Jesus Christ certainly is God's only
forgotten son today. We remember all the other sons –
those who reach the moon or sell a million records – but
the one who could possibly resolve many of the world's
problems lies largely forgotten by the men and women of
this generation.

The reason is quite simple. Having lost the knowledge
of God we have put man in his place. Dr Austin Farrer
said it would be as inevitable as that, 'If I have no other
God, how can I help being God to myself?'Such human-
ism really is the biggest take-over bid in history. In
modern times it all began in 1762 when Rousseau in his
book *Social Contract* made what he called his Copernicus
discovery namely, that it is not God, but man who is at
the centre of the living universe. And the take-over, having once been initiated, has gained momentum ever since,
until today it has the proportions and the force of a full-
scale invasion.

At least one of our political leaders has noticed the
strength of the invasion and has stated in quite uncom-
promising terms its effect on the nation. Lord Hailsham
once said:

Our country is being destroyed before our eyes by a conspiracy of intellectuals without faith, delinquents without honour, muck-rakers without charity or compassion, young men who are incapable of dreaming dreams, and old men who have never known what it is to see visions. In the public life of today a public man is mocked when he speaks about patriotism . . . A cynical sneer greets references to honour and integrity in political as in business affairs . . . And if someone by any chance says that he believes in a healthy family life as the foundation of civilization, or backs the traditional Christian ethic on sex and morals, we hear an awful lot of nonsense about the need for tolerance and charity in allowing the young to be taught to do as they please.

When you look at a statement like that, in spite of all the technological advances of the past decade, there is little point in singing with Swinburne, 'Glory to man in the Highest. For man is the master of things.' Perhaps it is time to look once more at the only forgotten son? After all, it is just possible that he is *the man* who is the master of things and therefore in rediscovering him we shall also find the key to life.

True history that actually happened

In John 2 we find Jesus at a wedding reception held at the little village of Cana in Galilee. It is a real place, a tiny wind-swept village three and a half miles farther away from the sea of Galilee than the village of Nazareth, and much higher in the hills. In Hebrew it is called *the place of the reeds*. It is also the home of the disciple Nathaniel.

One of the most interesting features of the Gospel narratives is that time and time again Jesus is linked with history. I am sure that the Gospel writers were not consciously writing for posterity, yet they seem to go out of their way to tie Jesus to people and events that were contemporary. The Gospel story begins when *Herod was king of Judaea* (Luke 1:5), at precisely that point in history when *a decree was issued by Caesar Augustus* (Luke 2:1). As though that was not enough historical reference the gospel writer Luke adds that it was also *the first enrolment when Quirinius was governor of Syria* (Luke 2:2). At the other end of the earthly life of Jesus we are told that he was seized and *led to Caiaphas the High Priest* (Matthew 26:57) and then *the whole company arose and brought him to Pilate* (Luke 23:1). In other words his whole life was surrounded by so many historical figures that in the end it is impossible to doubt his historicity. As one who would hardly call himself a friend of the Christian faith, Sir James Frazer, author of *The Golden Bough* (Macmillan), put it:

The doubts that have been cast on the historical reality of Jesus are in my judgment unworthy of serious attention. Quite apart from the positive evidence of history, the origin of a great moral and religious reform is incredible without the personal existence of a great reformer. To dissolve the founder of Christianity into a myth is as absurd as to do the same with Mohammed, Luther or Calvin.

One of the plays by George Bernard Shaw is called *In Good King Charles' Golden Days*. I noticed for the first time, when it was on television, that it is subtitled *A True History That Never Happened*. I found that title intriguing. I gather that it meant that the people involved, the events described, and the dialogue used were all in character. It could all have happened, but it did not. Now the gospel stories are much more than that, they are not merely people and events in character, something that could have happened but did not; the life of Jesus Christ is true history that actually happened. 'His life is not so much written as ploughed into the history of the world' (Emerson).

'A little baby thing'

On the other hand he did not storm history, simply charging on to the stage of time still wearing the clothes of godly splendour. Rather, he chose to identify himself with the creatures of this world even to the extent of entering their life in precisely the same way that they did.

That is why in the first place he was not recognized as the Christ. It needed that strange poet preacher of Scotland, George Macdonald, to put it most touchingly:

> They all were looking for a King
> To slay their foes and lift them high;
> Thou cam'st a little baby thing
> That made a woman cry.

9

I am sure it was always possible to mistake him for an ordinary man. For me it is significant that when Judas betrayed him he had to give the soldiers of the high priest a sign. Judas could not say to them that Jesus was the holy-looking one in the garden, or the one wearing the religious clothes. On the contrary, to distinguish him from all the other bronzed and dusty Palestinians Judas had to say, *the one I shall kiss is the man* (Mark 14:44).

His home life certainly does not betray him to be other than a normal Galilean of his period. Even in his late twenties, we see the well-preserved family relationships that we would expect from a society where the family unit was longer-lasting than it is today. It is the confirmation of a normal home life when we read that the mother of Jesus was also a guest at the wedding. But then his life has all the elements that we would expect. There was a natural birth. The virgin birth is not really an accurate description of what took place. His mother's confinement was perfectly natural, it was her conception of the child that was supernatural, and Jesus, having been born in a normal way grew as other children grew. His body was subject to tiredness and hunger, pain and death, and on an emotional level his life held in balance the usual tensions of love and anger, joy and sorrow.

It is only when we look at that part of his life that we would call his moral life that we find that he differs radically from all the other men who have ever walked on this planet. In his life there was no moral failure; he did not sin. He was perfectly human in that he could have sinned: not to admit this would be to make nonsense of his temptation; but that he did not sin is the testimony of both his life and the scriptures.

A gallant young man?

So Jesus was an ordinary young man; *but not merely that*. Again it is the wedding at Cana that reveals this so clearly. Two things happened at the reception that mark Jesus off from merely being a Palestinian of the time of the Roman occupation. The first is such an innocent remark, that it is not until you stop and think about it that you realize just how odd it is. John tells us that the mother of Jesus said to him, 'They have no wine'. It does not seem to have been a horrified whisper on her part, the sort that you would expect a guest to make when the champagne had run out before the first toast. In fact, rather than showing astonishment. Mary seems to be making such a firm statement that she expects some visible response.

To expect anyone but the host to do anything about the lack of wine would be to cast a slight on his hospitality and his ability to provide. Nevertheless it was to Jesus that she turned. Here is something else that we see throughout the gospel stories. That though on the outside Jesus has the appearance of being no more than an ordinary human being, he also has an aura of authority that commands people's attention and makes them come to him with the belief that he has the answer to their problem. An elderly statesman prince, who you would have thought had all the theological answers, came to him at night; a tax collector climbed a tree to catch a glimpse of him; a Centurion came to him about his son; just as a Syro-Phoenicean woman came to him about her daughter. The lepers came to him; the blind called after him; and they all believed that he could answer their need. In just the same way his mother came to him expecting him to answer the problem of a wedding feast without wine.

To find an adequate description of Jesus I think we need more than Dag Hammarskjold's '*a gallant young man*'. Because of his authority and of the obvious command he had of every situation I think I would call him as Samuel Rutherford did a '*kingly king*'.

He stands alone

The truly astonishing thing about Jesus Christ is not that he was clearly an historical figure, nor even that looking so ordinary he had such a powerful air of authority; the really astonishing thing about him is that his words and actions were so convincing that we are driven to the inescapable conclusion that he was either divine or a charlatan. Either he was a dreamer about God, deluding his followers by his words and actions, or his dreams were not the fantasy of a deranged mind, but were the truth and reality that he proclaimed them to be.

Jesus stands alone, in the loneliness of extreme pathological megalomania, or alone without peer or rival in time and eternity. C. S. Lewis said in *Mere Christianity* (Geoffrey Bles):

A man who was merely a man, and said the things Jesus said, would not be a great moral teacher. He would either be a lunatic – on a level with the man who says he is a poached egg – or else he would be the Devil.

That is the only way that you can look at the provision of wine for the festivities of this little village wedding. It was hardly a small deception, the secret provision of a dozen bottles of vintage wine that Jesus just happened to have in the saddle-bag of his donkey, which he somehow managed to have smuggled into the house. Jesus took the six stone jars standing at the doorway of the house for the Jewish rites of purification and he turned them into wine. There is some doubt about the actual size of the water jars, but that is not really important, because at the very least Jesus made 120 gallons of wine and at the most it was in the region of 180 gallons. So it was either a gigantic hoax or a magnificent statement of divinity. The latter of course was the opinion of the disciples, for by this *sign* they saw him to be *manifesting his glory*. This was the second thing at the wedding that marked him off from other men.

Look down to look up

There is a magnificent ceiling painting in Rome by Guido Reni that he has entitled *Dawn*, depicting light emerging from darkness. To study it in detail will bring a crick to the back of the neck so a mirror has been conveniently placed on a table beneath the painting. This great work of art can now be studied at leisure and in an attitude that comes easily to the human frame. So many people spend so much time trying to discover God by looking up. By doing so they bring theological cricks to the backs of their spiritual necks! To discover God it is not necessary to look up; rather, look down at Jesus, for in him is mirrored every detail of the Godhead.

Intoxicating religion

When Jesus took the water and turned it into wine, he gave us a picture of all that he longs to do for us. He wants to take the ordinary in our lives and turn it into the *heady* experience of a *life lived in God's era*. Which is what John's phrase *eternal life* means (John 3: 16). Jesus wants to take the coldly religious in our lives and turn it into the intoxicating experience of real Christianity. The flatness of those prayers, that cold worship, that ineffective witnessing can all go and the whole of our lives can begin to bubble with life.

The climacteric man

In a literary sense Francesco Petrarch is often called the *climacteric man* because his life marks the beginning of the Renaissance. Indeed Petrarch himself said, 'I stand as a man between two worlds, looking both forward and backward'. Yet it is difficult to see Petrarch in this rôle, because the Renaissance is hardly a peak or a climax of history. It is, as its name clearly states, a re-awakening to the past. Certainly there was a new spirit abroad in the fifteenth century which began in Florence when the past was re-discovered, bringing a new confidence to the human race; and from this confidence sprang great works of art. But the net result was that man discovered that he had not changed very much at all. The world that Petrarch looked forward to was precisely the same world that lay behind him.

The truly *climacteric man* is Jesus Christ. The real division of history comes not in the fifteenth century but at the beginning of the Christian era; even our dating system is a witness to that. The man who in fact stands between two worlds is the wedding guest at Cana of Galilee. Here within the span of this man's earthly life is the real climax of history. What the world desperately needs today is a new renaissance when it can rediscover *God's only forgotten son*.

He stoops to conquer

There is nothing that moves the human race more than someone who is willing to lay down his life for others. This is well illustrated by the fact that sacrifice is the constantly recurring theme of television drama and popular entertainment. It is the sacrifice that catches our attention in the epic story of a famous battle, just as in the massacre by one side or the other in a story from the American wild west. It's there just the same in the much more ordinary story of parents who hazard their own health for the sake of their children. In one sense the date, location and costume of the sacrifice are all irrelevant; if the plot contains some element of self-giving then it is bound to make compelling viewing. No matter whether we see it on the large screen of the local cinema or the much smaller TV screen in our own homes; the drama and the virtue of many of these sacrificial acts is easy to understand. If you are British, then the 'few' who laid down their lives at the Battle of Britain are clearly heroes. I presume that if you are an American you feel just the same way about General Custer's last stand at Little Big Horn in Montana on the 25th June in the year 1876, when the Sioux Indians massacred the General and his 264 men.

The sad thing is that sacrifice is attractive to the human race, no matter how irresponsible it may be. A good example is the famous charge of the Light Brigade at Balaclava in 1856, which has been described in a variety of ways. It's been called a military disaster, just as it's been called the most rash, culpable and criminally blameworthy military order ever given. And yet, if anyone ever talks about the charge of the six hundred, the word they nearly always use is the word of the French general who actually witnessed the charge – '*magnificent*'.

The same attraction to sacrifice is seen in the political thinking of young people today. Here is the reason for much of the posthumous success of Che Guevara; most university campuses somewhere have a poster from which his bearded, bereted face stares. He attracts the young because he was a politician who did not merely talk but also acted upon his beliefs. He went to live and fight in the jungle, although physically quite unsuited to that sort of life. In one sense when he went into the jungle, he was willing to lay down his life for things in which he believed. Just as older men said that the charge of the six hundred was '*magnificent*', so younger people look at the lonely death of this young revolutionary and say precisely the same thing.

Obviously, there is nothing new about the virtue of sacrifice. Presumably, it is as old as the human race. It has certainly been admired by men since long before Jesus was born. Five hundred years before his birth, a young prince called Gautama lived in India. His home was a palace full of gorgeous things. His days were spent in feasting and enjoyment. Yet somehow four signs were able to penetrate the security of his palace. The prince saw the unpleasantness of disease in the form of a leper, then he saw the tragedy of sin in a holy man lamenting his spiritual failures. The ugliness of death was brought to him by the sight of a funeral procession. Then a tottering, decrepit old man posed for him all the questions that surround old age. Such startling signs from the outside world could not be banished from the young prince's mind. He began to investigate the condition of those who were beyond the luxury of the palace walls. Soon he was to leave his palace to enter and to share the sorrow and the suffering of ordinary people. For fifty years he lived as a beggar wandering through India teaching others. His followers called him Buddha, meaning '*the enlightened one*'. And such a lasting impression was made by the young prince's utter self-sacrifice that millions still follow his teaching to this very day.

Having considered the fascination of sacrifice, we can now look at the death of Jesus. His self-giving was quite different from the examples that we have already seen. His death was not a defiant last stand such as General Custer's. Nor was his death a rash but magnificent all-or-nothing charge in an attempt to redeem the human race. Certainly Jesus was a young revolutionary like Che Guevara when he died. You could say that he was like Gautama in that he left the luxury of the palace to live largely on the hospitality of others, wandering through Palestine teaching and sharing the lives of ordinary people. However, as we shall see in a moment, his death has a much deeper meaning than simple self-sacrifice.

Crucifiction?

It was a printer's spelling mistake. He had been asked to print some posters announcing the preacher's subject as the *crucifixion*, but the preacher's theme appeared on the posters as *crucifiction*. However, the last thing that anyone can ever query about the death of Jesus is its authenticity. Jesus clearly lived and died. '*Christ died*' says Peter in his first letter (1 Peter 3: 18); and we know precisely whom he means by Christ, because he begins this letter: '*Peter, an apostle of Jesus Christ*'. The Jesus that died was the same Jesus that had called Peter to service three or four years earlier. It was the same Jesus that Peter had whole-heartedly·denied outside the high priest's house, a denial that caused him to go away and to weep with guilt and remorse. It was, in fact, the same Jesus about whom, only six weeks later, Peter was to preach with such authority and zeal.

Sometimes people bring into the story an element of fiction by not looking closely at the facts of the death of Christ as recorded in the Gospels. Several people have suggested to me recently that Jesus did not die on a cross-shaped cross, saying rather that the cross was shaped like a capital T or a capital x. Now certainly there were various ways of putting people to death by crucifixion; the word for *cross* in the New Testament simply meant a 'stake'. No doubt in the first place men were nailed or tied to an upright stake driven into the ground. A natural development of this would be to take two stakes driven into the ground at angles, forming what we sometimes call a St Andrew's cross. A cross shaped as a capital T was another known variation. But the more popular design was the traditional shape. My reading of the New Testament suggests to me that it was on a traditionally shaped cross that Jesus was executed. John tells us in his Gospel that a sign was printed in three languages with supposed irony, naming Jesus as the *King of the Jews*, and this was nailed above his head. There is only one known form of a cross that would provide a space for the notice; and that is the shape that for centuries has been accepted as the shape of the cross upon which Christ died.

A bloody, dusty, sweaty business

Dorothy L. Sayers says in the introduction of her book *Man Born to be King* (Gollancz):

His executioners made vulgar jokes about him, called him filthy names, taunted him, smacked him in the face, flogged him with the cat, and hanged him on the common gibbet – a bloody, dusty, sweaty and sordid business.

As Douglas Webster says in his book *In Debt to Christ* (Highway Press), 'the gospel is a murder story. It is a crime, and there is blood'. The marks of that sordid business were indelibly made upon the body of Jesus. Even after the Resurrection they were still there for all to see.

They are the scars of victory, the jewels of a crown. Jacob Epstein's majestically beautiful and compassionate figure of Jesus in Llandaff Cathedral fails to be the victorious figure of the Christian faith simply because all the marks of the crime have been removed. It is not that Christians have a morbid, sadistic curiosity that makes them want to look at the wounds of Jesus; the point is that those scars are the evidence of his victory.

Much ado about nothing?

If we are thinking merely about the physical death of Jesus then the whole affair is indeed '*much ado about nothing*', and the death of Jesus is no different from the death of any other man; and the centrality that his death holds in Christian worship and thinking is the same morbid curiosity that people have always had for accidents and executions. However, the situation immediately becomes much ado about something when we see actually what was happening on the cross and who it was who died.

It's God they ought to crucify

Sidney Carter in his song *Friday Morning* imagines one of the two thieves that was crucified at the same time as Jesus, saying to him:

> *Now Barabbas was a killer*
> *And they let Barabbas go.*
> *But you are being crucified*
> *For nothing, here below.*
> *But God is up in heaven*
> *And he doesn't do a thing:*
> *With a million angels watching,*
> *And they never move a wing.*
> *It's God they ought to crucify*
> *Instead of you and me,*
> *I said to the carpenter*
> *A'hanging on the tree.*

Indeed, it was God that they crucified that day. As we saw in the first chapter, Jesus was no mere man. If he was just a man then crucifixion would have been a just punishment received in advance for the colossal deception that he was to pull on the human race over the next two thousand years. However, the evidence of the New Testament does not point to his being a confidence trickster; but rather someone who was, as he claimed to be, the Son of the living God.

The good, the bad, and the ugly

The verse that I have already quoted from Peter's first letter goes on to say that Jesus '*died for sins . . . the righteous for the unrighteous, that he might bring us to God'* (1 Peter 3:18). Peter is saying that, when Jesus died, it was not simply a case of God being crucified, but that on the cross Jesus was dying in our place to take away our sin. Jesus was paying the ransom price for human failure. He who was spiritually clean became unclean that he might receive our just punishment. Such a deep truth can never be adequately illustrated, but one pale example comes from the First World War when there was great concern about the spread of trench fever which was thought to be carried by lice. A scientist called Bacot, who had made an exhaustive study of lice, was asked by the War Office to visit the front line and to see if anything could be done. The scientist acquired some lice and attached them to his own arm. As he went about his work, visiting the different battle areas collecting further specimens, he experimented with various cures upon himself. He became extremely ill with typhus and died. He who was clean became unclean to save others.

The bad and the ugly is a very good description of the spiritual state of the human race. Society today talks less about sin, but it is there just the same. William Prendergast, creator of the television series *Z Cars* and now police adviser to the programme, has said that we are all born with the tendency to evil. He served for the most part of his working life as a policeman in Liverpool so he ought to know what life is really like.

It used to be said that if you could find a truly primitive tribe in one of the unexplored corners of the earth then you would have found a people who were blissfully and innocently happy. When compared with so-called civilized people they would be unaware of sin and would be quite uninhibited, and entirely free from guilt and all the other consequences of sinful behaviour. Such a tribe has never been found. Even in the near-primitive tribes such as those of the South Seas there is obviously a profound awareness of the results of human failure. We see this in the story of Gauguin and his anger. When Paul Gauguin left his wife and his job in Paris to go and live and paint in the freedom of the South Sea islands he lived with a young native girl. Once, while out fishing with the men of the island, Gauguin was the first to catch a fish. When it was pulled from the water it was noticed that his hook was caught in the lower lip of the fish. At this, the South Sea islanders laughed, and at first refused to reply when asked to explain their amusement. When forced to, they said that that was a sign that his native woman was sleeping with another man while he was away. Gauguin was furious. Immediately he returned to the island. He questioned the girl who denied that any such relationship had taken place. Gauguin sulked through the rest of the day and at night, when the dusk had fallen and Gauguin was sitting in his hut, the young native girl came in with a heavy rod saying, *'Please beat me or your anger will make you sick'*. That primitive South Sea island girl seems to be making a statement that is full of psychological truth about anger and its consequences.

Would the real problem please stand up

Not long ago a lady came to see me to tell me about her dog. It had recently become a nuisance by continually snapping at tradesmen and callers. She took it to the local dog hospital where the dog doctor said that something was obviously wrong, and he suggested that a dog psychiatrist should be asked to call. Let me quickly say that I would not have believed the story either if I hadn't known the lady concerned and actually heard it from her own lips. Eventually the dog psychiatrist called and was invited into the sitting room of the lady's home. He asked for the dog to be allowed to walk freely around the room while he looked at it. For five minutes he examined the dog, then suddenly he turned to the lady and said *'Madam, there's absolutely nothing wrong with your dog, but there's an awful lot wrong with you'*. The lady came to see me to tell me that it was quite true: she was in fact the cause of all the trouble. Her bitterness and frustration had been transferred to her dog.

How often we blame everybody and everything but ourselves. We say it's the weather; it's the Russians; it's our environment; it's our job; when, in reality, we are the cause of all the trouble. War begins in the mind of a man. Murder is conceived in the heart of a man. World hunger is caused by the greed of individual man. We say 'what a sad society we live in with all its violence, and corruption'; and yet, society is only a collection of individual people. Society is never the cause of all the troubles; the cause is always the individual personality. Society is only an exact reflection of the individual.

We, then, are the cause of all the trouble. The death of Christ was the death of the *good one* dying in the place of the *bad and ugly*. By his death our badness and ugliness is taken away. That is the inner, spiritual meaning of his death which lies beyond the physical self-sacrifice of laying down his life on our behalf.

The last train home

There is one further aspect of the death of Jesus that we must consider. It comes again from those words that we have been looking at in Peter's first letter to the early Christian Church. Because the death of Jesus achieved its spiritual goal of being able to blot out our failures, the cross has a dynamic of its own. Peter put it like this: '*Christ also died . . . to bring us to God*' (1 Peter 3: 18). I have a friend who at the moment is one of the more successful of the young poets. At the time that I am referring to John Williams used to work for one of the large commodity firms in the City of London. Even at that time his interest in literature meant that he had a permanent order with his bookseller to be sent one copy of all Penguin Books published in the 'classic' series. One of the books that arrived for him was a copy of a new translation of the four Gospels especially prepared for the series by the editor, Dr E V Rieu. John Williams took the book for reading as he travelled to work to his office in Mark Lane. He had read his way through Matthew's Gospel and had started on the Gospel according to Luke. One day he had finished work in the office and then had stayed in town to help at a youth club, catching the 11:46 train home from Victoria. He settled in to a corner seat, opened the four Gospels and continued to read Luke's account of the crucifixion.

There were two other men in the compartment; one was an Englishman and the other an American. The Englishman suddenly fell on to the floor of the compartment and had a convulsive fit. The American leapt to help him, to loosen his tie and to put his handkerchief into the Englishman's mouth to stop him biting his tongue. The American said to John Williams, 'I'm awfully sorry; but this happens several times each week. You see, we were in the Korean war together and I was wounded and left in no man's land; and this Englishman came and carried me to safety. Just as we were arriving at a safe position a shell landed beside us, and the next thing that we knew was that we were in hospital. I was invalided out of the army back to America when I heard that the Englishman would never get better. I left my job, broke off my engagement and came to England to look after him. You see, *he did that for me. There is nothing that I cannot do for him.*'

He did that for me

The train had arrived at the next station. By that time the Englishman was much better and he and the American got out. John Williams was left alone in the compartment of the train as it swayed through the dark night. He continued to read the story of the crucifixion with a voice ringing in his ears *'he did that for me; there is nothing that I cannot do for him'*. Suddenly he closed the book, knelt in the compartment of the train and gave his life to Christ. Christ's death, the cross of Christ, has a dynamic all of its own. Peter says Christ died *'to bring us to God'*.

The story of Jesus is the story of God's Son who stooped to conquer, who came into this world to take away the sin of the human race. It was achieved on the cross. The young ex GI could say about the Englishman, *'he did that for me; there is nothing that I cannot do for him'*. As Jesus has stooped to conquer our sins, that should be our response too.

The surprise of your life

Among the most frightening wars that this country ever had to fight were the Napoleonic Wars. As a country, we felt we were not only fighting a political enemy, but a social enemy as well. If Napoleon won, then the mob rule and violence of the French revolution would quickly spread to this small island. Everything rested upon the Duke of Wellington as he set sail with his army to confront Napoleon; therefore the whole of England waited poised for news of victory or defeat. Without modern means of communication, news would arrive many days after the actual battle had taken place, and the result would be brought to this country by an already established system of signal ships and lookout towers. One of the main lookout points on this side of the Channel was the roof of Winchester Cathedral; from the top, the Channel could be seen; below a horseman waited to carry the news to London. Some time after June 18th 1815, the signal ship came in to view. A severe fog almost prevented the signal from being seen, but before the mist finally came down, the essentials of the message were received. They were '*Wellington defeated . . .*' There it was, the worst had happened, and the depressing news began to spread across this tiny kingdom; but when the fog lifted, the true message was discovered to be: '*Wellington defeated the French.*'

That story, often told by one of the old vergers of Winchester Cathedral, has striking similarities with the events of the first Easter. The message received on that

first Good Friday certainly appeared to be: '*Jesus defeated.*'
And that was the depressing news that began to filter out
from Jerusalem to such places as Emmaus. But when the
mists of the weekend cleared, the real message was seen to
be the reverse: '*Jesus defeated the grave.*'

A fundamental Christian doctrine

If Jesus did cheat the grave, it is obviously an important
doctrine; but its real importance is found in the fact that
this is the doctrine that underlies all other Christian truth.
If you remove this one truth, then the whole structure of
Christianity collapses. Only once in the New Testament is
there mentioned any real doubt about the Resurrection;
and it is done to make this very point. Paul says that, if
there is no Resurrection, then Christians are '*of all men
most to be pitied*' (1 Corinthians 15: 19).

The full force of this is seen if you look at the importance of the Resurrection in the lives of Christian people.
Take David Livingstone, talking to a group of students at
Glasgow University. As he stood to speak, the effects of his
struggles in Africa could easily be seen. Severe illness on
many occasions had left him gaunt and haggard; his left
arm, crushed by a lion, hung limp at his side. After describing his many difficulties he said, 'Would you like me
to tell you what supported me during all the years in exile
among a people whose language I could not understand,
and whose attitude towards me was always uncertain and
often hostile? It was this. "*Lo, I am with you always, even
unto the end of the world*"' (Matthew 28: 20 AV). If the
Resurrection did not take place, then those students were
looking at a pathetically tragic figure, whose life had
been sustained through many difficulties by a myth.

In our own time, Richard Wurmbrand, a Lutheran
minister working in the underground church in Rumania
was called to counsel a Russian officer who had never
attended a church service or seen a Bible. Richard
Wurmbrand read to the man part of the Sermon on the
Mount, which made the Russian exclaim that he could
not live without knowing this Christ. When the Russian
heard about the death of Christ, he fell in to an armchair

and wept bitterly, believing that the Christ that he longed to serve had died. Richard Wurmbrand, in his book *Tortured for Christ* (Hodder & Stoughton), goes on to say,

Then I read to him the story of the resurrection. He had not known his Saviour arose from the tomb. When he heard this wonderful news, he beat his knees and swore a very dirty, but, I think, a very 'holy' swear. This was his crude manner of speech. Again he rejoiced. He shouted for joy, '*He is alive! He is alive!*' And again he danced around the room, overwhelmed with happiness.

If that Resurrection did not take place, then Karl Marx was right: the Christian faith is no more than '*the opium of the people*'.

However, the contention of the whole Christian Church is that Jesus did rise from the grave three days after he was dead and buried. This is said by some to be the best-attested fact in history, but in spite of this, from time to time attacks have been made on this fundamental Christian doctrine by people suggesting that Jesus either fainted, or that his dead body had merely been stolen from the cave-like burial place. Because of the importance of the doctrine, we must look at the attacks on the Resurrection as carefully as we can.

Take a look at this

One of the major attacks against the Resurrection comes from a group of people who suggest that the body of Jesus was stolen. Of all the views of those who try to explain away the Resurrection, this is probably the most widely held at the moment. One of the latest to add his name to this theory is Malcolm Muggeridge in his book *Jesus Rediscovered* (Fontana). The suggestion is that the body of Jesus was either stolen by the Jewish authorities to stop any further development of what was to them a political and religious heresy; or that it was taken by the disciples who simply wanted to bury Jesus in a quiet place so that his body would not be disturbed. A further strand to the theory is that vandals, knowing the popularity of Jesus, broke into his tomb hoping that his followers had decorated the inside with valuables that could be stolen.

To believe that the Jews stole the body, and then did not produce it to discredit the rumours of resurrection, is to fail to understand the political tensions in Jerusalem. The spiritual prestige of the Jewish people was at stake. Without any doubt they would have looked for the body of Jesus. They probably even thought of finding a body or disguising a body to look like Jesus. The Jewish cabinet must have briefed the police to find the body at all costs.

A story that illustrates the pressure on the Jewish authorities comes from the Easter of 1966. Some time before that date the Americans had lost a hydrogen bomb off the coast of Spain. They began to search for it. At the same time, rumours began to spread that the Americans could not find their bomb or that they did not have the right sort of equipment to raise it from the ocean bed. However, they eventually recovered it and, on Good Friday 1966, security was lifted so that the world could see a photograph of a hydrogen bomb for the first time. It was a cigar-shaped metallic object, twelve feet long and rather battered and dirty. The force of the photograph was quite obvious. The Americans were saying, '*take a look at this: we've found what we were looking for*'. Now the same sort of political pressure must have been on the Jewish people to produce the body of Jesus. Unlike the Americans, the Jews could not say '*take a look at this*'. So far as we know at the time of the Resurrection there was only one who could say '*come and look at the facts*'; that was an angel, and he was pointing at the empty space where Jesus had been lying in the tomb (Matthew 28:6).

Look at their lives

Any suggestion that the disciples stole the body is immediately contradicted by their lives. Perhaps after the crucifixion they could have put on a brave face, and preached as though nothing had happened, but even that does not allow for the fact that after the death of Jesus the disciples preached with a liberty and an enthusiasm that they certainly did not have when he was alive. Also, it is impossible to believe that these men could live through the hardships of a long life preaching the Resurrection, knowing it to be a lie. They were, after all, only a tiny group of men. Their hardships were extreme and they were willing even to die for the truth in which they believed, yet when they were imprisoned, or shipwrecked, or stoned, or whipped, there was never even the slightest suggestion that their whole philosophy of life was built on a hoax.

So far as the rather ghoulish suggestion of a grave robber is concerned, the body of Jesus would have been an item of stolen property that the Jewish authorities would have bought at any price. That is always supposing that any thief would have dared to rob a grave with the Roman equivalent of *Securicor* on guard. We know from the New Testament narrative that the authorities were not averse to buying information or people when necessary. Because of the rumours of resurrection, the pressure on the Jewish authorities to show that Jesus was really dead was far greater than the pressure to kill him in the first place so, if someone had stolen the body, the authorities would have certainly bought it to put on view.

Alive and kicking

A further area of attack against the Resurrection comes from a group of people who suggest that Jesus did not really die at all; they say that the agonies of crucifixion merely caused him to lose consciousness, but that he was revived by the coolness of the tomb and the smell of the embalming spices working rather like smelling salts. Now this particular view does not take into account all that we know about the death of Jesus and the general pattern of the death of all the others who died by this particularly brutal form of capital punishment. Shortly before his crucifixion, Jesus was *scourged*. This does not mean that Jesus was whipped in an arbitrary fashion. To be *scourged* meant to receive a well-defined Roman punishment. The way it was to be received and the way it was to be administered was laid down in detail. We know that, under this particular form of punishment, many died. Still more lost their reason and for the rest of their lives were mentally deranged. Very few people remained conscious while they were receiving a scourging, and history suggests that most survived as completely broken men.

Recall then that we are thinking about a man who had been physically broken by scourging, and who then endured the effort of carrying a cross to the place of crucifixion. No wonder he could not manage it by himself. This was followed by the physical and psychological pain of being nailed to a cross. The cross was then lifted upright and fell into a hole cut into the rock of Golgotha, tearing at the body as it hung by nail-pierced hands. Because of the impending Sabbath, some effort was made to ensure that Jesus was dead, therefore before his body was removed from the cross a spear was thrust into his side. The body was then prepared for burial by being wrapped in bandage-like lengths of linen with spice between the folds. John tells us that the spice, a mixture of myrrh and aloes, weighed about 100 lbs (John 19: 39), so if the spices did act as smelling salts, then it would be to suffocate Jesus rather than to revive him! If there was no resurrection and Jesus somehow managed to walk out of that cave, then he walked out a sick man. He would have been a deformed cripple to the end of his days. The New Testament certainly says that there were scars on his body: Thomas put his hand into the hole in his side made by the spear; but the implicit suggestion made in the New Testament about his health is that, after his resurrection he was *radiantly* healthy: he was alive and kicking.

Seeing things

The last major attack against the Resurrection comes from a group of people who suggest that the early disciples were simply seeing things; that the Resurrection was a simple hallucination. The only thing that can be said here is that hallucinations are very rarely a group experience. Perhaps it is possible that ten men could see an hallucination, or eleven, but not, surely, five hundred at one time.

Royal reassurance

At the heart of the battle of Hastings in 1066, the rumour spread through the Norman lines that King William was dead. William took his horse and galloped through the ranks shouting '*I am alive! I am alive!*' The appearance of the King gave them the confidence for victory.

To the disciples, the events of that Passover had been decisive. Although they had not suffered physically, they were spiritually and emotionally drained. They had lost the will to fight. The events that followed that first Easter day were in the most literal way the events of a royal reassurance. Even the sceptic among them got the full force of that '*I am alive!*' presence, when he thrust his hand into the hole in the side of Jesus. The confidence engendered by that royal reassurance was to be with them to the end of their lives. It was so real, they could not forget it; it was so real, it almost became an obsession. So often did they preach about Jesus and his resurrection that on at least one occasion the people thought the disciples were preaching about Jesus and his wife! This is the point that Michael Green makes in his book *Man Alive* (IVP).

In a remarkable passage in Acts 17, we are told what the ordinary Athenian eavesdroppers understood Paul to be getting so excited about. Not politics, not bishops, not ecumenism, not even the cross. No, none of these things. He kept on talking about '*Jesus and Anastasis*'. The Authorized Version demurely renders this as 'Jesus, and the resurrection'; so do most of the other translations. That is to miss the whole point. The casual Athenian layabouts listening to Paul seem to have jumped to the conclusion that he was offering them an interesting couple of new gods for their pantheon, Jesus and his wife Anastasis. So great was his emphasis on Jesus and his resurrection.

In a way, Jesus is married to that doctrine. You cannot divorce Jesus from his resurrection; in the New Testament they are inseparable.

Living above
One of the interesting things about the Resurrection in the New Testament is the insistence that we can begin to share in it now. This is not an isolated thought, but is a recurring theme, especially in the letters of Paul. For centuries one of the traditional parts of the Bible read on Easter Day has been from the third chapter of Paul's

letter to the Christians at Colossae; it begins '*If then you have been raised with Christ . . .*' The same thought occurs in his letter to the church at Ephesus. '*You he made alive . . . made us alive together with Christ . . . and raised us up with him, and made us sit with him in the heavenly places*' (Ephesians 2: 1, 6). In any period of history men are cemented to ideas by what the historians call *ethos*. It is the spirit of any age or culture. It is that which gives life to any particular group of ideas. The *ethos* of the New Testament, the spirit of the New Testament age, is that of resurrection. In some strange way the early followers of Jesus, though still living quite ordinary lives, were *living above*, sharing in the resurrection of Christ. Over the door of an old cabinet maker in the City of London, where it would usually declare the proprietor's address, it simply said '*Living Above*'. Those early disciples were not quite as explicit as that. Perhaps that is because they did not need to be: they did not have to write it above their doorways because it was so obvious in their lives.

Would you please say that again?

It is so difficult to describe the spirit of *living above* that it is best to turn to the Bible for an example. Like all truly spiritual experiences, there is nothing magical or fantastic about it; rather, the reverse is true: it is intensely real and practical. By this experience of living above we certainly do not escape from the harsh knocks of life, but when those knocks come to us we have the spiritual strength to take them. The example that we are going to look at is perhaps the best-known piece of biblical literature in the world, the twenty-third psalm.

In all probability David wrote this psalm at the time of a family feud between himself and his son Absalom, a feud that resulted in David being driven from his own palace in Jerusalem. David's life at this point could hardly be described as being at an all-time spiritual high. This is indicated by his lack of creativity. One of the gifts that God had given David was the ability to translate spiritual experience and perceptions into song. Hence, the psalms. The psalms are a record of the depth of David's experience of God. David's spiritual life was so low at this point in time that he had nothing to sing about. Only twice in the past decade had he put pen to paper, and that was to write spiritual laments. He wrote psalms fifty-one and thirty-two to crystallize his thoughts of repentance, after the sad affair with Bathsheba.

Perhaps his spiritual life was low because he was a king. No longer did he have to rely on God, as he did when he looked after his father's sheep out on the rolling hills that surround Nazareth. As king, he didn't have to pray about the weather or provision for himself and his flock. In the palace he just said '*peel me a grape*' and it was done. The family feud worsened; Absalom had virtually taken the throne from him. David hurriedly escaped from Jerusalem with a tiny army. Most of the army were paid Gittites, rather than loyal men of Israel. There was only one escape route open to David and his men and that was down into the Jordan valley across the Jordan and up in to the hill country of Gilead. Apart from the handful of men, David had nothing. There were no provisions for the men, no tents in which to lodge them, no parched corn and cream cheese to keep their hunger at bay. If the situation had not been so serious it would have been quite farcical. The tiny group morosely hacked their way through the foliage of the hills of upper Gilead, acutely conscious that there was no bed and board at the end of their labours. David suddenly straightened his back, and with a new burst of inspiration and insight said, '*The Lord is my Shepherd*'.

A radical new theology

This certainly was the most radical of new theologies. The sacred name of God had been attached to godly attributes for centuries before David's time, but no one before this date had dared to attach God's name to such a personal and prosaic activity. God the Shepherd must have been a shattering new thought to Israelite and Gittite ears. Perhaps *living above* is best described as being a radical new theology. It is never an escapist attitude to life. All the hardships of a physical life remain, but there is an overwhelming consciousness of the presence and provision of the living God.

Not a creed but a conviction

Martin Luther once met a peasant farmer looking absolutely depressed. Luther asked him the cause of his gloom. The peasant replied that his house and stocks had been destroyed by fire. He had lost everything, therefore life was no longer worth living. Luther asked him if he knew the Apostle's Creed.

'Of course,' said the peasant.

'How does it go, then?'

Without any hesitation the man responded:

'I believe in God the Father Almighty, Maker of Heaven and Earth . . .'

'Stop,' said Luther, 'now say it again.'

'I believe in God the Father Almighty, Maker of Heaven and Earth . . .'

'My good man,' said Luther, 'if you really believe that, then there is absolutely no reason to be so gloomy. If God is the Almighty Father then he can easily provide you with a new farm.'

Luther's peasant needed to learn that Christian experience is not a matter of a creed but of conviction. Like Luther's friend, David and his men had lost absolutely everything. But suddenly David's concept of God changes from a purely credal statement to a personal conviction. God *is* his Shepherd, therefore he will not want. He will be led to green pastures; even if he has to traverse the valley of the shadow of death God will be with him.

That is exactly what it is like to *live above*. We have no reason to be despondent. The Easter message is not 'Jesus defeated' but '*Jesus defeated the grave*'.

Fire down below

Next door to Tokyo's main university is the little Anglican church of St Thomas. A story is told of a well-known preacher being invited to speak there while on a tour of the Far East. The invitation was for Trinity Sunday so he took as his subject the baptism of Jesus with its strong trinitarian theme. He spoke of the heavens opening and the Father speaking to the Son standing firmly on the earth, picturing the Spirit descending upon him in the form of a dove. It was a sermon of great skill; without any pressure on the text the full force of the Trinity was revealed. After the service the visiting preacher was invited to stand at the door and shake hands with the congregation as they left. A well-dressed Japanese gentleman paused in front of him and said, 'Honourable Father I understand. Honourable Son I understand. Honourable bird no understand.'

It must surely be an apocryphal story, but it does point to something that is so true of most Christian congregations. It is reasonably easy to understand the person and work of the Father and Son but our understanding immediately becomes blurred once we start to think about the Holy Spirit. The purpose of this chapter is to look at the Holy Spirit in as much detail as space allows.

Something irresistible
The old theologians used to speak about the *prevenient* work of the Holy Spirit. The same word is used in the

Anglican prayer that begins 'Prevent us, O Lord, in all our doings with thy most gracious favour'. When that prayer is used today most ministers translate it 'Go before us, O Lord'. That exactly sums up the first work of the Holy Spirit; he goes before us drawing us into the Christian experience. As you read Christian biography it is difficult to find Christians of any school of thought who have not been conscious of being drawn to God. Richard Wurmbrand, a Lutheran minister, put it like this in his book *In God's Underground* (W H Allen):

I was like the man in the ancient Chinese story, trudging exhausted under the sun, who came on a great oak and rested in its shade. 'What a happy chance I found you!' he said. But the oak replied, 'It is no chance. I have been waiting for you for 400 years.' Christ had waited all my life for me. Now we met.

In *Tortured for Christ* he described his conversion in a more practical way, but the emphasis is just the same. He tells how a Jewish carpenter living high up in one of Rumania's many mountain villages was praying that before he died he might have the joy of leading another Jew to Christ. With the improbability of another Jew going to that particular village it seemed to be a prayer that could not possibly be answered. Then, said Jewish-born Richard Wurmbrand, '*something irresistible drew me to that village*'.

Professor C S Lewis was an Anglo-Catholic, and yet in his biography *Surprised by Joy* (Geoffrey Bles) we see his experience was similar to Richard Wurmbrand's. He says: 'amiable agnostics will talk cheerfully about "man's search for God". To me ... they might as well have talked about the mouse's search for the cat.' And he adds, '*God closed in on me*'. An evangelical such as Brownlow North writes, 'It pleased God, one night when I was sitting playing at cards, to make me concerned about my own soul'. Even religious television personality Malcolm Muggeridge echoes this experience. In *Jesus Rediscovered* (Fontana) he says: 'I have never wanted a God, or feared a God, or felt under any necessity to invent one. Unfortunately I am driven to the conclusion that God wants me.'

Seeking asses and finding a kingdom

The history of Saul in 1 Samuel 9 would be a good place to look at the biblical background to this point, and to note that while the process of being led to God is going on we will almost certainly be entirely unaware of it. The young Saul, looking for the asses that belonged to his father, traversed the length of five small countries and thought he was looking for lost property, but the Spirit was drawing him to the place where he would meet the man of God. It is very easy in a Christian biography to look back and see God at work, whereas in reality when the events were actually taking place we were unconscious of them. Neither Brownlow North as he sat playing cards nor Richard Wurmbrand struggling up the last winding yards to that Rumanian mountain village felt the irresistible pull of God, but they were being pulled all the same. Like Saul, seeking asses, they found a kingdom.

Out of the shadows into the sunlight

If the first work of the Holy Spirit is to draw us to God then the second is to open our minds to God's truth. The Holy Spirit is the great illuminator of the minds of men. He brings light to man where intellectual darkness once reigned.

There is a most delightful illustration of this in the field of English literature which has puzzled the scholars for over 300 years. It concerns John Donne, the seventeenth century Dean of St Paul's who was one of the most powerful preachers and saintly men of his time. In 1630 as he lay dangerously ill, he was aware that it could well be his last illness, so having set his papers in order, he made his will. He made ample provision for his children, he gave the usual charitable gifts and a few of his more intimate mementoes were bequeathed to his friends. Almost the last item in his will was a picture of himself painted thirty-five years earlier:

Item, I give to my honourable and faithful friend Mr Robert Ker of His Majesty's bedchamber that picture of mine which is taken in shadows and was made very many years before I was of this profession.

The words that have intrigued men of letters for three centuries are contained in the phrase 'in shadows'. No one was ever certain if the phrase was to be taken literally or merely philosophically. Not until 1959, that is, for in that year the picture was discovered at Newbattle Abbey in Scotland, the home of the Marquis of Lothian and a direct descendant of Robert Ker. The painting depicts John Donne as a young Elizabethan courtier posing as a victim of lover's melancholy. Over the picture is the blasphemy 'lighten our darkness, mistress', being a parody of the prayer, 'lighten our darkness, we beseech thee, O Lord'. In the picture John Donne is seen to be a worldly young Elizabethan whose mind was clearly in shadows as he went the way of most young men in the world. But it was not to be so for very much longer, for the Holy Spirit was about to illuminate his mind, and the profession that would soon come easily to his lips was far from blasphemy.

Same skin but a different man inside

The mind of young Saul was enlightened when he was led through those five countries – Ephraim, Shalishah, Shaalim, Benjamin and Zuph – to meet the man of God.

However, something even more radical is about to happen to Saul. In 1 Samuel 10, Saul is told specifically that the Spirit will turn him into 'another man' (verse 6), and when the experience actually comes to him we are told 'God gave him another heart' (verse 9). Now here is the Holy Spirit's third area of work. He makes real in our lives all that Christ has achieved for us. Looking back from the cross this is seen in the Old Testament in the change of heart experiences which happened to Saul; it is summarized in the New Testament in the doctrine of regeneration, whereby through new birth we become a new creation in Christ. Christ can change a man so radically that when we meet him after the experience it is as though we are meeting a different man. In the last century a famous wealthy racing figure called Edward Studd became a Christian, and the change was so noticeable that his coachman remarked 'Although it is the same skin it is a different man inside'. It is the Holy Spirit's work to effect this change in us.

The miracle of new life

Some people will always try to take a short cut into this new life. They will endeavour to become *different* people by various means, but the end result will never be very convincing. Somehow they will always seem to be the same old people rather thinly disguised. The hollowness of these various methods of change will be seen at once if you imagine a European trying to become completely Chinese. The European could endeavour to effect the change by altering his behaviour, but I suspect his family will hardly be convinced that he is Chinese by the fact that he eats his cornflakes with chopsticks. Then he could try changing his beliefs and wave a little red book containing the sayings of Chairman Mao under the noses of everybody he meets. As a last resort he could even go to Peking, and at one of those vast military parades be formally initiated into the Chinese People's Republic. However, after all this, it would still be obvious that he was European and had in no way become part of the East.

In the same way you cannot become a Christian by a change of behaviour because a change of behaviour is the result, not the means, of Christian experience, and any emphasis on behaviour would only tend to produce the modern equivalent of a Pharisee. So far as belief is concerned the Bible points out that even the devil believes, so that there can be no virtue in that. Ceremonies of initiation are important as acts of testimony: through them the candidate is testifying to an inward experience that has already taken place, so that by themselves they have no meaning. For a European to become a Chinese it would need nothing less than a miracle. It needs a similar miracle for a man to become a Christian. It is the work of the Holy Spirit to effect this. He can change us into *another man* by putting a new heart within us.

Stop – royalty is speaking

Saul was led through five countries, his mind was illuminated, and a miracle of change took place because a crown was waiting for him; he was to become a king. In just the same way, the Holy Spirit is leading us towards the place where we really feel members of God's family. It is possible to experience the Fatherhood of God, not merely in the sense that he is Creator of all, but in the much more intimate sense of being part of his family. It is the Holy Spirit's task to make us aware of our position and of our inheritance.

A constant pageant of triumph

Paul uses one of the most startling ways of describing our family position when he likens it to sharing in the victory parade of a Roman general. Only great victories were celebrated by a *Triumph*. A *Triumph* was a wonderful, colourful procession through the streets of Rome to the temple of Jupiter, high on the Capitoline Hill. The procession was led by state senators and trumpeters, and included the captured leaders. There would be officials and musicians; and a white bull for a sacrifice.

Then would come the general in a chariot pulled by four white horses; apart from his personal servant he would be quite alone. On this day he would be clothed in a purple toga embroidered with golden palm leaves. In his right hand he would hold the ivory sceptre of Rome surmounted with the imperial eagle. Over his head his servant would be holding the crown of Jupiter. Behind the general would come his parents, his wife and children, and bringing up the rear of the procession would be the general's own troops, the troops that had gained the victory for him. As they marched through the streets of Rome they chanted '*Triumph! triumph! triumph!*' Paul put it like this: Jesus '*makes my life a constant pageant of triumph*' (2 Corinthians 2: 14 Moffatt).

Life is difficult for most people. It certainly will not be easier because we are Christian. Look at the soldiers marching behind the general. They have walked from the limits of the known world. Some are wounded, all are weary. Yet their faces shine with victory because they are sharing in the Triumph of their general. Jesus is the Victor; and no matter how life treats us the Holy Spirit can make us aware that we are sharing in the *Triumph of Christ*.

The Royal Pardon

We have spent most of our time so far looking at Jesus Christ, endeavouring to discover who he was and why he came to the earth. As we moved on we looked at the Holy Spirit and we began to see some of the spiritual experiences that man could enjoy. Yet, we have not actually stopped to look at man and to find out exactly who he is. This must be our next task.

Dust of the earth

If you have the coldly factual mind of a scientist then I suppose you could describe man in the terms of a shopping list. This is what Professor C E M Joad used to do in the days before he became a Christian. He used to say in *Philosophy for our Time* (Nelson) that man is:

Enough water to fill a ten-gallon barrel; enough fat for seven bars of soap; carbon for 9,000 lead pencils; phosphorus for 2,200 match heads; iron for a medium-sized nail; lime enough to whitewash a hen-coop; and small quantities of magnesium and sulphur.

Obviously it is quite amusing to describe man as merely being made of the basic elements of the earth, but of course it leaves out all those intangible qualities that make man quite different from the dust of the ground. Qualities such as life itself, or man's aspirations, or even man's strange ability to fail with such consistency, that, had he been a lesser animal he would never have survived. However, the really devastating descriptions of the human race come from the anthropologists of our time. Dr Desmond Morris, in his book *The Naked Ape*, subtitled *A Zoologist's Study of the Human Animal* and published by Corgi Books, describes man as:

Vertical, hunting, weapon-toting, territorial, neotinous, brainy, Naked Ape, a primate by ancestry and a carnivore by adoption.

One can go on, as there are literally thousands of definitions of man; so perhaps it is time we looked at the word the New Testament uses. The Greek word for *man* is simply *anthropos*. We still use this today to describe man in such words as 'anthropology', the science of the study of the human race. The popular etymology of the Greeks declared that *anthropos* literally meant the 'upward looker'. William Barclay, in *The All-sufficient Christ* (SCM Press), says that man's physical form is proof that he was designed by God to look up at him. The Puritans used to take this one step further by saying that it was not only man's upright stature, but also his unique ability among the animals to move his eyes upward which showed clearly that he was made to gaze at God.

Man wears God's image

God said 'Let us make man wearing our own image and likeness'. This is the Knox translation of Genesis 1:26, emphasising that the word 'image' refers to the fact that God has shared his *outward appearance* with man. This immediately lifts man above the rest of the created world, but of course there are the inward characteristics that God has also shared with man. Man has power of thought, and of feeling and of will; and is also like God in that he is self-conscious and is, to some degree, self-determining. Man, in the first place, even shared a moral likeness with God in that he was created *good* (Genesis 1:31).

Made and purchased by God

Man was created like God that he might be God's friend. For me this is delightfully expressed in a poem by James Weldon Johnson called *The Creation*. The poem begins by describing how God was lonely and he said 'I'll make me a world'. And after the creation of the sun and the stars and a world full of living things we find that God is still lonely, so the poem concludes:

> *Then God sat down –*
> *On the side of a hill where he could think,*
> *By a deep, wide river he sat down;*
> *With his head in his hands, God thought and thought,*
> *Till he thought: I'll make me a man.*

It must have been a heart-rending experience for God to find that his newly created friend so quickly rebelled against him, removing all possibility of an intimate friendship. However, God then took the initiative in repairing the friendship by sending his Son into the world. The death of Jesus paid the price of man's sin, so that the friendship could be re-established.

There is an old Scottish story of a crofter's son who lived on one of the more remote westerly isles, who spent the whole of one winter making a model sailing boat. On the first pleasant day of spring he took the boat to the water's edge and gently lowered it into the sea. So perfectly had he shaped the boat's hull and so well had he set the sails, that the breeze quickly took the boat from his grasp and out to sea. The next time he saw his boat, it was being offered for sale in a second-hand shop in a nearby town. He went into the shop only to be informed that the boat had been purchased from a fisherman, and that the price was five pounds. He saved his pocket money and did odd jobs over the next few months to raise the price of the boat. As he came out of the shop clutching the boat, he said to it: '*You're twice mine: I made you and I bought you.*'

In the same way we are twice God's. We were made by him. Man's disobedience has taken him away from God. Yet the death of Jesus was the place where the purchase price for man's redemption was paid. We are twice God's: *he made us and he bought us.*

Excuse me, your behaviour is showing

Where there is no friendship between God and man it is obvious in the way man behaves. Look at the history of

41

war. It has been said that in the last six thousand years there has not been one year without a war somewhere. In the last three hundred years there have been three hundred and eighty-six wars in Europe. Since the year 1500, eight thousand known peace treaties have been signed. Each one was signed with the intention that it should last for ever, and yet the average length of each one is a little over two years.

A leading article in the *Daily Telegraph* (1961) has linked man's behaviour with his rebellion from God. Commenting on the moral collapse in England since World War 2, it said 'We had better, as a nation, pick up the Gospels again and inwardly digest their message'.

Man is clearly not what he was created to be. His behaviour betrays his fallen nature. The possibility of forgiveness is there, yet man seems to have lost the way back to God. So we must look at the way of forgiveness.

The way of forgiveness

Psalm 51 gives an ideal example of someone coming back to God step by step. King David's behaviour prior to writing this psalm shows just how far he had drifted from God. While walking on the roof of his palace, David had seen the beautiful Bathsheba, bathing, and had desired to make love to her (2 Samuel 11:2 ff). Bathsheba could hardly be expected to refuse the king's desires. The authority of a king over his subjects made them virtually his possession. Without any hesitation, it seemed that David added murder to adultery in order to make Bathsheba his wife. If it had not been for Nathan the prophet showing David just how evil his actions had been, David might have remained unconcerned about his behaviour (2 Samuel 12:1 ff). But Nathan touched David's conscience, and in Psalm 51 we see the slow, painful steps of a man coming back to God.

The awareness of sin

The way of forgiveness begins with the awareness of sin. David, in the first two verses of this psalm used the three great Bible words for spiritual failure: *transgression*, that is, the breaking of God's law; as with the civil law of the land, ignorance of the law is neither an excuse nor a defence. *Iniquity* is the word that is used to describe the root of moral evil in our lives; and *sin* is the word that the Bible uses for our failure to attain all that God intended for us. God created us to be his friends, so we have sinned simply in our failure to be friendly with him.

Belief that we are responsible

It is so easy to blame our failure on the events or the people who surround us; to say that the cause of all the trouble is our job, or our environment, when in fact we are responsible. David spoke of *my* transgressions, *my* iniquities, *my* sins. A lady came to see me on the 15th July 1967 and she said she was conscious of being surrounded by evil. She said that at first she thought that the evil was in the wardrobe and she had taken it downstairs and burned it on a bonfire in the garden. Then she thought that it was in the sideboard and she had taken that outside and had dealt with it in a similar way. But then she said that she was aware that the evil was still there, and could I show her where it was. I looked up and was about to speak, and she said 'Ah, you're like all the rest: you're going to say that it's in me, aren't you.' I had to confess that she was right. The lady concerned was rather unfortunate, but the story does illustrate that it is so easy to say that evil is anywhere else than in us. The second step in the way of forgiveness is belief that we are responsible for our own failures.

Confession of our failure

In verse four of Psalm 51 David says '*Against thee, thee only, have I sinned*'. As with David, our failures may have hurt and harmed other people, but our confession in the first place is to God. Nothing can take the place of confession. Confession is not merely awareness of failure, nor the belief that we are responsible; it is confession only when we actually come to God and say, as the Prodigal Son said: '*Father, I have sinned against heaven and before you; I am no longer worthy to be called your son*' (Luke 15:21).

43

Desire to be made new

Our human nature is so perverse that if it feels it can get away with just the first three steps it will, and will then slide back into its old way. As we saw in the last chapter, what we are offered in Christ is the experience of *regeneration*, whereby we are given another heart and are turned into quite a different person. In Psalm 51:10 it says, '*Create in me a clean heart*'. We must desire to be made new. Bishop Stephen Neill in his book *On the Ministry* (SCM Press) said if you have not known the experience of new birth '*it is no use pretending that some other experience will do as well*'.

Experience of salvation

David, in verse 12, speaks of the '*joy of salvation*'. It is almost impossible to speak of salvation in any other way. C S Lewis called his autobiography *Surprised by Joy*; and his experience of salvation was so real that he could almost put a date on it. Writing to a lady on the 9th of July 1939, he said, '*Though I am forty years old, I am only about twelve as a Christian*' (*Letters of C S Lewis* ed. W H Lewis, Geoffrey Bles). It seems sad that people can go through all the other steps of the way of forgiveness and yet fail to experience this final point. There is a story told of Harrow parish church when the organist was Dr F W Farmer and the local Salvation Army band had been invited for a united service. Dr Farmer was slightly upset by the way that the Salvation Army drummer was banging his drum, and he asked the Salvationist if he could bang his drum a little more quietly. The drummer replied: 'Lord bless you, sir! Ever since I've been converted, I'm so happy I could bust me blooming drum!'

Freedom to testify

David says in Psalm 51:13: '*I will teach transgressors thy way*'. Paul, in Romans, links the experience of believing and testifying when he says 'for man believes with his heart and so is justified, and he confesses with his lips and so is saved'. This freedom or liberty to testify is an important part of the experience of forgiveness. By testifying about the new life we keep our experience real and fresh. The River Jordan supplies two large lakes. The Sea of Galilee is a sea full of living things, whereas the Dead Sea has nothing living in it at all. The only difference between these two areas of water is that the Sea of Galilee passes on all that it receives, whereas the Dead Sea does not. It is one of the laws of the spiritual life that the more we give out, the more we receive.

All the King's men

In many ways this is an ideal title for a chapter on the Church because it is a picture of the Church as it ought to be: royal children committed to the service of the King of kings. Unfortunately the phrase 'all the King's men' has other connotations which quickly spring to mind for they are a better description of the Church as it is, because it is a quotation from the nursery rhyme where we find that all the king's men could not put Humpty Dumpty together again. Mankind has fallen and got itself into a mess, and the King's men who ought to be able to do something about it find that they cannot. The Church of our age is certainly much more aware of its failure on earth than it is of its relationships in heaven.

Don't just stand there – do something

It was Cardinal Newman who said that the Church was like an equestrian statue. The front legs of the horse were lifted from the ground ready to leap forward; every muscle of the back legs stood out, throbbing with life, caught as it were in the act of springing. As you look at the statue you expect it to leap at any moment; unfortunately, when you come back twenty years later, you discover that it has not moved even a fraction of an inch. How like the Church: all the potential is there; with new preachers and new movements you think that it cannot fail to make an impact on the present generation. However, when you come back twenty years later you discover that it has not made any progress at all.

To find out what has gone wrong we must discover what the New Testament means by *the Church* and also find out what the Church's experience of God ought to be.

The Church belongs to God

Our word 'church' is a corruption of the Greek word *kuriake* which means 'that which belongs to the Lord'. We misuse the word when we make it refer to a particular kind of building. The Church is people, the group of people that belongs to God. The word 'Church' in the New Testament means 'a special gathering of people'. You can define those people as the Church, or you may prefer to use the much more striking picture that Paul uses in his letter to the Christians at Ephesus, when he calls that special assembly the body of Christ (Ephesians 1:23). Moreover, he adds that Christ is the head of the body. Now the phrase *the body of Christ* tells us quite a lot about the nature of the people that belong to God.

No spiritual Robinson Crusoe

The picture of the Church as the *body of Christ* emphasizes the group experience and the fact that there is no such thing as a freelance Christian. 'God knows nothing of a solitary religion' was the way that John Wesley put it. William Barclay says 'Christianity is unquestionably a personal experience. It is equally unquestionably not a private experience'. The Church consists of people who have experienced Christ and who are now linked together by that experience of him. They need each other in the same way that the various parts of a body need all the other parts. A healthy body works as a whole and responds not only to the head but also to the rest of the body. John Chrysostom, one of the early Christian Fathers, put it like this:

When a thorn is fixed in your heel, the whole body feels it, and cares for it. The back bends, the thighs contract, the head stoops, and the eyes examine. With the greatest care, the hands descend, the fingers draw out the thorn. So the whole church works together.

The human body is made up of cells, and it is almost inconceivable to think of one of those cells acting by itself without any reference to the head or the rest of the body. Unfortunately there can be such a rebellious cell. It is called a 'cancer' and, given half a chance, it will destroy the whole body. In a similar way, the body of Christ can be affected by the individual member who acts without any reference to either the head or the rest of the body.

Spiritual hypochondria

This phrase, the *body of Christ*, also shows us how absurd it is to be continually taking our own temperature and being over-concerned about the body's health. It is true that we get very depressed about the Church today and pessimistic about its future. If we translate this into the terms of the human body we see how silly it is. It is the head that worries; it is the body's task to obey. If the body is ill, then the head will do something about it. The group of Christians that belong to Christ are his body. We can be sure that he is even more concerned about his body than we are.

The royal body of a king

It is sometimes said of rather dreamy people that their head is in the clouds. Now that in a spiritual sense can be truly said about the Christian Church. Its head is in the clouds; Christ, the head of the body, has ascended. Allowing for the limitations of time and space, it must be correct to say that what is true of the head is also true of the body. One of the main themes of Ephesians 1 is that the Church is the body of Christ; this theme is continued in chapter two with the thought that the head and the body live a similar sort of life. You can say at least three things about Jesus, the ascended head of the Church. One, he is quite clearly alive and his life is the ascended life; two, without question he is holy; three, he now has access to the Father and to the vast, unnumbered community of godly people of all ages and races who occupy heaven. Paul is saying in Ephesians 2 that these three things ought to be experienced by the Church. The people that belong to God 'he made alive' and 'raised us up' with Christ. Clearly, holiness is part of the planned life of God for his people, for the Church is 'his workmanship created . . . for good works, which (he) prepared beforehand that (they) should walk in'. Further, just like the head, those people who are the body of Christ have 'access . . . to the Father' and are 'no longer strangers and sojourners, but . . . fellow citizens with the saints and members of the household of God'.

What is obviously wrong with the Church at the moment is bad circulation. The full life force which ought to be making its way down from the head to every member of the body is just not getting through; consequently, the Church is in a state of decline. However, there is hope. The Church is the royal body of a King.

The shape of the body
There is obviously a challenge too in the statement that the Church is the body of Christ, a challenge that will not let the present-day Christians rest until the body is healthy and active once more. The phrase that we have been looking at says: 'the church which is his body, the *fulness* of him who fills all in all' (Ephesians 1:23). That word *fulness* suggests that the body must not expect the royal head to do the things that it ought to be doing for itself. The word *fulness* is used to describe *the crew* of an ancient galley. No matter how royal and magnificent the ship was, without the crew to row it would make no progress at all. It is also used in another place to describe the *basic citizenship of the perfect city*. No matter how well the buildings were designed and the city laid out in attractive boulevards, without people there could be no city. Here again is the emphasis that the Church is people; and behind this emphasis is the fact that these people need to be spiritually healthy and active to *fill out* the body of Christ in the world today.

All fingers and thumbs?
It is only when you look at the Church as the *body of Christ* that you get the present movement towards unity into the

49

right perspective. Although all the different parts of the human body are not the same and have different functions, there is still an overall unity. Any movement that endeavours to make Christian people the same is like wishing that a human body consisted only of fingers and thumbs. It just is not possible: a body by definition is made up of different parts. Of course we cannot all be the same. There will inevitably be different forms of Church government and worship, as there will be different patterns of behaviour. And these will not necessarily destroy the overall unity of God's people. To think that there will ever come a time when all Christian people will worship and behave in exactly the same way is as naïve as to suppose that one day the whole of the human race will enjoy eating precisely the same sort of food. It can never be so.

Churches will never be like different branches of the same bank, with the buildings looking the same. We can hope that one day the churches will be like different homes of people belonging to the same family; each home reflecting the culture, the environment and the beliefs of the people who live there. It ought to be possible to invite, and to accept invitations to visit other members of the family. But even then, in a spiritual sense it will never be wrong to say of one's own particular denomination, *there is no place like home*.

Vaguely kept in mind

One reason for the lack of spiritual health in the Church today is our failure to grasp the importance of doctrinal truth. Paul Dehn, in his poem *A Modern Hymnal* (*Fern on the Rock* Hamish Hamilton), is not only stating the obvious lack of vitality in the Church today, but he is also setting down the reason for spiritual apathy and lassitude. He says:

> *Onward, Christian soldiers,*
> *Each to war resigned,*
> *With the cross of Jesus*
> *Vaguely kept in mind.*

In the past when the great doctrines of the Church have

become blurred, then the whole of Church life has declined and in some cases ceased to exist altogether. This is nowhere better illustrated than in the history of Christianity in China. In the year 1685 in north-west China at a place called Sianfu, evidence was discovered of the existence of a church in China in the seventh and eighth centuries. The evidence was on a stone, which has become known as the *Sianfu stone*, and it shows that the Christian influence lasted for a period of nearly a century and a half. It began in the year 635 when a Syrian missionary called Olopan arrived, and it lasted until the year 781 when the Sianfu monument was erected while Tihtsung occupied the Peacock Throne. It is clear from the stone that the Christians in eighth century China adjusted their doctrine to accommodate the views of the Chinese intelligentsia. The missionaries attempted to communicate the Christian gospel by truncating Christian doctrine. They wanted to win the Chinese Buddhist and Confucianist, and because the death and Resurrection of Christ was such a stumbling block they toned down their teaching. The cross of Christ was quite literally '*vaguely kept in mind*', but instead of winning the educated Chinese, the Christian Church vanished without trace in the land of China.

A poor pimping business

A second reason for the decline in Church life today could well be the poverty of Christian worship. We seem to have lost the way so far as worshipping and adoring the living God is concerned. Consequently most church services are a depressing rather than a lifting experience. They are not a vibrant, thrilling act of praise, but a limping, lisping liturgical wilderness. We cannot go as far as Robert Burns, who said, '*What a poor, pimping business is a Presbyterian place of worship, dirty, narrow and squalid.*' Yet some of his words certainly contain truth about Christian worship today. Our church services are squalid because we are so mean with our praise. They are sometimes narrow, too, in their failure to grasp the breadth of God's revelation of himself; just as they are certainly parochially narrow by hardly ever lifting up eyes to the horizon of human need. The gloom that Robert Burns obviously experienced in his day can still be found in our churches because of the lack of mind-grabbing truth that ought to come as the word of God is expounded.

Perhaps the body of Christ will remain weak until it really begins to exercise its lungs with praise and the limbs of its mind with the revealed word of God.

A dull habit or an acute fever

William James made the statement that religion was either a '*dull habit or an acute fever*'. If we look at Ephesians 3 and the message of the Church, we will see that it is so practical that it could never be described in feverish terms; equally, it is so relevant that it ought never to become merely a dull habit. To see this is so we will look at the picture that this chapter presents of the Triune God.

The unsearchable riches of Christ

Ephesians 3:8 speaks of the *unsearchable* riches of Christ, and the word here literally means *cannot be mapped out*.

Imagine a family on holiday on the south coast and one of the children has the bright idea of walking around the sea; so the whole family immediately turns sharp left and starts to walk. Many months later they will probably find themselves back on exactly the same spot, but they cannot congratulate themselves on having walked around the sea; because they will merely have walked around the British Isles. Even if they could walk around the great oceans of the world they would only have touched the periphery of those oceans. To map out the sea they would have to cover every bit of the surface and every bit of the ocean bed together with all the levels in between. The riches of Christ are unsearchable, they cannot be mapped out. You cannot walk around even the edge of them. You cannot even begin to experience the greatness of the blessing that there is in him. The word for riches refers to material wealth, so we may take it that it does not refer only to spiritual treasure. The physical, the mental, the intellectual riches that are in Christ are impossible to map. This means that every day of our life on earth it is possible to experience more of him.

The manifold wisdom of God

This phrase 'manifold wisdom' comes in verse 10 and the word 'manifold' means 'many coloured' or 'many patterned'. When I was vicar of a church in Chatham we used to have a bookstall in Rochester market place every Friday where we were always surrounded by stalls that sold remnants of materials. Imagine that someone found on one of the stalls just the material that they wanted for their new curtains. It was an orange material with a flower design. They took the remnant home, and made up the curtains for the front of their house, hanging two curtains in the first front bedroom, two curtains in the second front bedroom, and two curtains in the sitting room downstairs. When they came to the last room downstairs they found that they only had one curtain. So, with a tiny scrap of material as a pattern, they had to return to Rochester market where the man on the stall said that he could not match the pattern, as he only sold remnants. A very supercilious salesman of a large department store in London said that he could not help as it was last year's material which was out of stock. Even the manufacturers could not supply any more in the right colour. Whatever the colour, the pattern, the texture, the weave of our problem, as soon as we show a sample of it to God, he matches it exactly with his *many patterned* wisdom.

Strengthening of the Holy Spirit

Paul deals with the third figure in the Trinity in verse 16 when he refers to the *strengthening of the Holy Spirit*.

Lord Radstock used to go to Csarist Russia to preach to the royal family where many of them were won to the Christian faith through his work. At one time he became very tired and near to a breakdown, and he was sent to recuperate at a quiet hotel on one of the Norwegian fjords. There he met a famous Norwegian couple and their child. They were so important that no one could complain about the child who proceeded to sit at the piano in the hotel lounge and make a noise that could only be described as *plonk, plonk, plonk*. Poor Lord Radstock: if the child continued, he certainly was not going to get any rest.

Then the hotel pianist sat down beside the child. He was musically offended by the noise the child was making, but instead of complaining, he played chords which turned the 'plonks' into music that was acceptable to the human ear. Because the people of God are part of the human race, their service for God, whether it is worship, or prayer, or witnessing, is never really going to be better than *plonk, plonk, plonk*. Verse 16 tells us that the Holy Spirit can come alongside and turn the efforts of the Church into spiritual music. Each individual member of the Church can be '*strengthened by the Holy Spirit in the inner man*'.

When the saints go marching in

One of the famous journalists of our age is a lady called Marguerite Higgins. She received a Pulitzer prize for her coverage of the Korean War, in particular for her account of the exploits of the 5th Company of us Marines. At one time the marines, numbering a little over 18,000 men, were under fire from over 100,000 Chinese. Marguerite Higgins describes the scene. The backdrop for the fighting is one of the most beautiful countries in the world, often called the Switzerland of Asia, but now as the scene is described we see that the beauty of the once wooded slopes of the mountains has been ravaged by war. Shattered tree stumps are all that remain of the forests, the exact terraced symmetry of the rice fields has been destroyed by gaping shell holes, and the winter's snow, instead of concealing the devastation, seems to accentuate the scars that modern warfare inevitably leaves behind. Just back from the fighting line some of the marines are taking their breakfast; with trench knives they consume cold baked beans straight from the tin. The temperature is 42° below. A group of war correspondents surround a marine sergeant, whose clothes are frozen stiff and whose bearded face is encrusted with ice and mud. One of the reporters asks him, 'If I were God and could grant you anything you wished, what would you most like?' Without any hesitation the marine replies *'Give me tomorrow'*.

Sometimes when the sunshine goes out of life and the bright colours of living are dulled, we may think about

God's tomorrow and all that it has in store for us; or when our situation becomes as trying as it was for that American sergeant and we are faced with the cold and blatantly ugly evils of this world we may even say, 'give me tomorrow'. However, the task before us at the moment is to discover what God's tomorrow is going to be like, to find out all that the saints will see and experience as they go marching in.

Death is a thoroughfare

Or, to state the quotation of Victor Hugo's more exactly, '*Death is a thoroughfare, not a blind alley*'. It is not that some go down the roadway of death to emerge into the wonders of paradise while others never get further than the grave and consequently do not even know what they are missing. No, death is a thoroughfare down which all men must make their way. Some may do so unwillingly, even more may do so disbelievingly, but the same life-force that brought a man into this world will propel him into the next. This is the point that is behind the word that Peter uses in his second letter when he speaks about his *decease*. The Greek word is *exodus*, which of course is the same word that provides both a title for the second book of the Bible and is also a description of all that book is about: namely, the *exit* or *exodus* of the people out of Egypt. In the most basic terms the story of the exodus is merely the story of people moving from one place to another. In the same way if you describe death without qualifying or adding embellishments to your description you could say that it is the removal of people from one place to another.

Eternity in the minds of men

It is difficult to find a civilization or a culture that does not possess a strong belief in life after death. The Bible teaches us to expect this when Solomon tells us that God '*has put eternity into man's mind*' (Ecclesiastes 3: 11). At creation we are told that God breathed *lives* into man (Genesis 2: 7); the word is plural, and many would see in this that eternity was not only put within man's intellectual grasp but that he also had a built-in mechanism preparing him for the next life.

Once we look back into history we find that ancient man was certainly aware of eternity. One of the earliest books in existence is called *The book of the dead*: it contains a collection of prayers and formulae to help the dead to communicate and to find their way about; and the oldest known name for a coffin, again coming from ancient Egypt, is *a chest of the living*.

Beyond the exit

It cannot be taken as an exact parallel, of course, but at least the book of Exodus can be used as a picture of all that happens to us as we make our exit from this world. The people of Israel, having made their exodus from Egypt, found two further areas of experience before them, *the wilderness* and *the promised land*. For them, these two experiences were to be consecutive, they were to pass through one to enjoy the other. However, leaving aside the consecutive nature of their experience, every person that leaves this world will find two similar areas before them. As they pass down the thoroughfare of death they will see the scenery either of *the wilderness* or of *the promised land*. It will be one or the other, but not both.

The wilderness

The Bible uses two main words to describe the experience that we summarize with the one word *hell*. Both have the same idea of a wilderness. The first one is found in the Old Testament and is the Hebrew word *Sheol*; it is simply the place of the departed. Sheol is a grey pit, a shadowy place, where men move about like ghosts in an environment entirely devoid of colour or joy. The main New Testament word is *Gehenna* which paints the frightful picture of *Ge Hinnom*, Jerusalem's largest public incinerator and rubbish dump tucked away from sight in the *Valley of Hinnom*. Ge Hinnom was a desolate place that perpetually smouldered, where the rubbish and the heat encouraged a vile species of worm to live and breed rapidly.

Both the pit of Sheol and the Valley of Hinnom suggest places that are hidden away, silent places put in the depth of the earth from whose nauseating surroundings there is no escape. These thoughts would seem to be confirmed by our Anglo-Saxon word *hell* which comes from the verb '*to hele*' or '*to hide*' – a word that gardeners still use today when they speak of 'heeling in' the roots of a plant, their suggestion being that the roots of the plant should be *hidden* or covered by the earth.

We may not be able to escape from hell but we will certainly be conscious of the awfulness of our surroundings whether it is the drab oppressiveness of Sheol or spine-chilling Gehenna. Jesus makes this quite clear in the story that we call *The rich man and Lazarus*, where the rich man in hell sees, feels, speaks and with regret recalls the past. This point is emphasized in the number of times that Jesus says there will be '*wailing and gnashing of teeth*'.

An awfully big adventure

Before we begin to look at heaven we must first look at death from a Christian point of view. Victor Hugo's statement about the thoroughfare is hardly adequate because it fails to give the sense of release, of purpose and of excitement that is always part of the New Testament meaning of the word death. In fact, after reading the New Testament you almost find yourself saying with James Barrie's Peter Pan, '*to die will be an awfully big adventure*'.

Paul in his second letter to Timothy says that the time for his departure has come (2 Timothy 4:6). His use of that word *departure* conjures up three vivid pictures of death for the Christian.

It is a word that was used for the freeing of a slave. The slave makes his departure from slavery and then he is free. You would hardly expect the slave to regard such an event with morbid introspection. His mind, instead of being gripped by the momentary experience of his release, would race on ahead to begin to savour the broad expanses of liberty. With regard to death we find just this point being made by John Fletcher of Madeley, when he says:

What is it to die, but to open our eyes after the disagreeable dream of life. It is to break the prison of corrupt flesh and blood.

In this century we see eagerness for the liberty that death brings in the last postcard of Dr F B Meyer in *Four Score . . . and More* A Lindsay Glegg (Marshall, Morgan & Scott). He was lying ill at Boscombe and addressed a postcard to Mr A Lindsay Glegg with a very shaky hand. He said, 'I have raced you to Heaven. I am just off – see you there. Love, F B Meyer.'

How different this is from the deathbed of those outside the Christian faith such as the American short story writer O Henry. As he lay dying on the 5th June 1910, he called to his nurse for a candle. When she asked why he wanted such a thing, he replied, 'Because I am afraid to go home in the dark.'

This word 'departure' is also used by the philosopher for a problem that has been resolved. The problem has departed and the answer has come: intellectual light now shines where there had been darkness. That is why Professor C E M Joad once said that he was looking forward to death because it would bring the answer to many of the perplexing things that had puzzled him. Christians of every age have regarded death in this way. 'Now for the morning and the King's face. No more night and no more darkness', was the passionate cry of Donald Cargill just before he was martyred in Edinburgh in 1681.

By far the most interesting use of this word *departure* in New Testament times is the one connected with shipping. It is the word for the last rope to be cast off, freeing the ship to begin its voyage. The ship is held by that one last rope to the quay and as her bows swing out towards the harbour mouth, then the rope is cut and the ship is free to leave the restriction of the harbour for the liberty of the great waters of the sea. The picture quite clearly says that departure is not the end, but the beginning; not journeys past, but journeys yet to come. The whole atmosphere of the word speaks of exotic adventure.

But we must add to this the fact that death is not a new route that we are about to sail. This is the point that Michael Green makes in his book *Man Alive* (IVP) when he speaks of Vasco da Gama. That great sailor was the first to circumnavigate the Cape at the southernmost tip of the continent of Africa, which in his day was as formidable as Cape Horn is for us. As Vasco da Gama sailed around the Cape he changed its name from the Cape of Storms to the Cape of Good Hope. The picture of the ship being untied may smack to some of the terrors of the sea rather than the possibility of new lands to be explored, but we take heart from the fact that Jesus has already died and has risen again; death has been circumnavigated and for us it is no longer the Cape of Storms but the Cape of Good Hope.

Bury me if you can catch me

One problem that arises here could be called the *problem of sleep*. Death may seem to be the start of an exciting voyage to some, but to others it is clearly a false start, because before the ship reaches the harbour limits they feel it is whisked into a dry dock and may have to wait a million years for the voyage to continue. They would say that after death we sleep until Christ comes before we actually go to enjoy heaven. Such a view is encouraged by our word *cemetery* which comes from the Greek word meaning *sleeping places*.

When we turn to the New Testament we certainly find that Paul makes some reference to *those that sleep* (1 Corinthians 15:20). One obvious reason for this would be Paul's Jewish background; the time before he became a Christian would have provided him with a view of survival after death that was closely akin to sleep. It is likely that he was simply making a statement about death that was so strongly coloured with Old Testament thought that it had the effect of overriding any other picture within the word.

On the other hand, the New Testament clearly speaks of immediate resurrection after death. Jesus said to the penitent thief as they were both dying after crucifixion, '*Today you will be with me in paradise*' (Luke 23:43). To encourage us the writer to the Hebrews tells us that we *are surrounded by a great cloud of witnesses* (Hebrews 12:1). The encouragement would immediately be removed if there was any suggestion that they were asleep! Article XL of the xlii Articles of the Church of England, issued during the reign of Edward vi says:

> The souls of them that depart this life do neither die with the bodies nor sleep idly. They which say that the soul of such as depart hence do sleep, without all sense, feeling, or perceiving, until the Day of Judgement . . . do dissent from the right belief declared to us in Holy Scripture.

That seems to sum up the situation well; even though the question of sleep can remain a problem, it is an even greater problem to find a doctrine of a bodiless soul in the Bible. On balance the New Testament says that when we make our *exodus* or *departure* we go straight to paradise, so I think I will say with Socrates '*bury me, if you can catch me*'.

Traveller, what lies over the hill?

We now turn to look at *heaven* and there is hardly a better question to have in mind than George MacDonald's '*traveller, what lies over the hill?*' Reinhold Niebuhr said that 'it is unwise for Christians to claim any knowledge of either the furniture of heaven or of the temperature of hell'. Yet when we look at all that Jesus has to say in chapter fourteen of John's Gospel we find that we are provided with an amazing wealth of detail about heaven.

We are going to run into difficulties straight away if we try to interpret the phrase '*in my father's house are many rooms*' (John 14:2) to mean western-style housing with twentieth-century-style rooms. Dr Westcott in his *Commentary on St John* begins to lead us back to the picture that Jesus must have had in mind, when he tells us that the word *rooms* has the meaning of *resting places or stations on a great road where the travellers found refreshment*. Archbishop Temple in his *Readings in St John's Gospel* (Macmillan) adds to this by telling us that the word means a *wayside caravanserai*. Looked at like this it is a very clear picture. The caravanserai was the motel of the camel caravan which the merchants used to cross the great land masses of the ancient world. A caravanserai may have consisted of a single building where the proprietor and his family lived, but the main feature would be space to park. Within that area would be a place to water the animals and somewhere to pitch one's own tent. If the caravanserai was in the desert then it would have the atmosphere of the oasis, the trees providing shade from the relentless glare of the sun. At night when all the guests had arrived and the animals were secured an exciting convivial spirit would prevail.

No admission except on business

When Florence Nightingale was told that a loved one had died and had gone to be at rest she very quickly replied, 'Oh, no! I am sure that the next life is immense activity.' That certainly is the view that the New Testament holds. It is often our hymn books that give us the notion of inactivity or boring repetition. John Hadham, in his book *Good God*, tells us that, as a child, he was fascinated by the line in the hymn that spoke of the saints *'casting down their golden crowns around the glassy sea'*. He says his mind was given to endless speculations on how the crowns got back on their heads for further casting. At first he thought that cherubs were retained as heavenly ball-boys; this was followed with the fearful idea that the new crowns grew continuously. Then he had the nasty feeling that, like his sailor hat, the crowns were secured by elastic and therefore always sprang back into place with a ping. Whether from our hymns or not, the idea of inactivity and boredom still prevails. Keith de Berry in his book *The Making of a Christian* (Hodder & Stoughton) emphasizes just how widespread this view is with the story of the young girl in South London who was asked what eternal life meant to her. She replied, 'If yer bad, yer goes to 'ell to frizzle and fry; and if yer good, yer sits on a cloud for ever and ever. It's so dull.' The New Testament view is the opposite to this when it says that over the hill lies *Paradise*, a fertile garden that could well be part of a caravanserai in the middle of the desert. It was a place in which you would find men engaged in all the activities of relaxation. To think of heaven as dull is as absurd as to think the same of our summer holidays. We hardly recoil from a few days away because it will mean having nothing to do.

Your reservation, sir!

As a caravan made its slow and tortuous journey across the desert it would be hindered from making reasonable progress by slipping loads and escaping children. Therefore the prospect of all that the caravanserai offered would be even more eagerly awaited by the weary travellers. However, the vision of welcomed refreshment may well have been dulled by the depressing thought that the lateness of the day might mean that a 'no vacancies' sign would await them at the end of a hard day's ride. To ensure that this would not be so, sometime early in the day the caravan master would send his servant on ahead to secure the appropriate number of *rooms* at the caravanserai. This whole process of a secure place is also part of the teaching of Jesus in John 14 concerning heaven: he clearly tells his disciples that he has *gone ahead to prepare a place for them*.

All roads do not lead to heaven

With so much detail it is a wonder that the disciples listening to Jesus in the upper room could want more information, so perhaps it needed a doubter like Thomas to raise the last necessary question and point to the one flaw in all that Jesus had said so far. You can almost hear Thomas saying, 'We are glad that heaven is just like a caravanserai and is therefore as real as a place on a map. And we are delighted that our reservations there are as secure as if we had personally sent someone on ahead to make them. But how are we going to find our way to the heavenly resting place? There are neither roads nor signposts in the desert, much less on the way to heaven. We shall not know if you have gone north, or south, or east, or west; so how can we follow you?' Jesus replies, '*I am the way, the truth and the life. No one comes to the Father but by me*' (John 14:6).

This remark squashes for the last time the illogical thought that all roads lead to heaven. Roads, after all, go in two directions at once; both to and from the place that you have in mind. So once we have chosen the right road we must also choose the right direction. Jesus said that he is the Way, *the right road to heaven*; he went on to say that he was the Truth, *the right direction along the right road*; he adds that he is also the Life, *so here is motive power down the right road in the right direction*. We can hardly ask for more than that.

Nothing profane shall enter in

Almost at the end of the Bible, in the last chapter but one, we find a forceful reminder that must conclude any teaching on heaven; that is, the statement that *nothing unclean* shall enter God's kingdom (Revelation 21:27). Christianity is an ethical religion. It lays down a standard of behaviour and requires that one day we shall be measured against that standard. Each action of life, every uttered word will be measured against the exactness of the divine yardstick. The recording angel is always at work, nothing escapes his notice. Put away the childish picture of an angel scratching away with a quill pen at a giant sized ledger. The account book is not really necessary since every thought, whether it is expressed in action or not, is recorded accurately in our own nature. We may excuse ourselves for each failing, kind heaven may be forgiving, but the record is made nonetheless, and even a cursory inward glance will tell us that we have fallen short of heaven's high standard. As Isaiah says, with both quiet wit and wisdom, *'all our righteousnesses are as filthy rags'* (Isaiah 64:6, AV).

The day when we are measured against God's standard is the Judgment Day, but if we then experience God's wrath it could well be that we have failed to experience all that God offers us in Christ. God is holy, therefore he cannot lower his holy standard, but he can change us. Paul puts it so clearly: *'if any one is in Christ he is a new creation, the old has passed away, behold, the new has come'* (2 Corinthians 5:17).